Indigenous Global Politics

A DISSERTATION
SUBMITTED TO THE FACULTY OF THE GRADUATE SCHOOL
OF THE UNIVERSITY OF MINNESOTA
BY

Sheryl Rae Lightfoot

IN PARTIAL FULFILLMENT OF THE REQUIREMENTS
FOR THE DEGREE OF
DOCTOR OF PHILOSOPHY

Raymond Duvall, Advisor

November 2009

UMI Number: 3387281

UMI

Dissertation Publishing

ProQuest®

ProQuest LLC
789 East Eisenhower Parkway
P.O. Box 1346
Ann Arbor, MI 48106-1346

Acknowledgements

A dissertation is never a solo effort, and so I must extend thanks to those who have played a variety of roles in bringing it to completion. While they all deserve credit and thanks, I am solely responsible for any errors. Several organizations provided financial support for the research and writing of this project. Dissertation support, including field research trips, were funded by an ICGC-MacArthur Fellowship (2008-2009), a Ford Foundation Diversity Dissertation Fellowship (2007-2008) and a University of Minnesota Diversity of Views and Experiences Summer Dissertation Research Fellowship (2007). Pre-dissertation funding was also generously provided by the University of Minnesota's Graduate Research Partnership Program (2006), and a Diversity of Views and Experiences Fellowship (2004-2005).

I wish to extend my sincerest thanks to the expert scholars who served as my dissertation committee members. I feel so fortunate to have had the opportunity to work with them these past few years: Professors Raymond Duvall, David Wilkins, Kathryn Sikkink and August Nimtz. I want to extend my deepest thanks to David Wilkins, not only for convincing me that I should return to graduate school but also for providing never ending advice and support along the journey. Special thanks also to Raymond Duvall for his patience, counsel and endless intellectual energy in support of both me and my project. Thank you for taking a chance on me in the beginning and for never wavering in both your professional and personal support.

My special thanks also go to others from the University of Minnesota who have read various portions of this dissertation and have offered critical suggestions, comments and direction, in addition to encouragement. My gratitude goes to my International Relations dissertation writing group, my ICGC Dissertation Development Workshop, and the American Indian Workshop. Special thanks to Professors Michael Barnett and Jean O'Brien who have read various parts of the dissertation and provided valuable insights. My deepest thanks also go to Jenny Lobasz and Lauren Wilcox, who are not only the greatest friends and colleagues I could have ever imagined finding in graduate school, but are also the ones whom I could count on and lean on during an "IR emergency."

Deep gratitude must also go to the numerous individuals and organizations that each played a role in my field research. Special thanks go to the International Indian Treaty Council staff and board, and especially to Bill Means, who helped provide valuable direction and moral support for this project. Thanks to doCip in Geneva for assistance with archives and documentation. Many thanks to the Indigenous Caucus in Geneva and the United Nations Permanent Forum on Indigenous Issues in New York for allowing me to attend your meetings. I also owe gratitude to the board and staff of the American Indian Policy Center for allowing me to serve as your chair for so many years and for extending me the privilege of representing you at international meetings. Many thanks to all of those who graciously gave me their time for interviews and conversations in Geneva, New York, the USA, and Canada. A special thanks to all those in Aotearoa-

New Zealand who shared their time and their country with me for an all-too-short period of time. I am deeply grateful.

Most importantly, I cannot find adequate words to express my thanks to my friends, my family, my community, my tribe, and my ancestors. I am who I am, and am able to do what I do, only because of all of you. I give this project back to you, with the hope that I bring honor to you. I want to especially thank my husband, Ken Thomas, my mother, Jennie Lightfoot, my sister, Julie Downwind and my aunt and uncle, Sharon and Don Edwards for their love, support and patience during the dissertation process. I would also like to thank my friend Lori Allison, for her unwavering belief in my abilities, and my nieces, Milayka and Alyssa, for always bringing smiles and sunshine into my life. A special word of gratitude goes to my daughters, Emma and Chloe, the absolute lights of my life. They always helped keep me in balance and provided daily reminders of what is most important in life. They were wonderful fieldwork travel companions, and it has been a sheer delight watching them grow during these years, along with me. I want to thank them, from the bottom of my heart, for their never ending and unconditional love and support.

Table of Contents

List of Tables

iv

List of Figures

Chapter 1

Introduction

The morning of 13 September 2007 was clear and sunny, a beautiful day in New York.[1] At the United Nations, diplomats and representatives from UN member states, dressed in suits and carrying briefcases, looking very serious and businesslike, took their places in the General Assembly, behind the name plates which identified them by country. That morning, dozens of indigenous delegates also arrived at the UN General Assembly. The indigenous delegates, however, while also businesslike and carrying large briefcases, were joyful. Many arrived that morning in their traditional clothing, a colorful sea of garb, representing diverse cultures from all over the world, from the Cree in Canada, to the Navajo in the United States, and the Saami in northern Europe, from the Maasai to the Hmong, to the Quechua. Hugs were freely shared among the indigenous delegates as they took their places in the back and in the side galleries of the UN General Assembly chamber. There were no official engraved name plates for the indigenous nations and organizations these delegates represent, although a few such name plates began to appear in front of some of the indigenous delegates, hand written on pieces of paper, indicating that they represented the Saami Council, or the Navajo Nation, or CISA, the Spanish acronym for the Indian Council of South America. The indigenous delegates looked truly happy; some had personally labored for over thirty years to reach this day.

---

[1] This narrative of the adoption of the Declaration on the Rights of Indigenous Peoples by the United Nations General Assembly has been compiled from a number of interviews and private conversations with indigenous delegates who were present in the UN General Assembly on 13 September 2007. I have also relied on draft footage prepared for a documentary film on the Declaration by Rebecca Sommer, Sommer Films.

At approximately 10:30 am, Sheikha Haya Rashed Al Khalifa, the President of the 61st Session of the General Assembly, announced that the General Assembly had before it a draft resolution, entitled the "United Nations Declaration on the Rights of Indigenous Peoples" and the voting process on the resolution would begin. One-by-one the representatives of the UN member states pushed green, yellow or red buttons on their desktops, indicating their vote on the indigenous rights Declaration ("the Declaration.") Green was a vote in favor, while red indicated a vote against, and the yellow button was pushed for an abstention. The indigenous delegates in the back and on the sides of the room, by and for whom this Declaration was written, through whose efforts this day was possible, did not have a vote. They could only sit and watch the screen on the wall, a scoreboard of member state votes on the Declaration. The scoreboard lit up as the member state votes were tallied. The final vote showed 143 votes for the Declaration, 11 abstentions, and 4 votes against. After thirty long years of struggle, the Declaration on the Rights of Indigenous Peoples had passed the United Nations General Assembly by an overwhelming margin and the world's indigenous peoples now had an international standard which specifically articulated their human rights. Only Australia, New Zealand, Canada and the United States had registered votes against it. Each of these four countries issued statements immediately following the vote, to clarify the reasons why each of these four states, known in indigenous circles as the CANZUS (Canada, Australia, New Zealand, US) group of states, had stood in such opposition to the Declaration. All four articulated that while they had various concerns about language, process, and even opposition to collective rights (US), the primary obstacles for them were land rights and self-determination.

Even with the opposition from CANZUS states, it did not detract from the absolute jubilation among the indigenous delegates as handshakes and hugs were again freely shared. Andrea Carmen (Yaqui), Executive Director of the International Indian Treaty Council, described the experience, "I was so privileged to sit in the Chamber that day, on the floor of the General Assembly, to see the voting on the scoreboard go up and realize that, after all of these years, we got the Declaration adopted."[2] The website of the International Indian Treaty Council declared, "History is made for Indigenous Peoples at the United Nations!" as "Treaty Rights, Land Rights and Self-Determination of Indigenous Peoples are recognized internationally with the adoption of the Declaration."[3] Les Malezar, Chairman of the Global Indigenous Caucus, declared that "The adoption of the Declaration...marks a momentous and historic occasion for both Indigenous Peoples and the United Nations."[4] Another indigenous delegate, from Guatemala, said, "It was great. We really are very happy!"[5] An indigenous delegate from Africa was so moved by the event that he could not speak.[6] Grand Chief Edward John from the First Nations Summit, said, "It's a tremendous day. It's all over now and we have in our hands a Declaration we helped construct and one on which we proudly stand. Notwithstanding

---

[2] Interview by author with Andrea Carmen, 26 September 2007, Mille Lacs Nation.
[3] www.treatycouncil.org, accessed 14 September 2007.
[4] http://censored-news.blogspot.com/2007/09/les-malezer-indigneous-declaration.html, accessed 20 September 2007.
[5] "Adoption of the Declaration on the Rights of Indigenous Peoples," a film by Rebecca Sommer, Sommer Films, 2007.
[6] Sommer, 2007.

3

Canada's 'NO' vote...we should all be proud in our collective achievement."[7] In a press

release issued the day the Declaration passed in the General Assembly, Victoria Tauli-

Corpuz, Chairperson of the UN Permanent Forum on indigenous Issues, stated that

> the 13th of September 2007 will be remembered as an international human rights
> day for the Indigenous Peoples of the world, a day that the United Nations and its
> member states, together with Indigenous Peoples, reconciled with past painful
> histories and decided to march into the future on the path of human rights.[8]

Meanwhile, Tonya Frichner (Onondaga), American Indian Law Alliance and member of

the UN Permanent Forum on Indigenous Issues, commented in a more muted tone, "It

was interesting. It was very interesting."[9]

Over the next year, the Declaration on the Rights of Indigenous Peoples began to

have some international impact. Within five weeks after the passage of the Declaration

by the UN General Assembly, the Belize Supreme Court ruled on a case, *Cal vs. Attorney*

General, which was the world's first judgment to be rendered which referenced the UN

indigenous rights Declaration. The Belize Supreme Court ruled that the national

government must recognize the customary land tenure of the Maya in Belize. The Court

asserted that the indigenous peoples had collective rights to their lands, resources and

environment and found that the Maya had their own "complex set of land tenure

regulations."[10] More specifically, the Supreme Court found that the Mayan "rights to

occupy their lands, farm, hunt and fish predate European colonization and remain in force

---

[7] www.treatycouncil.org, accessed 14 September 2007.
[8] Press release, 13 September 2007, New York, Message of Victoria Tauli-Corpuz, Chairperson of the UN Permanent Forum on Indigenous Issues, on the Occasion of the Adoption by the General Assembly of the Declaration on the Rights of Indigenous Peoples.
[9] Sommer, 2007.
[10] Kim Petersen. 23 January 2008. "Indigenous Rights and the Mayan Victory in Belize." *The Dominion.*

today."[11] In other words, the state of Belize had no right to unilaterally abrogate indigenous land rights.

Meanwhile, in Bolivia, President Evo Morales' dream of a "plurinational" state with territorial and administrative autonomy for indigenous peoples got a significant boost from the passage of the indigenous rights Declaration in the General Assembly. A news article in September 2007 observed that the Declaration "might call for a reorganisation of the Bolivian state and a reversion to the scheme of productive communities and regions, which was in operation at the time of the Spaniards."[12] In fact, on 7 November 2007, President Evo Morales announced the passage of National Law 3760, the Rights of Indigenous Peoples, which inscribed the UN Declaration on the Rights of Indigenous Peoples into national law in Bolivia.[13] Bolivia was thus the first country in the world to adopt the Declaration as national law. In his address announcing the passage of this law, Morales said, "From the passage of this declaration, I feel that the indigenous movement has gone from one of resistance to one of power, ...a power that, at it's core (sic), is a way of living in a community ...it is the power of resolving problems equally for all, not only in Bolivia but in the entire world."[14]

On 8 April 2008, the Canadian House of Commons passed a resolution calling on the Government of Canada to endorse the Declaration and "fully implement the standards contained herein," even though Prime Minster Stephen Harper refused to sign the

---

[11] *Ibid.*

[12] Frank Chavez, 10 September 2007. "Bolivia: Morales Gets Boost from UN Declaration on Indigenous Rights." http://ips.news.net.

[13] Kearns, Rick. "UN Declaration Becomes Law of the Land in Bolivia." *Indian Country Today.* 12 December 2007.

[14] *Ibid.*

resolution.[15] By May 2008, the US states of Maine and Arizona had passed resolutions

supporting the indigenous rights Declaration. The city of Phoenix also passed a

resolution of support.[16]

What exactly is this document called the Declaration on the Rights of Indigenous

Peoples, and what is it attempting to accomplish? The Declaration is a document which

sets out the individual and collective rights of indigenous peoples as well as their rights to

identity, language, health, education and other issues. It emphasizes the right of

indigenous peoples to maintain and strengthen their own institutions, cultures and

traditions. It also prohibits discrimination against them, while simultaneously

maintaining their right to remain distinct and to pursue their own visions of development.

It is a United Nations declaration, and not an international treaty, and so it is not a legally

binding instrument under international law. Nevertheless, it does now form part of the

international human rights consensus, and according to a UN press release, represents a

"major step forward towards the promotion and protection of human rights and

fundamental freedoms for all...(through)...the General Assembly's important role in

setting international standards."[17] In a separate press release, the former UN Special

Rapporteur on Indigenous Issues, Rodolfo Stavenhagen, noted the important shift this

Declaration forged in the international human rights system, when he stated that "the

---

[15] Joint Press Release issued by ten indigenous and non-indigenous organizations, including the Assembly of First Nations, Amnesty International Canada, Grand Council of the Crees, Inuit Circumpolar Council and the Native Women's Association of Canada. "UN Declaration on the Rights of Indigenous Peoples: Canadian Parliament Calls for Implementation of Critical Universal Human Rights Instrument." 9 April 2008.

[16] Kara Briggs. "UN Declaration on Rights is Gaining Momentum." *Indian Country Today.* 14 May 2008.

[17] United Nations. General Assembly. Department of Public Information. Press Release. "General Assembly Adopts Declaration on Rights of Indigenous Peoples." 13 September 2007.

Declaration reflects a growing international consensus concerning the rights of indigenous peoples."[18] It took more than thirty years of effort by indigenous peoples at the United Nations to reach this point, including numerous working groups and sub-committees, many arguments over definitions and other issues, a hunger strike and even an eleventh-hour attempt by certain states to change the text of the Declaration. But, in September 2007, the declaration passed the UN General Assembly, to the delight of some, while others remained steadfast in their opposition.

There were certain states (the US and Australia) that opposed this Declaration in nearly every possible way and at every critical juncture throughout the Declaration's thirty year history. They tried to block it in its various committees and fought it right down to the final vote on the floor of the General Assembly. Other states, like Canada and New Zealand, which are widely considered to be on the forefront of international human rights, also worked vigilantly against the Declaration.

Why did the transnational indigenous rights movement need to fight so hard and so long to secure passage of a bare minimum standard on indigenous rights? Why is it that certain countries are so threatened by an emerging international indigenous rights regime? How does the emerging indigenous rights regime challenge the international status quo, and how are nation states responding to these changes? I aim to address all of these questions in this dissertation by engaging in two lines of analysis: international change and country-specific responses to such change. Following a presentation of my research methodology later in this chapter, I will begin in Chapter 2 to build a theory of

---

[18] United Nations. Press Release. "Adoption of Declaration on Rights of Indigenous Peoples a Historic Moment for Human Rights, UN Expert Says." 14 September 2007.

how indigenous politics at the global level compels a new direction of thought in international relations by challenging some of its fundamental tenets. I argue that indigenous global politics is a perspective of international relations that, through the pursuit of land, self-determination and other collective rights, complicates the structure of international politics in new and important ways, challenging both traditional notions of state sovereignty and liberalism in the international system and the international human rights consensus. In Chapter 3, I engage in an original historical analysis to demonstrate that the Indigenous Rights Declaration process took more than thirty years and was so difficult because indigenous global politics was more than a typical transnational rights movement, but rather, by constituting itself in terms of land and self-determination rights, it represents a real and direct threat to both the existing international system of sovereign states and the contemporary liberal world order.

In Chapters 4, 5, and 6, I will examine how states have responded to these tremendous and foundational changes in international discourse regarding indigenous rights. Chapter 4 will present a data set which demonstrates the various types of state response to the emerging indigenous rights regime, including compliance, partial compliance, under-compliance. I will also introduce a new concept, which I call "over-compliance." I am referring here to a puzzling pattern of state response to the emerging indigenous rights regime which has not yet been explored in international relations or in compliance theory. I have termed this pattern "over-compliance" by which I mean that a state's behavior vis-à-vis indigenous rights goes above and beyond its international treaty commitments while it simultaneously resists the articulation of such international

8

standards. By over-compliance, I do not imply that these states are models of indigenous rights compliance, because they are certainly not. My intent is to examine their puzzling and paradoxical compliance behavior in the area of indigenous rights. Chapters 5 and 6 then engage in a comparative case study of indigenous rights over-compliance in two cases: New Zealand and Canada. Through my original field research in North America and New Zealand, I have identified several mechanisms which I hypothesize create conditions of indigenous rights "over-compliance" in these states. The conditions I identify are: 1) highly vocal domestic indigenous movements which are connected to and invoke the principles of indigenous global politics, 2) the country's concern for its human rights reputation and identity within the international community, and 3) a search for national identity which is shifting to define itself in terms of liberal multiculturalism. I find that these three conditions have propelled these countries toward a reconciliation effort with indigenous peoples, but that these reconciliation efforts remain firmly rooted in colonial, rather than post-colonial, ideology and thought-processes. I suggest that these countries are over-compliant in indigenous rights not because they are in any way progressive in indigenous rights but because they are actually *resisting* the emerging indigenous rights discourse. Indigenous global politics is pushing the international community toward a new vision of self-determination, territoriality, and sovereignty which is post-colonial, while over-compliant states are attempting to remain fully rooted in colonial discourses both domestically and in the international system. Chapter 7 will explore some of the implications of indigenous global politics and state over-compliance and also suggest some avenues for future research.

9

Research Methodology

In my dissertation, I have integrated international relations theory, qualitative case studies in comparative perspective, and indigenous methodologies in order to investigate the international change brought forth by indigenous global politics, as well as state resistance to such change. Because this is a theory-generating and not a theory testing project, I have utilized a qualitative case study approach.[19] At the same time, I am an indigenous researcher[20] engaged in an emancipatory project involving indigenous subjects, making indigenous methodology not only appropriate, but necessary. The post-positivist turn in political science, and especially in international relations research, has opened up a space for the insertion of indigenous perspectives.[21] Integration of these various methodologies in practice means that "we can begin with all the maps of qualitative research we currently have, then draw some new maps that enrich and extend the boundaries of our understandings beyond the margins. We need to draw on all our maps of understanding."[22] One of the "maps" that I bring to this project is my experience in indigenous nations and urban communities. I have almost fifteen years of experience working in various volunteer and contract capacities for a number of organizations in the American Indian community of Minneapolis-St. Paul, including more than a decade in a leadership position of an American Indian non-profit research institute which specialized

---

[19] John Gerring. 2007. *Case Study Research: Principles and Practices.* Cambridge: Cambridge University Press.

[20] I am Anishinaabe (Ojibwe), an enrolled citizen of the Lake Superior Band, Keweenaw Bay Community, in northern Michigan. I grew up primarily in Minneapolis during the 1970s and 1980s and have always been active in the American Indian community in the Minneapolis-St. Paul area. I am married to a Mdewakanton Dakota man, and have lived on his reservation in southern Minnesota since 1995.

[21] Linda Tuhiwai Smtih. 2005. "On Tricky Ground: Researching the Native in the Age of Uncertainty." In *The Sage Handbook of Qualitative Research, Third Edition.* Norman K. Denzin and Yvonna S.Lincoln, ed. Thousand Oaks, CA: Sage, p. 85-108.

[22] *Ibid.*, p. 102.

in community-based and indigenous-driven research.[23] Therefore, I have chosen in this project in order to fuse qualitative international relations research with indigenous community-based participatory research methods and perspectives.

Qualitative Case Study Approach

I have employed a qualitative case study approach in my research for several reasons. First, in the spirit of critical constructivism and other critical theories, my goal is to understand the constitutive processes and relations of power of both indigenous global politics and the states which over-comply with their indigenous rights commitments rather than make, or systemically test, generalizable predictions. This is therefore a hypothesis-generating study, and I employ a case study methodology where it is strongest, that is, in an exploratory mode rather than a confirmatory/disconfirmatory mode.[24]

Second, I have a small universe of cases for analysis in both the study of the transnational indigenous rights movement and the cases of state over-compliance. The transnational indigenous rights movement is a singular case and, as Chapter 4 will uncover, the universe of countries which exhibit over-compliance in indigenous rights is three, and these three cases deviate substantially from what is expected in extant compliance theory. Because of this small universe, I selected cases in adherence with

---

[23] American Indian Policy Center, St. Paul, MN.

[24] Gerring, 2007.; Andrew Bennett. 2004. "Case Study Methods: Design, Use, and Comparative Advantages." Pp. 19-45 in Detlef F. Sprinz and Yael Wolinsky-Nahmias, eds. *Methods, Numbers, and Cases: Methods for Studying International Relations.* Ann Arbor: University of Michigan Press.; Jack S. Levy. 2008. "Case Studies: Types, Designs, and the Logics of Inference." *Conflict Management and Peace Science* 25:1-18.; Dawson R. Hancock and Bob Algozzine. 2006. *Doing Case Study Research: A Practical Guide for Beginning Researchers.* New York: Columbia University Teachers College.

Mill's method of agreement so that I could look for the conditions that are common between two cases with the same outcome.[25] In other words, I examined the universe of three cases of over-compliance (New Zealand, Australia and Canada) and then selected two cases for this study which were most comparable in background variables to achieve as much control as possible.[26] Because New Zealand and Canada are both treaty-based settler countries in terms of their relationships with indigenous peoples,[27] I selected these two cases for this study. Both countries have also initiated treaty settlement processes in recent decades. Both countries also find themselves in the "younger, smaller sibling" position to a larger and more powerful, English speaking neighbor. Canada and New Zealand also both assert themselves as world leaders in human rights. So, there are many background variables in these two cases that are similar.

Third, the use of qualitative case studies, including field work, is consistent with indigenous methodology. My aim here is to integrate indigenous perspectives into the study of the transnational indigenous rights movement and to the patterns of state responses to those changes that movement is forging in the international order. Linda Tuhiwai Smith advocates qualitative approaches for the study of indigenous communities because these approaches offer tools which can not only insert indigenous perspectives and alternate storylines into international relations but can also "create spaces for

[25] Bennett, 2006, p. 30.; David A. Bositis. 1990. *Research Designs for Political Science: Contrivance and Demonstration in Theory and Practice*. Carbondale, IL: Southern Illinois University Press, p. 24-25.
[26] Arend Lijphart. 2006. "The Comparable Cases Strategy in Comparative Research." Pp. 156-170 in Matthew David. *Case Study Research, Volume III*. London: Sage.
[27] Australia never signed a treaty with indigenous peoples, but settled the country strictly on the basis of *terra nullius*, or "empty land."

decolonizing"[28] as well as "create spaces for dialogue across difference"[29] and help understand shifting identities, experiences and realities.[30] By using indigenous methodologies, I also aim to keep academic research relevant to the lives of indigenous peoples and communities, following the path set forth by Vine Deloria, Jr., who was one of the first to call for academic research in indigenous contexts to seek not just "knowledge for knowledge's sake" but rather, produce outcomes that are relevant and useful to tribal communities.[31]

The case study approach has a number of benefits but also some limitations. Qualitative case studies are particularly useful for "how" and "why" questions like I am asking in this study.[32] Some scholars even argue that case studies may be best, if not the only, way to discover causality.[33] The aim of a case study approach is to develop a rich theoretical framework to find conditions under which a phenomenon is likely to be found.[34] In this approach to research, one cannot begin with a theory but rather with specific research questions. Then, the researcher gathers a range of different data and makes a theoretical explanation which follows the data.[35] The process is descriptive, inferential, subjective, and participatory, based on real-life phenomena.[36] The aim is to gain an "in-depth understanding of an individual example" and the desired end product is

---

[28] Smith, 2005, p. 103.

[29] *Ibid.*

[30] *Ibid.*

[31] Vine Deloria, Jr. 1969/1988. *Custer Died for Your Sins: An Indian Manifesto.* Norman, OK: University of Oklahoma Press.

[32] Yin, 1994, p. 20.

[33] Alexander L. George and Andrew Bennett. 2005. *Case Studies and Theory Development in the Social Sciences.* Cambridge, MA: MIT Press.; Lijphart 2006.

[34] Yin, 1994.

[35] Bill Graham. 2000. *Case Study Research Methods.* London: Continuum. p. 1-2.

[36] *Ibid.*, p. 10.

rich, detailed insight, a situated understanding,[37] based on a holistic approach.[38] In

addition to identifying new variables and hypotheses, a case study methodology is also

advantageous for exploring complexities where little is already known[39] and are also a

good tool to locate "intermediate factors lying between structural cause and purported

effect."[40] While investigating causal pathways, case studies also help provide "insight

into intentions, reasoning and information-processing procedures"[41] utilized by actors

within those cases. Because there is such a paucity of scholarship on indigenous politics

in international relations, the case study approach allowed me to explore the richness and

complexity of the transnational indigenous rights movement and domestic indigenous

politics in New Zealand and Canada.

Problems with the case study approach include case selection issues and selection

bias.[42] Often case studies are criticized for selecting on the dependent variable, which I

have admittedly done, although according to Lijphart, this is not always a problem

especially in hypothesis generating research.[43] Other scholars have even argued that in

case study methods, selecting on the dependent variable is actually beneficial, in

discovering whether a variable is necessary for an outcome[44] and identifying the causal

---

[37] Willis, 2007, p. 189-190.

[38] John Gerring. 2007. *Case Study Research: Principles and Practices.* Cambridge: Cambridge University Press, p. 1,4,7, 49-50.

[39] Graham, 2000, p. 11.

[40] Gerring, 2007, p. 45.

[41] *Ibid.*

[42] C. Achen and D. Snidal. 1989. "Rational Deterrence Theory and Comparative Case Studies." *World Politics* 4(2): 143-169.; B. Geddes. 1990. "How the Cases You Choose Affect the Answers You Get: Selection Bias in Comparative Politics" *Political Analysis* 2:31-50.; Bennett 2004.

[43] Lijphart 2008, p. 8

[44] D. Dion, 2003. "Evidence and Inference in the Comparative Case Study." In *Necessary Conditions: Theory, Methodology, and Applications*, edited by G. Goertz and H. Starr, 95-112. Boulder: Rowman and

14

paths and causal mechanisms leading to the dependent variable, findings which can be tested on a more general basis at a later date.[45] Also, case studies are said to be inherently indeterminate,[46] meaning that there is no way to exclude all but one explanation,[47] also called the degrees of freedom problem, which is when there are more potentially explanatory variables than cases.[48] Again, this issue appears in my project as I have identified more explanatory variables for over-compliance than the number of my cases. While it can be argued that this is a weakness of the case study approach, others have argued that case studies do not necessarily suffer from a lack of determinancy because each case actually has a large number of observations on intervening variables,[49] which also occurs in my cases. Another major limitation of case studies is that they lack a precise way to interpret findings,[50] and findings are usually contingent and limited in scope.[51] Eisner, however, argues that qualitative research should be evaluated not on its ability to make broad generalizations but rather on its coherence, consensus and instrumental utility,[52] and Willis adds another criterion, insightfulness.[53] I aim for these goals in this project.

Littlefield.; D. Collier. 1995. "'Degrees of Freedom' and the Case Study." *Comparative Political Studies* 8(2):178-194.

[45] Bennett, 2004, p. 40.

[46] *Ibid.*, p. 41.

[47] O. Njolstad. 1990. "Learning from History? Case Studies and the Limits to Theory-Building" in *Arms Races: Technological and Political Dynamics*, edited by O Njolstad. Los Angeles: Sage.

[48] Achen and Snidal, 1989, p. 156-157.

[49] Gary King, Robert O. Keohane, and Sidney Verba. 1994. *Designing Social Inquiry: Scientific Inference in Qualitative Research*. Princeton, NJ: Princeton University Press, p. 225; Donald T. Campbell. 1975/1988. "'Degrees of Freedom' and the Case Study." In E. Samuel Overman, ed. *Methodology and Epistemology for Social Science*. Chicago: University of Chicago Press, p. 377-388.

[50] Yin, 1994, p. 26.

[51] Bennett, 2004, p. 19.

[52] E. Eisner. 1997. *The Enlightened Eye: Qualitative Inquiry and the Enhancement of Educational Practice*. Columbus, OH: Merrill., p. 39-59.

[53] Willis, 2007, p. 167.

Indigenous Methodologies

Indigenous methodologies are approaches to research that privilege indigenous voices, experiences, knowledges, reflections and analyses.[54] These are approaches to research which are deliberately and unapologetically activist, and counterhegemonic in the tradition of critical theories and emancipatory research.[55] Smith describes these methodologies as "involving the unmasking and deconstruction of imperialism, and its aspect of colonialism in its old and new formulations alongside a search for sovereignty,"[56] as well as the transformation of colonial relations.[57] Indigenous methodologies situate research programs and approaches firmly within a decolonization framework[58] while attempting to build and maintain connections between the academy, indigenous communities and wider political struggles.[59] Indigenous approaches to research recognize that research is never neutral but reproduces a certain set of power relations[60] and so indigenous methodologies attempt to channel their transformative agenda to the benefit of indigenous communities. While some scholars argue that indigenous research is defined as that which is carried out by indigenous researchers with and for indigenous communities,[61] Aboriginal professor Lester Rigney, (Narungga Nation, in South Australia) who first named this approach to research as "Indigenist,"

---

[54] L. Rigney. 1999. "Internationalization of an Indigenous Anticolonial Cultural Critique of Research Methodologies. A Guide to Indigenous Research Methodology and Its Principles." *Wicazo Sa Journal of American Indian Studies Review* 14(2):109-121, p. 117.
[55] Smith, 2005, p. 88.
[56] *Ibid.*
[57] Linda Tuhiwai Smith. 2002. *Decolonizing Methodologies: Research and Indigenous Peoples*. Dunedin, New Zealand, University of Otago Press, p. 4.
[58] Smith, 1999.
[59] Smith, 2005, p. 88.
[60] Smith, 2002, p. 5.
[61] F. Cram. 2001. "Rangahau Māori: Tona Tika, Tona Pono--The Validity and Integrity of Māori Research." In M. Tolich, ed. *Research Ethics and Aotearoa New Zealand*, pp. 35-52.

refined the approach further, arguing that it centers on three principles: resistance, political integrity and privileging indigenous voices.[62] As a transformative project, Indigenist research is critical of power relations and inequality and recognizes that, while research has been used as a tool of colonization, it is now a way to reclaim indigenous language and culture, voices and knowledges and "give voice to an alternative way of knowing and of being,"[63] although it admittedly also "weaves in and out" of Western and indigenous ways of knowing.[64] In the New Zealand context, this research is called Kaupapa Māori, an approach that Smith describes as "the ability by Māori as Māori to name the world, to theorize the world, and to research back to power"[65] while also remaining firmly grounded within the wider project of self-determination struggles[66] and based on the assumption "that research that involves Māori people...should set out to make a positive difference for the researched."[67]

Indigenist approaches to research also require particular sets of ethics, protocols and methodologies. Three principles are central. First, reciprocal and respectful relationships must be established and maintained. Second, trustworthiness and integrity must be absolute. Third, researchers need to be accountable to the indigenous communities being researched and engaged in "culturally responsive research practices,"

---

[62] Rigney, 1999.
[63] Smith, 2005, p. 91.
[64] Smith, 2002, p. 190.
[65] *Ibid.*, p. 90.
[66] Graham Smith. 1992. "Research Issues Related to Māori Education," *The Issue of Research and Māori*, Auckland, New Zealand: Research Unit for Māori Education, University of Auckland.
[67] L.T. Smith, 2002, p. 191.

especially humility.[68] This also means that research questions should emanate from the indigenous community and results should be reported back to the community, in a comprehensible way. Smith lays out the specifics of appropriate research conduct in Kaupapa Māori settings, although these practices are easily applicable to other indigenous contexts as well. Smith mentions seven values and practices which should be followed when utilizing indigenous methodologies:

1. Aroha ki te tangata (a respect for people.)

2. Kanohi kitea (the seen face; that is, present yourself to people face to face).

3. Titiro, whakarongo ... korero (look, listen ...speak).

4. Manaki ki te tangata (share and host people, be generous.)

5. Kia tupato (be cautious).

6. Kaua e takahia te mana o te tangata (do not trample over the *mana*[69] of people).

7. kaua e mahaki (don't flaunt your knowledge.)[70]

These are the guiding values and principles that I adopt in my research, not only in Māori settings, but in all indigenous settings. At the more pragmatic level, Smith articulates a set of eight questions which should be addressed when adhering to indigenous methodologies in research:

1.   What research do we want to carry out?

---

[68] L.T. Smith, 2005, p. 97; Russell Bishop. 2005. "Freeing Ourselves from Neocolonial Domination in Research: A Kaupapa Māori Approach to Creating Knowledge." In *The Sage Handbook of Qualitative Research, Third Edition.* Norman K. Denzin and Yvonna S.Lincoln, ed. Thousand Oaks, CA: Sage, p. 109-138, p. 111.

[69] *Mana* is a Māori word that does not easily translate into English. The word denotes an individual's pride, and more accurately, their spirit. When one shows respect to another, one is honoring their *mana*. At the same time, a person who is well respected in the community is said to have great *mana*.

[70] L. T. Smith, 2002, p. 120.

2. Whom is that research for?

3. What difference will it make?

4. Who will carry out this research?

5. How do we want the research to be done?

6. How will we know if it is a worthwhile piece of research?

7. Who will own the research?

8. Who will benefit?[71]

While engaging in my academic work focused on indigenous politics in international relations theory and aiming to make a contribution there, I must also, at the same time, keep my work grounded in this set of questions. While I am asking research questions relevant to international relations theory, I am also bringing forward questions that I have heard voiced in Native American communities, questions which are relevant to indigenous activism and politics not only in my communities but on the global level as well. At each stage of this project, I have paused to revisit these questions and make sure that my research reflects these practical concerns. Mine is a dual approach to research, but I aim for an output that is more integrated. My findings and implications should speak simultaneously to international relations and to indigenous politics in both theory and practice.

---

[71] Linda Tuhiwai Te Rina Smith. 2000. "Kaupapa Māori Research." Pp. 225-247 in *Reclaiming Indigenous Voice and Vision*, Marie Battiste, ed. Vancouver: UBC Press, p. 239.

Data Sources and Research Process

In a search for both validity and reliability in my qualitative work, I have utilized

five sources of evidence to construct my three case studies, looking for corroboration

across sources.[72] I have used documentation (e.g. internal documents, formal studies,

newspaper clippings, speeches), archival records, interviews, direct observation and

participant observation to research my case of the development of the Declaration on the

Rights of Indigenous Peoples, and the two country cases of indigenous rights "over-

compliance."

The emergence and development of the Declaration on the Rights of Indigenous

Peoples remains largely undocumented in the scholarly literature, so I conducted original

archival and field research in Geneva, New York and other locations in North America,

and New Zealand in order to document the birth of indigenous global politics in Chapter

3, through an original historical analysis of the Declaration. I relied on several specific

sources of data in this historical analysis. First, I utilized United Nations documents on

the Declaration process which are housed in the collection of doCIP in Geneva. DoCip is

an NGO, based in Geneva, whose mission is "to support Indigenous Peoples as they

defend their rights, particularly within the framework of international institutions."[73] In

addition to assisting indigenous organizations with language translation and other

technical services, doCip serves at the documentation and information center for

indigenous delegations attending United Nations meetings. Since 1977, doCip has

collected and housed all official UN documents associated with indigenous peoples'

---

[72] Yin, 1994; Willis 2007; Hancock and Algozzini 2006.
[73] From doCip's website, docip.org/Our-Organization.26.0.html, accessed 10 May 2009.

participation at the UN as well as many memos, letters and statements made by indigenous organizations. As an indigenous person, I was able to go to Geneva and gain free and unrestricted access to all of these documents.

I supplemented these official documents with a set of interviews with key individuals involved in the Declaration process and with my direct observations of UN meetings in New York and Geneva,[74] and my participant observation of Indigenous Caucus meetings in Geneva.[75] I was also able to directly observe a Board of Directors meeting of the International Indian Treaty Council as well as a human rights training session for indigenous nations and organizations conducted by the International Indian Treaty Council, both hosted by the Mille Lacs Nation of Ojibwe, located near Onamia, Minnesota in September 2007.[76]

Interviews, direct observations and participant observations of international indigenous activity for Chapter 3 took place over a twelve month period of time between mid-2007 and mid-2008. Interviews with participants in the transnational indigenous rights movement were conducted between September 2007 and mid-2008. In total, eleven interviews were conducted during this time period in a variety of locations both in

---

[74] I attended two official UN meetings as an observer: 1) an Informal Meeting to Discuss the Most Appropriate Mechanisms to Continue the Work of the Working Group on Indigenous Populations, 6-7 December 2007, Palais des Nations, Geneva, and 2) the Seventh Session of the United Nations Permanent Forum on Indigenous Issues, 21 April - 2 May 2008, New York.

[75] This closed meeting of the Indigenous Caucus was held 4 - 5 December 2007, Palais des Nations, Geneva.

[76] The Board of Directors Meeting of the International Indian Treaty Council was held at the Mille Lacs Indian Museum 24-25 September 2007 at Grand Casino Mille Lacs on 26 September 2007. The Human Rights Training session conducted by the International Indian Treaty Council was held at the Mille Lacs Indian Museum on 27 September 2007. I am grateful to the International Indian Treaty Council board members for allowing me to observe over the course of these four days. Your kindness, hospitality and, most of all your willingness to allow me to be present is most deeply and sincerely appreciated.

the US and abroad. These interviews were semi-structured,[77] with a focus on a particular

set of questions, but interviewees were allowed the freedom to talk about indigenous

global politics as they saw it and understood it.[78]

Much of the transnational indigenous political activity I was able to directly

observe during my fieldwork is closed to outsiders, and I was able to gain access only

because of the leadership position that I held in an indigenous organization at that time. I

thus became a participant observer in the transnational indigenous rights movement and

part of the process, rather than remaining simply an observer outside the process.[79]

While I always disclosed my university affiliation and never hid my academic research

agenda during any part of my fieldwork, there are several meetings that I was allowed to

attend only as an indigenous person holding a leadership position in an indigenous

organization. I also needed permission from the Board of Directors of my home

organization to travel and represent them while I was doing my fieldwork.[80] Because of

the delicate issues of representation and accountability involved in this process, and in an

effort to maintain the confidentiality of the Indigenous Caucus, I do not cite or disclose

any content from those meetings, but rather, I attended them to observe and gain an

understanding of the internal dynamics of the transnational indigenous rights movement.

---

[77] Steiner Kvale. 1996. *Interviews: An Introduction to Qualitative Research Interviewing.* Thousand Oaks, CA: Sage., p. 124.

[78] *Ibid.,* p. 124.

[79] Bositis, 1990, p. 86.; D. Schuler and A. Namoika. 1993. *Participatory Design: Principles and Practices.* Hillsdale, NJ: Erlbaum.

[80] I with to express my deep gratitude to the Board of Directors of the American Indian Policy Center for allowing me to represent them internationally during this time. I also wish to express my sincere thanks to the Indigenous Caucus for allowing me to attend meetings wearing both my activist and academic "hats."

The case studies of indigenous rights compliance in Chapters 5 and 6 were also constructed using multiple sources (triangulation)[81] which aim to "weave a chain of evidence"[82] through holistic, non-experimental, historical and textual fieldwork.[83] Both case studies of indigenous rights compliance behavior are bounded geographically in the state context, as is common practice in political science, and also bounded temporally, restricted to an analysis of indigenous rights policy behavior between 1977, the beginning of the transnational indigenous rights movement, and 30 June 2008, the somewhat arbitrary end date of my research.[84] My fieldwork for these two cases (New Zealand and Canada) relied primarily on documentation (letters, memos, speeches, formal government studies, newspapers, mass media) and interviews. Seventeen interviews were conducted for these two cases. Interviewees included both elite and grassroots activists, as well as government officials. I also incorporate observations and experiences from fieldwork time spent in New Zealand during the first half of 2008 and in Canada during the end of 2007 and June 2008. Because individuals involved in indigenous global politics are transnational activists, interviews took place at varied locations and not necessarily in the country under study. Because I was adhering to indigenous methodologies and cultural practices, some of these interviews were lengthy. Typically, interviews with government officials and elite activists were approximately an hour in length while interviews with other activists and grassroots participants went up to three to four hours. Again, because

---

[81] Yin 1994, Graham 2000.

[82] Yin, 1994.

[83] Gerring, 2007, p. 17.

[84] This date was determined by the end date of my research funding (generously provided by the Ford Foundation) rather than any significant event in those states or in the transnational indigenous rights movement.

I adhere to indigenous (and Kaupapa Māori) values and principles of respect and reciprocity in my research, I always offered a gift from my home culture to my interviewees, in return for their participation. I have also checked back with interviewees to make sure that I understood and represented their comments correctly. I have also promised each participant a full and complete copy of the completed chapters.

Analysis of the data in my cases followed a nonlinear, recursive process of data collection, analysis and interpretation.[85] In order to develop an understanding of the causal paths and mechanisms for why the Indigenous Rights Declaration took so long and confronted such difficult challenges, and why some states engage in unexpected behavior in the face of the emerging indigenous rights regime, I used an inductive method of analysis, scanning the data for patterns in explanatory variables.[86] For all three case studies, I worked through the data as I collected it, developing "emerging insights, hunches, and tentative hypotheses" which then directed the next phase of data collection and refinement of specific questions.[87]

Chapter 4, which focuses on the patterns of state compliance with the emerging indigenous rights regime, is the most analytically linear of all the data chapters. In this chapter, I present a data set on state patterns of compliance with indigenous rights, which I compiled using primarily data from the Indigenous Work Group on Indigenous Affairs, a Copenhagen-based NGO, and from the 2008 CIA World Factbook. Again, the

---

[85] S. Merriam. 1998. *Qualitative Research and Case Study Applications in Education.* San Francisco: Jossey-Bass.
[86] Yin, 1994, p. 108; W. Phillips Shively. 1990. *The Craft of Political Research, 3rd Edition.* Englewood Cliffs, NJ: Prentice Hall.; Bennett and George, 2005.
[87] Willis, 2007, p. 310.

analytical approach I employed is largely inductive, scanning the data for patterns in the explanatory variables.

Issues and Dilemmas in Research

There was a set of clear advantages that I brought to this research project based upon my identity and my professional background working in the American Indian community. I had access to meetings and situations which I would not have enjoyed as a non-indigenous person or solely as an academic. I had personal and professional connections which helped open doors for me and made my qualitative research a much faster process than others may have experienced. I also possess a set of cultural knowledge, including how to act in certain situations, ethics and protocols, and the unstated meanings behind particular statements and actions. However, while this set of advantages is substantial in a research project of this kind, I must emphasize that each one of these advantages has an associated set of disadvantages and dilemmas which I also had to work through.

First of all, my presence and participation in meetings presented dilemmas, some of which have been touched upon already. While I was able to gain access to meetings as a representative of an indigenous organization, I always had to be clear about who I was and what my agenda was in these meetings. In the spirit of recognizing and acknowledging my biases as a researcher,[88] I did not wish my presence at any of these meetings to disrupt or impede the process in any way, and so I often adopted a quiet and

---

[88] Willis, 2005; Bruce Berg. 2009. *Qualitative Research Methods for the Social Sciences, Seventh Edition.* Boston: Allyn & Bacon.

unobtrusive posture in my observations and participations. Such a posture can present a disadvantage in gathering data and seeking out potential interviewees. Also, since a strong negative legacy is tied to research among indigenous communities, the "most researched" people on the planet,[89] participants were often unsure of me, or even suspicious of me and my motivations as an academic researcher. Even though I am an indigenous person, in some instances I was still not able to overcome this burden which was left behind by researchers that came before me. Finally, even though my Native American background provided some degree of privileged access, it is also important to note that I came to these meetings with a certain set of biases, family histories, and kinship connections which rendered me simultaneously an insider and an outsider to the process, in a highly complex and always dynamic relationship.[90]

Second, during the course of my fieldwork, meeting attendance and interviewing, I was often provided with information which was confidential, and I was sometimes provided information which was completely irrelevant to my research questions. I refer to this as the "gossip factor," and it occurred on more than one occasion, especially during long and detailed interviews and conversations. Broad issues of confidentiality were sometimes difficult to navigate, even outside of the ordinary risks of gossip. The circles in the transnational indigenous rights movement are small, and it is often easy to identify interviewees by geographic location, date, or even by the interviewee's manner and style of speaking; however, many interviewees did not wish to be publicly identified.

---

[89] Smith, 2005, p. 87.
[90] Both Smith, 2002 and 2005, and Bishop, 2005, discuss this complex terrain of inside/outside positioning of indigenous researchers involved with indigenous subjects.

26

I have therefore sometimes been extremely vague in identifying the location and/or the date of an interview. Another issue of confidentiality is that people talk about other people and other communities and then wish to keep their comments confidential out of concern for being accused of speaking for another person or community.

Fourth, and related to the issues of confidentiality, is that the topics examined in this project are inherently highly political and often controversial and volatile. Many of these issues are deeply threatening to other actors, particularly to those invested in the dominant world order. In both Canada and New Zealand, outspoken indigenous activism has been met in recent years by police action and attempted repression, and so issues of confidentiality are extremely salient.

Finally, and most importantly, I have felt the heavy burden of meeting both indigenous and non-indigenous criteria for research[91] and performing to multiple levels of accountability: the academy, my home communities and the larger indigenous world.[92] On occasion, these criteria and accountabilities are in direct conflict. In order to adhere to the cultural standards of indigenous methodologies, I had to make some deviations from standard political science research practices. As mentioned earlier, I always presented a gift to interviewees. Also, in making contact with a new person, a potential interviewee, I would mention how I was connected to that person, disclosing the path of connections which brought me to them. Often, this is the only way to establish trust and credibility in indigenous contexts.

---

[91] L.T. Smith, 2002, speaks to this dilemma as well.
[92] Graham Hingangaroa Smith. 2000. "Protecting and Respecting Indigenous Knowledge." Pp. 209-224 in *Reclaiming Indigenous Voice and Vision*, Marie Battiste, ed. Vancouver: UBC Press, p. 213.

In sum, my research process has attempted to strike a balance between effective qualitative political science research and indigenous-driven, community-based research methods and procedures. While I make no particular claims about objectivity, I have tried to employ a multitude of methods in order to make my research as complete and informative as possible. My goal is to make simultaneous contributions to international relations theory, to the global political struggle for indigenous peoples' rights, and, ultimately, to indigenous communities.

Chapter 2

Towards a Theory of Indigenous Global Politics

For more than three decades, the indigenous rights movement has been engaged in a struggle on the international level for recognition of indigenous peoples' rights. Almost universally, indigenous peoples[1] have not demanded secession from states, but instead have asked states to recognize and secure indigenous rights. Again almost universally, indigenous peoples desire recognition of their rights to land and self-determination, rights which when protected together enhance the cultural integrity of indigenous peoples and thus their ability to survive as distinct peoples.

At the same time, the transnational indigenous rights movement also sees the Westphalian system of sovereign independent nation-states as a construct that privileges certain Euro-centric societies over other societies in the international sphere. The Westphalian system of independent, territorial sovereign states is the norm in international relations (IR) and is one of the central assumptions in all mainstream IR theories. The current international system emanates from the European state system conventionally associated with the Treaty of Westphalia that ended the Thirty Years War in Europe in 1648.[2] This international system traveled the globe by means of the

---

[1] The definition of indigenous peoples is an important issue and will be discussed in more detail later in this chapter. The UN Working definition of indigenous people relies on several components. Indigenous peoples are defined by the United Nations as meaning a group of people who were: 1) the first occupants of the land, 2) colonized, 3) subordinated by or incorporated into alien states in their original territory and, as a result, became marginal to or dominated by the state that claims jurisdiction over them, and 4) remain culturally distinct from the dominant society. Because some of these criteria can also apply to other national minorities which are not indigenous, both the UN and the ILO rely on self-definition as an essential element of indigeneity.

[2] This theory of state sovereignty pre-dates the actual Treaty of Westphalia; the significance of the 1648 treaty is more symbolic than substantive. See Andreas Osiander (2003) "Sovereignty, International

Doctrine of Discovery[3] which gave only European sovereign states the right to "discover" and colonize non-European territories and peoples. The Doctrine of Discovery is "the theory that guided colonial practice."[4] The underlying assumption in the Doctrine of Discovery is that "Europeans were higher ...in intelligence than the Indians, and also suggests that the Europeans, by virtue of a 'superior' intelligence, possessed a higher position of power in relation to the lands of the (American) continent and in relation to the indigenous peoples living there."[5] A similar doctrine held sway as Europeans colonized peoples worldwide after concentrating initially on the Americas.

Discovery and colonization under this theory of international law also meant property rights that European nations claimed for themselves. As Deloria wrote, "in practice, the theory meant that the discoverer of unoccupied lands in the rest of the world gained a right to the land titles as against the claims of other European nations."[6] Robert J. Miller also wrote about property and other rights that Europeans claimed for themselves under the Doctrine of Discovery,

---

Relations, and the Westphalian Myth," *International Organization* 55(2) for further discussion of the Doctrine of Discovery and its related Doctrine of Conquest.

[3] See Vine Deloria, *Behind the Trail of Broken Treaties: An Indian Declaration of Independence* (University of Texas Press, 1985), for further discussion of the Doctrine of Discovery and its related Doctrine of Conquest. Vine Deloria and David E. Wilkins, *Tribes, Treaties, and Constitutional Tribulations* (University of Texas Press, 1999), Steven T. Newcomb, *Pagans in the Promised Land: Decoding the Doctrine of Christian Discovery* (Fulcrum Publishing, 2008), David E. Wilkins and K. Tsianina Lomawaima, *Uneven Ground: American Indian Sovereignty and Federal Law* (University of Oklahoma Press, 2002), Robert A. Williams, "Like a Loaded Weapon: The Rehnquist Court, Indian Rights, and the Legal History of Racism in America," *Perspectives on Politics* 4, no. 03 (2006). Simply stated, the Doctrine of Discovery, which was likely the first international law, was based on medieval Papal Bulls which stated that European powers had the right to claim newly discovered territories as their own. Under the Doctrine of Discovery, only European powers held this right. Other peoples were not deemed civilized enough to exercise rights under the Doctrine of Discovery.
[4] Newcomb, *Pagans in the Promised Land: Decoding the Doctrine of Christian Discovery*, ix.
[5] *Ibid.*, 78.
[6] Deloria, *Behind the Trail of Broken Treaties: An Indian Declaration of Independence*, 86.

30

The Doctrine provided, under established international law, that newly arrived Europeans immediately and automatically acquired property rights in native lands and gained governmental, political, and commercial rights over the inhabitants without the knowledge nor the consent of the indigenous peoples.[7]

This right of discovery was even transferable to other nations, as long as they were European. "When colonial areas changed hands, it was believed that the successful nation acquiring the colony inherited the original claim under the doctrine of discovery of the nation they had defeated."[8] Miller also notes that the Doctrine of Discovery remains valid international law today and has been relied upon in a United States Supreme Court case as recently as 2005.[9] Furthermore, the seminal case which articulated the Doctrine of Discovery in the United States has also been cited at various times by courts in Canada, Australia and New Zealand.[10] In one of the most recent expressions of the theory, Russia sent a pair of submersibles two miles under the polar ice cap in August 2007, specifically to plant a Russian flag on the seabed at the North Pole. A New York Times writer noted that "the dive was a symbolic move to enhance the government's disputed claim to nearly half of the floor of the Arctic Ocean."[11] In other words, Russia was invoking the Doctrine of Discovery to claim property rights in the Arctic vis-à-vis other nations.

When the European powers retreated during decolonization, they left independent sovereign territorial states behind, often as settler states, which then became part of the

---

[7] Robert J. Miller, *Native America, Discovered and Conquered: Thomas Jefferson, Lewis & Clark, and Manifest Destiny* (Westport, CT: Praeger, 2006), 1.

[8] Deloria and Wilkins, *Tribes, Treaties, and Constitutional Tribulations*, 5.

[9] Miller, *Native America, Discovered and Conquered: Thomas Jefferson, Lewis & Clark, and Manifest Destiny*, 1. The case referred to is the *City of Sherrill v. Oneida Indian Nation of New York*, 544 U.S. 197 (2005).

[10] *Ibid.*, 1-2. The case referred to here is *Johnson v. McIntosh* 21 U.S. (8 Wheat.) 543 (1823).

[11] C.J. Chivers, "Russia Plants Underwater Flag at North Pole," *New York Times*, August 2 2007.

international system. As Bull argues, the modern system of states originated in Europe, expanded from Europe and then became universal.[12] The Westphalian international system thus continues to privilege Euro-centric conceptions of state and society over all other forms of society. The transnational indigenous rights movement seeks a reconfiguration of this norm toward a more pluralistic conception. In order to protect the culture, society and political organization of each distinct indigenous nation, the right of self-determination for indigenous nations must be secured at both the international and domestic levels. Under the dominant Westphalian system, nation-states are the only entities which may maintain external and internal sovereignty over their territories. The indigenous rights movement however, has asserted that indigenous rights protection, specifically land rights and self-determination, need not take place only through the Westphalian state system. Indigenous rights to land and self-determination can be secured through a set of standards which exist, either within states,[13] and/or outside of the bounds of Westphalian states. Securing indigenous rights to land and self-determination through a less state-centric and more multi-faceted view of sovereignty thus offers a new and particular challenge to the hegemonic, though increasingly pressured, Westphalian international system.[14]

The transnational indigenous rights movement's push for indigenous self-determination also challenges the global norm toward liberal conceptions of governance.

---

[12] Hedley Bull, "The Importance of Grotius in the Study of International Relations," in *Hugo Grotius and International Relations*, ed. H. Bull, B. Kingsbury, and A. Roberts (Oxford: Clarendon Press, 1992).

[13] This can be accomplished through mutually recognized and respected treaties or other agreements with indigenous nations.

[14] The Westphalian international system is increasingly under pressure from many societal changes and new sources of global governance including such developments as international human rights treaties, multinational corporations and globalization, international tribunals such as the International Criminal Court, and supranational organizations such as the European Community, to name a few.

While some of the demands of the indigenous rights movement revolve around non-discrimination, poverty and the disadvantages that indigenous individuals around the world experience when compared to other citizens of their host states,[15] the demand for self-determination and its correlate, land rights, pushes the bounds of the liberal state to its outer limits and normatively challenges its hegemony. First of all, indigenous demands for land rights and self-determination are group rights and not rights of the individual. From its beginnings in the post World War II period, the international human rights consensus had operated solely within a liberal framework, in which human rights adhere to individuals and not to groups.[16] Secondly, the concept of self-determination rests upon the liberal principle of consent of the governed, meaning that people have the right to determine their own form of government, and that a government established without the consent of the governed is illegitimate.[17] If indigenous nations are to have the right of self-determination, then no form of government, be it liberal democratic or otherwise, should be imposed upon them. When the liberal concept of consent of the governed is adhered to, indigenous nations may or may not choose liberal democratic forms of government. True self-determination requires that they must be free to choose their own government, even if that government departs from liberal democratic principles

---

[15] For example, seventeen of the forty-five articles of the Declaration revolve around discrimination and the disparities between indigenous peoples and other citizens.

[16] See Jack Donnelly, *Universal Human Rights in Theory and Practice* (Cornell University Press, 2003), Paul Gordon Lauren, *The Evolution of International Human Rights: Visions Seen* (University of Pennsylvania Press, 2003), for a description and justification for the exclusion of group rights and the reliance on individual rights in human rights law and discourse.. Until the passage of the Declaration on the Rights of Indigenous Peoples by the UN General Assembly in 2007, the only group right which formed part of the international consensus was self-determination (i.e. decolonization). Note that the international consensus on self-determination deliberately excluded indigenous peoples from the right of self-determination in the 1950s with the passage of the "blue water" or "saltwater" thesis which stated that only overseas colonies qualified for decolonization and self-determination.

[17] This assertion is based on the social contract theory of Hobbes and Rousseau.

as would be the case in many traditional forms of indigenous governance. Therefore, the transnational indigenous rights movement leaves liberal states in a quandary. In order for liberal states, which are committed to the equal rights of each of their individual citizens, to fully practice the liberal principle of self-determination by consent of the governed, they must allow for the possibility of an autonomous, illiberally governed territory within their state. Therefore, the indigenous rights movement is also pushing for a fundamental change in the liberal state towards a more pluralistic vision of state and society.

The field of international relations (IR) has been largely blind to these transformational moves by the transnational indigenous rights movement. There is a nascent IR literature pertaining to transnational indigenous politics, but so far it does not have a name or a recognized place within the discipline. Those who have written about indigenous nations in IR have classified themselves as either "critical constructivists,"[18] "world society theorists,"[19] "international society" theorists based in the English School tradition,[20] or "post-structuralists,"[21] while the indigenous voice in global politics has also been cast at times as part of social movement theory.[22] Is there something unique about transnational indigenous politics, including the international indigenous rights movement and the Declaration on the Rights of Indigenous Peoples, that resists classification into the existing intellectual framework of international relations? In this chapter, I will

---

[18] Allison Brysk, *From Tribal Village to Global Village: Indian Rights and International Relations in Latin America* (Stanford: Stanford University Press, 2000).

[19] Franke Wilmer, *The Indigenous Voice in World Politics* (Thousand Oaks, CA: Sage, 1993).

[20] Paul Keal, *Conquest and the Rights of Indigenous Peoples* (Cambridge: Cambridge University Press, 2003).

[21] Sean Patrick Eudaily, *The Present Politics of the Past: Indigenous Legal Activism and Resistance to (Neo) Liberal Governmentality* (Routledge, 2004).

[22] Erick D. Langer and Elena Muñoz, eds. *Contemporary Indigenous Movements in Latin America* (Wilmington, DE: SR Books, 2003.)

demonstrate how transnational indigenous politics could represent a new perspective of IR, akin to critical theory and post-colonial IR, but when taken together is sufficiently different from other perspectives. Most important to its theoretical distinctiveness is that the transnational indigenous rights movement is an *explanatory* and *normative* project which places pressure on two hegemonic ideas within the discipline of IR: the Westphalian system of sovereign nation-states and the liberal world order, foundational to principles of governance, rights, and property ownership.

This chapter will first explore the existing IR literature to demonstrate the distinctiveness of the transnational indigenous rights movement. After demonstrating the limitations of existing IR theory to account for the features and limitations of the transnational indigenous rights movement and the Declaration on the Rights of Indigenous Peoples, I will propose a new concept, which I am terming indigenous global politics. In the second part of the chapter, I will begin to build a theory of how indigenous politics at the global level compels a new direction of thought in international relations by challenging some of its fundamental tenets. I will sketch out the parameters of indigenous global politics as a perspective of IR that, through the pursuit of land, self-determination and other collective rights, complicates the structure of international politics in new and important ways, challenging dominant notions of state sovereignty and liberalism in both the international system and the international human rights consensus.

Indigenous Global Politics in International Relations Theory

The existing literature on transnational indigenous politics within the discipline of IR focuses on the transnational movement of indigenous peoples. This movement, which is centered on the concept of a globally shared indigenous identity,[23] seeks to secure both internationally and domestically the right of individual indigenous nations to exist as self-determining sovereigns within the boundaries, or across the boundaries, of existing nation states.[24] Within the current international system, political self-governance and self-determination require territorial integrity, and so this movement also necessarily seeks to secure land rights for indigenous nations. The transnational indigenous rights movement differs from other minority group movements in that it does not seek secession from states and does not necessarily or only seek equality for individuals or groups within states. The transnational indigenous rights movement and the IR perspective of indigenous global politics which I am proposing both hinge on a globally shared indigenous identity which emanates from a shared experience: indigenous peoples' localized spiritual attachment to and responsibility toward their lands. The movement wishes to preserve distinctive cultures and political organizations through the recognition of indigenous nations—nations which exist outside of the current Westphalian

---

[23] Ronald Neizen, *The Origins of Indigenism: Human Rights and the Politics of Identity* (Berkeley: University of California Press, 2003).It should be noted that this global indigenous identity is a supranational layer of indigenous identity which has been added to the already complex web of kinship, tribal and national identities that indigenous people maintain. It is important to note that this indigenous identity, while global in scope, is not intended as a universalizing forces but rather, it aims to collectively secure the distinctiveness and singularity of individual indigenous nations, cultures and communities on a more local level.

[24] There is a sizable literature pertaining to indigenous peoples global struggle for self-determination within the international human rights system. Some prominent examples are S. James Anaya, *Indigenous Peoples in International Law*, Second ed. (New York: Oxford University Press, 2004), Cynthia Price-Cohen, "Human Rights of Indigenous Peoples," (Transnational Publishers, Incorporated, 1998), Patrick Thornberry, *Indigenous Peoples and Human Rights* (Manchester: Juris Publishing, 2002).

international state system. Indigenous nations are not states and generally do not aspire to become independent states, but rather, they exist either within a state or across state boundaries but are or wish to be territorially distinct and, often, politically autonomous.

The transnational indigenous rights movement has achieved certain notable successes in the international sphere and suffered from a particular set of limitations. The existing literature and theories of IR can either account for the successes of this movement or it can explain its limitations, but there is no single IR perspective which can simultaneously account for both the successes and limitations present in transnational indigenous politics.

Successes of the Transnational Indigenous Rights Movement

The transnational indigenous rights movement, which developed as a worldwide response to five centuries of colonization and exploitation, first emerged as an issue of global governance during the 1960s and 1970s and has achieved some notable successes over the years, particularly achieving passage of the Declaration on the Rights of Indigenous Peoples, establishing the United Nations Permanent Forum on Indigenous Peoples and successfully altering the behavior of several important states. In a broader sense, the transnational indigenous rights movement has helped to constitute "indigenous peoples" as subjects of global politics and has also been a contributor to an emerging conceptualization of sovereignty which is non-statist in character. It also forged an important shift in the international human rights consensus which now includes collective rights for indigenous peoples.

The Declaration on the Rights of Indigenous Peoples was intended to establish minimal international standards for the recognition and protection of the rights of indigenous people. The fact that these numerous indigenous groups, which represent indigenous peoples with widely divergent interests, situations and histories from across the globe, could reach consensus on a single document, the Draft Declaration, is a remarkable achievement in the realm of international politics. Then, the fact that the document was passed by an overwhelming majority of states in the General Assembly, when states themselves have been the targets of the movement for almost three decades, is also nothing short of remarkable.

Another significant achievement of the transnational indigenous rights movement, an achievement which was fundamental and verging on revolutionary in the international system, was the recognition of indigenous rights to land. This was notable for two reasons. First, when indigenous people seek land rights, they often mean collective rights to the land.[25] While certain states had previously had provisions for collective indigenous land ownership, indigenous peoples had never enjoyed broad recognition of collective land rights and ownership internationally. Second, indigenous peoples' self-determination was specifically excluded from the decolonization regime by the 1950s "saltwater" or "blue water" thesis, which had asserted that only overseas territories were

---

[25] This is necessitated by indigenous conceptions of land ownership and title which are distinct from dominant liberal conceptions. While the liberal model of land ownership means that an individual has a property right to buy, sell and control land as a commodity, indigenous conceptions of land have a cultural and spiritual character. They invoke a mutual responsibility and relationship between the land and the people. Indigenous conceptions, therefore, require collective land rights in order to secure the survival of indigenous peoples' culture, spiritual life and identity.

38

eligible for decolonization and self-determination.[26] Yet, even though indigenous rights

to self-determination and land had been deliberately excluded from international regimes,

the transnational indigenous rights movement asserted these rights at the international

level for decades and finally witnessed their international recognition with the passage of

the Declaration in 2007. The inclusion of indigenous self-determination as an

internationally recognized right, along with collective land rights, represents an important

shift in the international system which is now expected to accommodate indigenous

demands for plural sovereignty arrangements within states.

Another remarkable success of the transnational indigenous rights movement was

its ability to pull and hold together a strong caucus at the United Nations. There are more

than 300 million indigenous people, living in about 5000 distinct groups spread over six

continents,[27] representing an incredible diversity of languages, culture, historical

experiences, contemporary situations and goals. Yet, even with this incredible diversity

of backgrounds and aspirations, the indigenous rights movement was able to maintain a

fairly unified movement at the United Nations for the better part of thirty years. Even

considering the disagreements which occurred regularly within the Indigenous Caucus

over the years, it does not detract from the fact that holding together such a diverse

caucus for most of three decades is a highly unusual feat in international politics.

Another notable achievement by the transnational indigenous rights movement

was the establishment of the Permanent Forum on Indigenous Issues, an advisory body to

the United Nations Economic and Social Council. The Permanent Forum was proposed

---

[26] Thornberry, *Indigenous Peoples and Human Rights*, 874-75.
[27] Data from the International Work Group on Indigenous Affairs (IWGIA), a Copenhagen-based NGO.

by indigenous groups during the 1993 World Conference on Human Rights which recommended that such a forum could provide an avenue for effective indigenous participation within the state-centric United Nations organization. The first meeting of the Permanent Forum took place in 2002 and yearly sessions take place in New York each May.[28] With the establishment of such a permanent institution for indigenous peoples at the United Nations, the transnational indigenous rights movement could claim success in helping to constitute indigenous peoples as subjects, rather than objects, of international relations.

Regarding nation-state behavior and indigenous rights, the results of the indigenous rights movement are mixed. Strangely enough, certain states (Australia, New Zealand and Canada)—states which vehemently opposed the Draft Declaration and were, along with the United States, the only states to vote against the Declaration on the floor of the General Assembly—enacted, during this same period, some reforms to recognize indigenous peoples' rights to land and self-determination. Meanwhile, other states have enacted limited constitutional reforms (Colombia, Venezuela, Ecuador, Bolivia) while others (United States, most Latin American states) have remained fiercely resistant to such domestic reform of their relationship with indigenous peoples. The "over-compliant"[29] behavior of Australia, New Zealand and Canada regarding indigenous rights

---

[28] See www.un.org/esa/socdev/unpfii/en for more information on the U.N. Permanent Forum.

[29] I will take up the issue and concept of "over-compliance" in greater detail in Chapter 4. For now, I will define an "over-compliant" state as one that paradoxically takes constitutional, legal and/or policy actions which recognize certain rights or a category of right that go beyond that state's international human rights treaty obligations or its normative international commitments. Australia, New Zealand and Canada are "over-compliant" in indigenous rights because they have each made reforms to their relationships with their indigenous peoples, effectively recognizing some collective land and/or self-determination rights of indigenous peoples. They made these changes all the while either a) declaring that they are complying with human rights standards that did not even exist under the conception of human rights as adhering to the

40

can be attributed at least in part to the participation of domestic indigenous movements in international politics, a finding which will be explored in greater detail in Chapters 4, 5 and 6.

Limitations of the Transnational Indigenous Rights Movement

While there have been notable victories for indigenous rights during the past several decades, the indigenous rights movement has also suffered from a unique set of limitations. First of all, the Declaration experienced a long and arduous road from its inception to adoption on the floor of the UN General Assembly in September 2007. The Draft Declaration, which had been completed by the UN Working Group on Indigenous Peoples in 1994, and was sent to the UNCHR[30] Intercessional Working Group, where it spent many years in discussion without significant progress. In a huge defeat to the transnational indigenous peoples' movement, the International Decade of Indigenous Peoples ended in December 2004 without adoption of the Draft Declaration, leaving the basic rights of the world's 300 million indigenous people officially unspecified at the international level. During the Second International Decade on Indigenous Peoples, which began in January 2005, the Draft Declaration successfully passed the UNCHR and was presented on the floor of the General Assembly where it underwent several important changes to the text, most of which were inserted to enhance protections for state sovereignty. Even with those protections for state sovereignty and territoriality, four

---

individual, or b) that these states were not obligated to adhere to because they had not ratified any treaty that requires it, or c) that these states had no normative obligation to adhere to, in their eyes, because they publicly opposed the Declaration as an international normative standard of indigenous peoples.

[30] UNCHR stands for the United Nations Commission on Human Rights. The Draft Declaration needed to pass through this body before it could advance to the General Assembly.

states felt that the document still went too far in these areas, and they voted against the Declaration. Despite 143 states voting in support of the Declaration, these four reticent states continued to assert that they would not be subject to the principles put forth in the document. So, the Declaration's path from inception to adoption was long, arduous and ultimately tempered by states' demands for protection from indigenous rights demands.

Secondly, the transnational indigenous rights movement sought fundamental international change in the areas of collective rights and the nature of state sovereignty, yet the indigenous rights movement went to the UN as NGOs, not as nations or as states, and thus had limited influence at the United Nations. Because the UN Charter established the UN strictly as an organization of member states, indigenous nations, even those with treaties, could only participate at the UN as NGOs, side by side with and holding equal status as *bone fide* indigenous and non-indigenous NGOs. Thus, they also had limited influence and power within the UN system, and could often be excluded from participation in certain Working Groups and committees due to their non-state status. Furthermore, the movement spent thirty years seeking a non-binding and unenforceable document as an articulation of indigenous rights. As a non-binding document, the Declaration on the Rights of Indigenous Peoples is strictly a political and moral tool which then needs to be implemented on a state-by-state basis.[31] So, even though the indigenous rights movement sought huge changes in the international system, their methods and strategies remained constrained by the structures of that system.

---

[31] A discussion on April 29, 2008 at the United Nations Permanent Forum on Indigenous Issues focused on the implementation of the Declaration on the Rights of Indigenous Peoples on a country-by-country basis. A statement made by outgoing Special Rapporteur on the Situation of Human Rights and Fundamental Freedoms of Indigenous Peoples, Rodolfo Stavenhagen, on that day highlighted the imperative of such a pattern of implementation. From author's notes.

Finally, the "over-compliant" states of Australia, New Zealand and Canada, while having made sometimes substantial reforms to their relationships with indigenous peoples and nations, remain far from global champions of indigenous rights. The land and self-determination provisions called for in the Declaration continue to be a stumbling block for these states which do not wish there to be any such international standard for indigenous land or self-determination rights. As stated earlier, all four of these states have publicly asserted that since they voted against the Declaration they are not bound by it, a position which flies in the face of standard UN practice on declarations which is that, once passed, UN declarations apply to all states regardless of an individual state's voting status. Furthermore, the actual behavior of these states concerning the full spectrum of indigenous rights is far from fully respectful of the rights to land and self-determination. The Canadian province of British Columbia has reluctantly and unenthusiastically participated in a treaty negotiation process. The government of Australia has paid occasional lip service to the idea of a treaty with the Aborigines, but has made no real progress toward that end. In New Zealand, Maori protests continue over unsettled land claims in the Waitangi Tribunal, and the Auckland Transit Authority refuses year after year to fly the Maori sovereignty (*Tino Rangatiratanga*) flag on the Auckland Harbour Bridge on Waitangi Day, even though it flies hundreds of flags of other nations and aspiring national groups on their respective national holidays.

So, the transnational indigenous rights movement went to the UN, as a set of NGOs in a strong Indigenous Caucus, which for three decades, sought a non-binding and unenforceable indigenous rights Declaration as well as a Permanent Forum for

Indigenous Issues within the UN system. The Declaration, which was supported by 143 states and opposed by four, represented a major challenge to the international status quo, complicating existing conceptualizations of sovereignty and territoriality. It also represented an important shift in indigenous subjectivity in international politics as well as an expansion of the international human rights consensus into the area of collective rights for indigenous peoples thereby challenging the liberal foundations of the existing human rights consensus. At the same time, the road to this non-binding document was long, arduous and, in the end, limited by states which felt the need to protect their sovereignty and territorial integrity; much state policy and behavior remains notably ambivalent to indigenous rights. Can any existing theory of IR adequately explain this full set of paradoxes?

IR Theory and the Transnational Indigenous Rights Movement

Realism is often seen as the foundational paradigm of IR theory in that all other IR perspectives seem to answer to it or look for its failings in order to put forward alternative explanations for international behavior. The realist approach to IR theory[32] assumes that sovereign nation-states are the core unit of analysis,[33] that all states,

---

[32] The Realist School of IR Theory includes such prominent works as Edward H. Carr, "The Twenty Years' Crisis: An Introduction to the Study of International Relations," (London: Macmillan, 1946), Hans J. Morgenthau, *Politics among Nations*, ed. Kenneth J. Thompson (New York: Knopf, 1948; reprint, 6th). Kenneth N. Waltz, *Man, the State, and War: A Theoretical Analysis* (New York: Columbia University Press, 1959), R. Jervis, "Cooperation under the Security Dilemma," *World Politics* (1978), John J. Mearsheimer, *The Tragedy of Great Power Politics* (New York: WW Norton & Company, 2003).
[33] Morgenthau, *Politics among Nations*, Kenneth N. Waltz, *Theory of International Politics* (London: Addison-Wesley, 1979).

regardless of their type of government, will behave similarly across time and space,[34] acting in their own interests, with their primary normative concern being power and security[35] in a world characterized by anarchy, meaning the lack of a central authority in international politics.[36] The imperatives for states under the realist paradigm are self-preservation and increasing their national power.[37]

Realist theory, in its various forms, can therefore explain state resistance to indigenous rights which would be perceived as threatening a state's territorial integrity (and its power resources) since an indigenous peoples' demand for self-determination would naturally be interpreted by a state as a push for territorial secession. Realism could also account for the reluctance of the transnational indigenous rights movement to push for independence from existing states since the military and economic power imbalance between states and indigenous groups is massive and indigenous peoples recognize this reality.[38] The decision by the indigenous rights movement to work through existing international institutions and regimes, even though they subjugated and excluded indigenous peoples and indigenous rights, could be explained by a realist as a recognition by the indigenous rights movement of global power politics and the marginalization of indigenous groups within it. What realism fails to explain are the successes of indigenous global politics. How did a group of numerous indigenous nations with vastly different interests and histories come to a consensus on global indigenous rights? How

---

[34]Robert Gilpin, *War and Change in World Politics* (Cambridge: Cambridge University Press, 1983), Waltz, *Theory of International Politics*.

[35] Morgenthau, *Politics among Nations*.

[36] Waltz, *Man, the State, and War: A Theoretical Analysis*.

[37] Morgenthau, *Politics among Nations*.

[38] See Waltz, *Theory of International Politics*, for an explanation of a realist structural theory of international politics which focuses on capabilities and power.

did this consensus hold together over a difficult thirty-year struggle? Why did the United Nations agree to a Permanent Forum on Indigenous Issues, if such a Forum represents a departure from the interests of powerful states? Also, how do emerging international norms of indigenous rights begin to alter certain states' behavior, even when they resist it? Realism fails to account for any of these important aspects of transnational indigenous politics. Realism's ontology of sovereign nation-states and preeminent concern with violent conflict means that the successes of transnational indigenous politics are outside of its realm of concerns.

Liberal theory in IR encompasses both explanatory and normative theorizing. Normative liberal theorizing in IR is concerned with the spread of democracy and international institutions that will strengthen peace around the world. Normative liberalism in IR also advocates individual freedom and the spread of human rights and free trade in particular as the rational means to increase happiness and prosperity.[39]

Explanatory liberal approaches to IR take individuals and interest groups to be the primary actors in international relations.[40] States represent a subset of those actors—that is, the state is pluralist rather than unitary, serving as an area for repeated competition between interest groups. Interests groups determine state preferences, which, unlike realists, can include goals besides security. Drawing on the work of philosopher

---

[39] Christian Reus-Smit, "The Strange Death of Liberal International Theory," *European Journal of International Law* (2001) 12:3, 573-593. Michael W. Doyle, *Ways of War and Peace: Realism, Liberalism and Socialism* (New York: W. W. Norton and Co. 1997)

[40] A. Moravcsik, "Taking Preferences Seriously: A Liberal Theory of International Politics," *International Organization* 51, no. 4 (1997), Michael W. Doyle, *Ways of War and Peace: Realism, Liberalism and Socialism* (New York: W.W. Norton, 1997), John M. Owen, "How Liberalism Produces Democratic Peace," *International Security* (1994).

Immanuel Kant, liberals have paid particular attention to the potential for pacific relations among liberal republics, known as the Democratic Peace.[41] For liberals, humanity is perfectible: through the use of reason, freely expressed, states can realize their common goals of peace and prosperity and need not be condemned to the perpetual threat of war.

Explanatory liberalism can account for some of the successes of the transnational indigenous rights movement, especially the high level of consensus in the Indigenous Caucus and the success of achieving an international minimum standard on indigenous rights by working through international institutions. Liberal IR expects that harmonization and/or coordination are possible among groups with common interests. Liberal IR also predicts that outcomes in international politics occur through bargaining and the configuration of preferences across the international system, so it views the passage of the Declaration after thirty years of effort to be simply the eventual outcome of tenacious bargaining between indigenous groups and states which eventually altered the preferences of the majority of UN member states to favor the indigenous rights Declaration.

What liberal IR cannot adequately explain is the puzzling "over-compliant" yet underachieving pattern of indigenous rights behavior by certain states because if the states are already following the standards, then by liberal IR logic they should not resist codification of those standards at the international level. Liberalism holds that state preferences are a function of societal interests, and state behavior is dependent upon the

---

[41] Michael W. Doyle, "Liberalism and World Politics," *The American Political Science Review* (1986).

distribution of state interests internationally.[42] This framework fails to account for the refusal of the three over-compliant states to vote for the indigenous rights Declaration, while over-complying with the language of the Declaration in some of their national laws and policies. From the perspective of explanatory liberal IR theorizing, this would suggest that there were costs internationally for voting in favor of the Declaration that were not borne domestically—which is not the case. The indigenous rights declaration is a non-binding declaration which is not enforceable at the international level. This framework also fails to explain the activism of indigenous groups at the international level, rather than state level, since under liberal IR logic, indigenous groups would seek to alter their host state's preferences through interest group politics.

The normative concerns of liberal IR are also challenged by the indigenous rights movement. While normative liberal theorizing holds that international peace can be obtained not only through an increased reliance on international institutions which help focus expectations in international politics[43] but also through the spread of democracy, especially liberal democracy. A core liberal belief is that governments are only legitimate if they express the will of the people. However, adherence to the principle of self-determination for indigenous peoples means that indigenous nations may choose a liberal democratic form of government or they may choose a form of self-government which is traditional, and thus illiberal, and possibly non-democratic as viewed from a

---

[42] Andrew Moravcsik, "Taking Preferences Seriously: A Liberal Theory of International Politics," *International Organization*, Vol 51, No. 4 (Autumn 1997), pp. 513-554.

[43] Stephen D. Krasner, *International Regimes* (Ithaca: Cornell University Press, 1983), Robert O. Keohane and Lisa Martin, "The Promise of Institutionalist Theory," *International Security* Vol. 20. no 1. (Summer 1995), pp. 39-51.

Western liberal perspective. Liberal IR theory has no available framework to deal with this potentiality. There is thus a tension within liberalism between two of its constitutive principles, self-determination and liberal democracy. On its own, liberalism cannot resolve that tension with regard to indigenous peoples.

There is a small literature on transnational indigenous politics which falls primarily into the liberal IR framework.[44] This group of scholars all write from the perspective of belief in the progress of humanity and the international system, especially through changes in international law and institutions which move to accommodate indigenous peoples. Anaya writes that "international law developed to facilitate empire building and colonization, but today it promotes a very different model of human encounter and provides grounds for remedying the contemporary manifestations of the oppressive past."[45] Cohen, Thornberry and Rodriguez-Piñero all agree with Anaya that progress in international human rights law in particular has helped the situation of the world's indigenous peoples and that further enhancements in international law vis-à-vis indigenous rights are both possible and desirable. At the same time, however, both Anaya and Thornberry also recognize the incompatibility of the liberal rights framework with indigenous self-determination. Thornberry notes that liberal democracy, focused on the rights of the individual, creates "apparent limits to the kind of social practices embraced"[46] since the "individual rights 'grid' or syntax of human rights makes difficult

---

[44] S. James Anaya, *Indigenous Peoples and International Law, Second Edition* (New York: Oxford University Press, 2004), Cynthia Price Cohen, *Human Rights of Indigenous Peoples* (Ardsley, NY: Transnational Publishers, 1998), Luis Rodriguez-Piñero, *Indigenous Peoples, Postcolonialism, and International Law* (Oxford: Oxford University Press), Patrick Thornberry, *Indigenous Peoples and Human Rights* (Manchester: Juris Publishing, 2002).
[45] Anaya, 2004, p. 289.
[46] Thornberry, 2002, p. 428.

49

the case for the collective."[47] Anaya adds that a particular challenge of working through the human rights system is to get players within that system to recognize that "self-determination for indigenous peoples--including the enjoyment of nondiscrimination, cultural integrity, land rights, social welfare and development, and self-government--is context-specific, given the vast diversity of circumstances of indigenous peoples."[48]

Constructivism in IR[49] concerns itself primarily with the role of ideas in shaping the international system. Constructivists see social reality as a social construction--that is, the meanings associated with the material world are socially constructed and not objective, and therefore they can change temporally or situationally through meaningful human practice. In constructivist IR, social groups at all levels of analysis (families, ethnic groups, churches, interest groups, NGOs, states and communities of states) are the central actors in international politics. Because the world is complex and behavior is thus also complex, agents categorize objects, giving them labels or identities and then ascribing specific meanings to them. Agents also categorize behavior as "legitimate or illegitimate," "desirable or undesirable," etc. International rules and norms are thus a continually dynamic process. As Wendt argued, even one of the central features of realist IR is socially constructed, because "anarchy is what states make of it."[50]

---

[47] *Ibid.*

[48] Anaya, 2004, p. 187.

[49] Numerous IR theorists utilize a constructivist framework, including Alexander Wendt, *Social Theory of International Politics* (Cambridge: Cambridge University Press, 1999), Martha Finnemore and Kathryn Sikkink, "Taking Stock: The Constructivist Research Program in International Relations and Comparative Politics," *Annual Review of Political Science* 4, no. 1 (2001), Michael. N. Barnett and Martha Finnemore, *Rules for the World: International Organizations in Global Politics* (Cornell University Press, 2004).
[50] A. Wendt, "Anarchy Is What States Make of It: The Social Construction of Power Politics," *International Organization* (1992).

Constructivist ontology is capable of explaining the shared global indigenous identity that has emerged with the indigenous rights movement[51] as well as the movement of diverse indigenous nations that successfully reached a normative consensus on indigenous rights at the international level outside the purview of nation-states.[52] Constructivism can explain the contested process of "meaning-making" in the creation of new norms of indigenous rights. It can also effectively theorize about the identity politics that the indigenous rights movement has brought about on the global level.[53] The explanatory difficulty with constructivism is the frequent assumption of a certain degree of normative and logical convergence in international politics rather than accounting for the continuation and (re)production of multiple logics, and enduring unresolved contestations. The more problematic aspect of constructivist approaches occur at the normative level. What constructivist IR does not sufficiently theorize is the indigenous movement's underlying resistance to the existing international system in which it takes part and the fundamental changes which would be necessary in the international system in order to fully accommodate indigenous peoples' rights. For example, while the transnational indigenous rights movement does behave in many respects like the transnational advocacy networks described in the work of Keck and Sikkink,[54] I contend that since this is a movement of indigenous nations and centers around a global identity of indigenousness, seeking fundamental international change, the indigenous rights

---

[51]Neizen, *The Origins of Indigenism: Human Rights and the Politics of Identity*..

[52] Allison Brysk, *From Tribal Village to Global Village: Indian Rights and International Relations in Latin America* (Stanford: Stanford University Press, 2000.)

[53] Deborah J. Yashar, *Contesting Citizenship in Latin America: The Rise of indigenous Movements and the Postliberal Challenge* (Cambridge: Cambridge University Press, 2005).

[54] Keck and Sikkink, *Activists Beyond Borders*.

movement extends the Keck and Sikkink argument into territory which makes it distinct from the transnational advocacy networks of NGOs and individuals described therein.

The 'society of states' approach, also called the English School tradition, with its roots in the work of Wight and Bull,[55] argues that there is an international society of states because states behave as if there is such a society of states. This approach focuses on the shared norms, social institutions, and values of states operating within the international society, and their historical development. States exist in anarchy, but there are relatively few wars because of this international society.[56] Wight describes the English School as a tradition of rationalism which serves as a 'via media' between the two extremes of the violence of realism and the utopian vision of various idealist theories of IR.[57] Broadly speaking, members of the English School hold that violence is always a possibility, but customs, laws, morality, and other social features of international society structure the world so that a high degree of order exists, despite the existence of anarchy.

In discussing the explanatory and normative shortcomings of the international society approach, I want to draw explicitly on the work of Paul Keal, one of the few IR scholars to devote a book-length treatment to indigenous rights and international relations and the only IR scholar to approach transnational indigenous politics from the English School perspective. Recognizing the history of dispossession and genocide brought about

---

[55] Martin Wight, "Western Values in International Relations," in *Diplomatic Investigations: Essays in the Theory of International Politics*, ed. H. Butterfield and M. Wight (London: Allen & Unwin, 1966), Hedley Bull, "The Grotian Conception of International Society," in *Diplomatic Investigations: Essays in the Theory of International Politics*, ed. H. Butterfield and M. Wight (London: Allen & Unwin, 1966).
[56] Hedley Bull, The Anarchical Society A Study of Order in World Politics (New York: Columbia University Press, 1977).

[57] Martin Wight, *International Theory: The Three Traditions*. Eds. G. Wight and B. Porter. (Leicester: Holmes and Meier Publishers, 1991).

by the European Doctrine of Discovery, Keal questions the very foundations of both the international society and settler states.[58] He argues "that the moral legitimacy of states with unresolved indigenous claims, like those that abuse human rights, is in question, and it follows from this that the legitimacy of international society as a defender of such states is also questionable."[59] In order for the society of states to gain moral legitimacy, Keal maintains that two actions are required. First, indigenous peoples should be recognized as peoples with the right of self-determination. Second, the recognition of indigenous peoples' self-determination must be accompanied by the sharing of political and territorial space within states.[60] He thus advocates for an uncoupling of the concept of self-determination from the state.[61] In addition, Keal provides a route for international society to redeem itself from its history of dispossession. He writes,

> This would be decisively reversed by the recognition of indigenous peoples as 'peoples' with the right of self-determination. The adoption of indigenous rights, including self-determination, would provide a set of standards supporting indigenous peoples in their claims against dominant peoples, redress the role of international society in their dispossession, and contribute to world order.[62]

Much of Keal's normative theory is consistent with the transnational indigenous rights movement. Keal recognizes the ugly history of colonialism that still infects the international system of states as well as the foundational (il-)legitimacy of settler states. Like the indigenous rights movement, Keal sees that international standards must change in order to accommodate indigenous rights within the international society of states.

---

[58] Paul Keal, *Conquest and the Rights of Indigenous Peoples* (Cambridge: Cambridge University Press, 2003).
[59] *Ibid.*, 2.
[60] *Ibid.*, 217-218.
[61] *Ibid.*, 219.
[62] *Ibid.* 223.

Keal's international society approach, however, suffers from a strong explanatory weakness in terms of indigenous rights. Like liberalism, the international society approach fails to explain why several states (Canada, New Zealand and Australia) which typically find themselves at the center of the international society of states on all other human rights issues operate as rogue states where indigenous peoples' rights are concerned.

There is another feature of Keal's international society approach which is neither explanatory nor normative yet still deserves mention. While Keal claims to support indigenous rights, including the rights of land and self-determination, he does so from a strictly state-centric perspective, discounting and/or dismissing any indigenous perspectives or agency in the process. His focus lies strictly on what actions states and the society of states must take to reconcile their moral illegitimacy. In that fundamental respect, Keal defends Westphalian sovereignty and the existing liberal world order in his analysis.

Post-structuralists and other critical theorists,[63] on the other hand, are more normatively compatible with the discourses of resistance that are ever-present in

---

[63] This admittedly broad category includes post-modernism, Marxism and other marxian approaches, post-colonialism, post-structuralism and feminist IR, all the while recognizing that there are substantial differences between these various approaches to IR. Such writers include Ashley, "The Poverty of Neorealism." in Robert Keohane, ed. *Neorealism and Its Critics* (New York: Columbia University Press, 1986), Steve Smith, "Positivism and Beyond," in *International Theory: Positivism and Beyond*, ed. Steve Smith, Ken Booth, and Marysia Zalewski (Cambridge: Cambridge University Press, 1996). James Der Derian and Michael J. Shapiro, *International-Intertextual Relations: Postmodern Readings of World Politics* (Lexington Books, 1989), Robert W. Cox, "Gramsci, Hegemony and International Relations: An Essay in Method," *Millennium: Journal of International Studies* 12, no. 2 (1983), J. Ann Tickner, *Gendering World Politics* (New York: Columbia University Press, 2001). Roxanne L. Doty, *Imperial Encounters* (Minneapolis: University of Minnesota Press 1996), Franz Fanon, *The Wretched of the Earth*, trans. Constance Farrington, vol. 39 (New York: Grove Press, 1963). Gayratri Chakravorty Spivak, *A Critique of Postcolonial Reason: Toward a History of the Vanishing Present* (Cambridge: Harvard University Press, 1999).

transnational indigenous politics, discourses that challenge the legacies of colonialism, racism, sexism, etc. still present in the international order. Like these myriad critical approaches to IR, the indigenous rights movement asserts that it deserves to have a voice in global politics even though indigenous nations are marginal to the existing international system.[64] Also, like these critical approaches to IR, the transnational indigenous rights movement challenges the power of international hierarchy and colonial discourses in the international system,[65] which are ignored by most mainstream theories of IR.

While highly normatively compatible, these critical theories, fail to explain why the transnational indigenous rights movement deliberately recognizes the existing power politics of the international system and also chooses to work strategically within the system, rather than seek to overturn the system. Given the opposition of indigenous groups to the political structure of the nation-state as it has developed and spread through colonialism through the world, it would seem paradoxical for indigenous groups to want to work within the state system and the United Nations to further their own goals, as it would seem impossible to challenge the founding rules of the system from the inside.

In sum, no existing perspective of international relations can adequately explain transnational indigenous politics while simultaneously maintaining normative compatibility with its objectives. While realism and liberalism explain either the limitations or the successes of transnational indigenous politics, neither perspective can adequately explain the other side of the coin. Alternative perspectives of IR can also

---

[64] Wilmer, *The Indigenous Voice in World Politics* (Thousand Oaks, CA: Sage, 1993).
[65] Taiaiake Alfred, *Peace, Power, Righteousness: An Indigenous Manifesto* (Oxford: Oxford University Press, 1999).

offer only partial explanations for transnational indigenous politics, and only critical perspectives find themselves normatively compatible with the objectives of transnational indigenous politics.

A Theory of Indigenous Global Politics

Since no standing IR paradigm or theory can adequately explain the paradoxes of indigenous political activity at the global level, I propose a new concept, which I call indigenous global politics. I argue that indigenous global politics should comprise a research program in IR that not only theorizes the full spectrum of indigenous politics on the global level but that also necessarily integrates indigenous agency and considers the potential impact of indigenous global politics on international relations both in theory and in practice. Indigenous global politics shares many elements with other research programs in IR, but it combines these elements in a distinctive way and for a unique normative purpose. It also exerts a particular transformational force upon international relations which deserves closer analysis.

Indigenous global politics bridges the gap between explanatory and normative theorizing in International Relations by moving away from a sole focus on indigenous practices in IR to also include an indigenous way of theorizing global politics. Indigenous global politics largely focuses on the global movement of indigenous nations and organizations represents itself on an international level outside of the purview of states and seeks a degree of sovereignty (or autonomy) either within or across the borders of nation-states. To do this, not only do indigenous activists participate in numerous ways

56

in global politics, but in doing so, indigenous activists and scholars have articulated a vision of global politics that challenges the structure of the international system. Practitioners of indigenous global politics use tactics and strategies on both the domestic and international levels to induce change at both the domestic and international levels simultaneously. Like critical IR theory, indigenous global politics seeks to expose the hierarchical structure of the international system but, at the same time, it also recognizes existing power politics, within the international structure in commonality with realism or liberalism. Indigenous global politics works within existing structures, making use of available tools and existing institutions and generally does not wish to threaten the sovereignty of existing states. At the same time, it shares a close kinship with the decolonizing and resistance impulses of post-colonial theory.

In order to discuss the distinctiveness of indigenous global politics, however, it is first necessary to touch upon the question of identity and scope, by specifically addressing who are the world's indigenous peoples and what brings them together in a unique form of transnational politics. According to data from the International Work Group for Indigenous Affairs (IWGIA),[66] a Copenhagen-based international human rights organization for indigenous peoples, there are more than 300 million indigenous peoples in the world, representing approximately 6% of the world's population, stretching across six continents. There are more than 5000 distinct peoples living in 72 countries which are recognized by the IWGIA as 'indigenous.'

---

[66] International Work Group for indigenous Affairs (IWGIA). Data from IWGIA's website, www.iwgia.org, accessed October 14, 2008.

A precise and objective definition of indigenous peoples has been exceedingly difficult to achieve due to the vast diversity of indigenous peoples in the world, including diverse historical experiences with colonialism. Furthermore, the issue of indigenous definition has proved to be a constant issue of contention in transnational indigenous politics, which is unsurprising given the fundamental nature of indigenous identity, as distinct from settler identity, to indigenous politics. Some indigenous groups in UN fora have argued that a lack of a formal definition of indigenous peoples could be used by governments to deny recognition of peoples as indigenous, while many other indigenous groups opposed such a definition on the grounds that governments have utilized such definitions in a discriminatory way.[67] For the most part, indigenous groups in various UN fora have insisted on the right of indigenous peoples to define themselves and their membership. This, in particular, is unique to indigenous global politics, as recognition of states and other groups rests upon external recognition. Other theories rest on assumptions of external definitional standards for subjects. As Aboriginal and Torres Strait Island Social Justice Commissioner Mick Dodson stated in the UN's Working Group on indigenous Populations, "there must be scope for self-identification as an individual and acceptance as such by the group."[68]   During the 13th Session of the Working Group on Indigenous Populations, José Bengoa (alternate for Working Group member Alfonso Martínez) also "stressed the fact that the principle of self-identification was inalienable and had to be part of the definition."[69] Furthermore, Bengoa noted, "the character of being the first people and the strong relation to the land also constituted

---

[67] E/CN.4/Sub.2/1995/24, para. 41, 43.
[68] *Ibid.*, para 43.
[69] *Ibid.* para 48.

important elements of a definition."[70] Linda Tuhiwai Smith has defined indigenous peoples simply as "the assembly of those who have witnessed, been excluded from, and have survived modernity and imperialism."[71] Smith also connects the desire to be self-defining and self-naming to a desire to be free, complicated and, ultimately, fully human.[72]

In response to growing government concerns about the definition of indigenous peoples at the Working Group on Indigenous Populations, Chairperson-Rapporteur Erica-Irene A. Daes, presented a "Working Paper on the Concept of Indigenous Peoples"[73] in June 1996. This Working Paper examined and reported upon some of the common international definitions of indigenous peoples, including the definitions developed previously for ILO No. 169 and the Cobo definition. The definition utilized in ILO No. 169 had three components. Indigenous peoples, under ILO No. 169, are those who: 1) are socially, culturally and economically distinct from the rest of the national community, 2) were descended from those present at the time of conquest or colonization, and 3) self-identify as "indigenous."[74] The Cobo definition, developed in the 1986 "Study of the Problem of Discrimination Against Indigenous Peoples"[75] emphasized an element of colonialism, or "historical continuity with pre-invasion and pre-colonial societies,"[76] and an element of distinctiveness from the dominant societies around them, including the fact

---

[70] *Ibid.*

[71] Linda Tuhiwai Smith, "On Tricky Ground: Researching the Native in the Age of Uncertainty," in *The Sage Handbook of Qualitative Research*, ed. Norman K. Denzin and Yvonna S. Lincoln (Thousand Oaks, CA: Sage, 2005), 86.

[72] *Ibid.*

[73] E/CN.4/Sub.2/AC.4/1996/2.

[74] See ILO Convention No. 169.

[75] E/CN.4/Sub.2/1986/7.

[76] E/CN.4/Sub.2/1986/7./Add.4, para 379.

that indigenous peoples continue to preserve their distinctive "cultural patterns, social institutions and legal systems."[77] In this Working Paper, Daes developed a working definition, based upon these prior definitions as well as the statements made by indigenous representatives in the Working Group, which came into use at the UN Working Group on Indigenous Populations and eventually became the UN's working definition of indigenous peoples. This UN working definition centers on three primary elements: 1) a pre-colonial presence in a particular territory, 2) a continuous cultural, linguistic and/or social distinctiveness from the surrounding population, and 3) a self-identification as "indigenous" and/or a recognition by other indigenous groups as "indigenous."[78]

These three elements together not only comprise the UN's working definition, they also coalesce into a set of experiences that indigenous people all over the world share. These common experiences bind indigenous peoples together in a transnational movement, distinguish them from other minority groups and have also formed much of the basis for how indigeneity had constituted itself on a global level. First, indigenous people experience *discrimination or marginalization*. Indigenous people are often the poorest, least educated and with the lowest health status of any other group in their host states. Second, indigenous peoples are also subjected to *assimilative forces* as a result of colonialism. Assimilative forces can vary from overt forced assimilation on the high end, as was the case in Canadian residential schools which literally attempted to "beat the Indian out of the child," to subtle, yet subversive pressures to assimilate into the

---

[77] *Ibid.*

[78] E/CN.4/Sub.2/AC.4/1996/2.

60

surrounding society, as is often the case with indigenous peoples in China and Southeast Asia. Indigenous global politics begins with these two common experiences. Smith notes that indigenous identity itself helped create unity in an atmosphere of extreme diversity. The term "indigenous peoples," she notes

> has enabled the collective voices of colonized people to be expressed strategically in the international arena. It has also been an umbrella enabling communities and peoples to come together, transcending their own colonized contexts and experiences, in order to learn, share, plan, organize and struggle collectively for self-determination on the global and local stages.[79]

Indigenous global politics, then, is a transnational response to the two common experiences of indigeneity and the shared definition of what it means to be indigenous. As I define it, indigenous global politics is theory which focuses on a transnational movement of indigenous nations, conducting international relations in an indigenous way, which aims to secure international and domestic rights for indigenous peoples so that they can continue to survive as distinct peoples. Brysk describes the indigenous movement as being simultaneously global and local.[80] I take her argument a bit further. This is a global struggle to preserve local distinctiveness and the individual indigenous community's right to maintain difference. This transnational movement, which is centered on the concept of a globally shared indigenous identity layered over national, tribal and kinship identities, seeks to secure both internationally and domestically the right of individual indigenous nations to exist as self-determining nations within the boundaries or across the boundaries of existing nation states. Indigenous global politics differs from other minority group movements in that it does not generally seek secession

---

[79] Linda Tuhiwai Smith, *Decolonizing Methodologies: Research and indigenous Peoples* (Dunedin, New Zealand: University of Otago Press, 2002), 7.

[80] Brysk, *From Tribal Village to Global Village: Indian Rights and International Relations in Latin America*.

from states and does not necessarily or primarily seek equality for individuals or groups within states.

The human rights regime that grew up after World War II, which was based exclusively on an individual rights understanding of human rights[81] did already offer numerous protections to indigenous peoples under the first experiential category mentioned above, *discrimination*, although it was felt by many indigenous peoples that the anti-discrimination provisions of existing human rights instruments were not adequately protecting them as indigenous peoples. So they sought enhancements and reinforcements for these protections which would apply specifically to indigenous peoples as groups, not just as indigenous individuals. It is the second experiential category, *assimilation*, where indigenous peoples felt most vulnerable, and also where indigenous peoples met their most continual and fiercest resistance from states, indicated visually in Figure 2.1 by the explosion graphic. Based on the collective indigenous experience of *assimilation*, the transnational indigenous rights movement sought certain collective rights to directly combat assimilation, in addition to individual rights to protect against discrimination.

Prior to the passage of the Indigenous Rights Declaration in 2007, international human rights law and discourse specifically and deliberately excluded the two elements which are critical to the indigenous quest for rights. First, the international human rights regime did not include collective rights to maintain such things as their culture, language, religion, identity, or their own educational systems in the face of assimilative pressures.

---

[81] See Donnelly, *Universal Human Rights in Theory and Practice*, Lauren, *The Evolution of International Human Rights: Visions Seen*.

These rights, which I will call, "soft rights," are indicated visually in Figure 2.1 by a box with rounded corners. Second, indigenous peoples' self-determination and their

Figure 2.1 Indigenous Global Politics

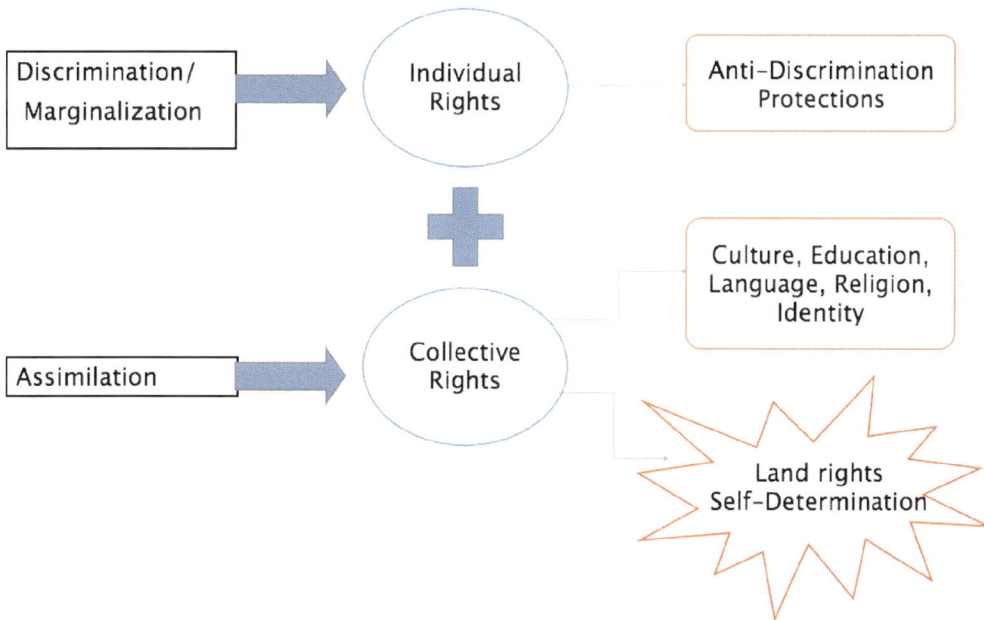

collective right to maintain their lands were specifically excluded from the post-World War II decolonization regime by what was referred to as the "salt water" or "blue water" thesis, which asserted that only overseas territories were eligible for decolonization and self-determination.[82] These were the "hard rights," the explosion, which states,

---

[82] See Anaya, *Indigenous Peoples in International Law*, 75-76. The salt water, or blue water, thesis developed in opposition to efforts by some colonial powers (especially Belgium) to expand the scope of the UN Charter to include indigenous populations. The thesis was placed into G.A Res. 1541 in 1960. The

especially colonial settler states, resist most fiercely. The decolonization meaning of self-determination meant independent statehood; the transnational indigenous rights movement aimed to change this and, as Keal asserts, uncouple self-determination from the state.[83]

Indigenous global politics exerted a particular pressure on the international system to accept a new, non-state-centric interpretation of self-determination, grounded in a self-definitional logic of subjectivity. Indigenous global politics had changed the meaning of self-determination so that it can also be "interpreted as the right of ...peoples to negotiate freely their political status and representation in the states in which they live."[84] Indigenous global politics seeks this interpretation of self-determination, a freely negotiated political status, and not typically secession as independent states.

Therefore, the quest for rights launched by the transnational indigenous rights movement ignited a thirty-year battle with states, largely over land and self-determination. While the indigenous rights movement had demanded a rearticulation of the international consensus on human rights to include collective rights, it was the demand for land rights and self-determination which proved the most threatening to states and the international system since they were reshaping the existing meanings of state sovereignty, self-determination and territoriality.

In essence, indigenous global politics seeks to do three major things, several of which are distinctive and some verge on revolutionary (see Figure 2.2.) First, indigenous

resolution stated that decolonization was only required for "geographically separate" territories administered by a colonial authority.

[83] Keal, *Conquest and the Rights of Indigenous Peoples*.

[84] Erica-Irena A. Daes, "Some Considerations on the Right of Indigenous Peoples to Self-Determination," in *International Law and Indigenous Peoples*, ed. S. James Anaya (Burlington, VT: Ashgate, 2003).

global politics seeks better protections for the individual rights of indigenous peoples. This is not particularly unique and is also of little threat to states. In fact, the transnational indigenous rights movement has found little to no resistance from states in this area.

Figure 2.2   Objectives of Indigenous Global Politics

Objectives of Indigenous Global Politics
1) Enhance individual rights protections for indigenous peoples.
2) Add collective rights to the international human rights consensus.
a) Soft rights: Culture, language, identity, religion
b) Hard rights: Land, self-determination
3) Conduct international relations in an indigenous way.

It is the next two objectives of indigenous global politics that require international change, some of which is extremely threatening to states. Collective rights had to be included in the international human rights consensus in order to meet the needs of indigenous peoples. This was a major shift in international human rights discourse away from a strictly liberal construction, but again, as long as it involved "soft rights" areas such as culture, language, education, identity and religion, states could accept it without much resistance.[85] Furthermore, the third objective, conducting international relations in

---

[85] The main exceptions are the United States and the United Kingdom, both of which are governments founded on the centrality of the rights of individuals. Both vehemently opposed to the collective rights provisions of the Declaration throughout its 30 year history. Right down to the end, even though the UK ended up voting for the Declaration and the US voted against, both countries registered their continued opposition to the international recognition of collective rights in official statements issued on the day the Declaration passed the General Assembly.

an indigenous way, centered on consensus decision making and grounded in cultural and spiritual practices and which will be explored in greater depth in Chapter 3, required some change in international practices and UN standing rules, but these were not insurmountable. It was the "hard rights" of land and self-determination that have been most problematic. Demands for indigenous sovereignty, self-determination, and plural sovereignty arrangements present a powerful threat to state sovereignty and territoriality, the underlying structure of the international system. And, for particular settler states like the United States, Canada, Australia, and New Zealand, international recognition of indigenous rights to land and self-determination present a threat to these states' very foundation, since all of these states rely to varying degrees on the Doctrine of Discovery for their foundation and legitimation and indigenous global politics seeks to dismantle not only the colonial project but also force a recognition and a rethinking of its underlying doctrines and patterns of thought which enable colonialism.[86]

Chapter 3 will elaborate on the features of indigenous global politics which grew out of the thirty year UN process for the Declaration on the Rights of indigenous Peoples. Chapters 4 through 6 will then explore how states, especially certain settler states, have responded to the changes in the international system that have been forged by indigenous global politics.

---

[86] Newcomb, 2008, xi.

Chapter 3

The Declaration on the Rights of Indigenous Peoples: Forging International Change

During the past several decades, human rights regimes have experienced

tremendous and unprecedented expansion. Ever since the mid-1960s, when three major

International Covenants turned the concept of human rights into binding international

law,[1] the number and scope of human rights instruments has increased exponentially in

the U.N. system. During this period of time, eight major treaties have passed through the

U.N. system and been widely ratified by states. In addition, dozens upon dozens of

declarations, proclamations and the like[2] have also passed through the U.N., indicating a

continual broadening of the international human rights consensus. These treaties,

declarations, proclamations and other documents pertain to such issues as genocide,

torture, apartheid, human trafficking, the rights of prisoners, the rights of women, and the

rights of children, among numerous others. While most arguments over human rights at

the U.N. have come to revolve around areas like treaty ratification, or state compliance

with already-ratified treaties, or even concern over the heavy monitoring burden that the

U.N. system sustains due to its tremendous success in articulating human rights norms,

the notion of utilizing the U.N. system for the articulation of human rights principles is

---

[1] The International Covenant on Civil and Political Rights (1966), the International Covenant on Economic, Social and Cultural Rights (1966) and the International Convention on the Elimination of All Forms of Racial Discrimination (1965).

[2] The distinction between conventions and declarations is noted throughout United Nations documents. For example, Pamphlet No. 1 of the UN Guide for Minorities states that "neither the UN General Assembly nor other UN bodies have the authority to create rules of law that are legally binding on States, but they have adopted a wide range of *declarations, proclamations, recommendations, guidelines,* and *principles*. These statements, particularly when they are adopted unanimously or by consensus, represent important political and moral commitments by States that may influence their conduct of international relations" (http://www.ohchr.org/Documents/Publications/GuideMinorities1en.pdf, p. 7).

now well established and largely uncontested.[3] As human rights norms emerge in

international political discourse, they get added to the burgeoning human rights

consensus fairly efficiently and expeditiously, typically working their way through the

U.N. system in ten to fifteen years, and occasionally even quicker.

The Declaration on the Rights of Indigenous Peoples ("The Declaration" or

DRIP) represents a particular exception to this prevailing pattern. The United Nations

General Assembly passed the DRIP on 13 September 2007, more than thirty years after

its conception. The DRIP represents the now internationally accepted minimum standard

of Indigenous peoples' rights and state relationships with Indigenous peoples. As a

United Nations declaration and not a convention, the Declaration on the Rights of

Indigenous Peoples is not legally binding on states, but rather, it is a political document

that became part of the international human rights consensus and its principles are, in

some sense, morally binding on all state conduct whether or not an individual state voted

for it.[4] But, unlike other UN human rights declarations and proclamations, such as the

Declaration on Race & Racial Prejudice,[5] the Declaration on the Protection of Women

and Children in Emergency and Armed Conflict,[6] the Declaration on the Elimination of

---

[3] Schmitz, Hans Pater and Kathryn Sikkink (2002) "International Human Rights." In Walter Carlsnaes, Thomas Risse, and Beth A. Simmons, Eds. *Handbook of International Relations*. London: Sage.
[4] The distinction between conventions and declarations is noted throughout United Nations documents. For example, Pamphlet No. 1 of the UN Guide for Minorities states that "neither the UN General Assembly nor other UN bodies have the authority to create rules of law that are legally binding on States, but they have adopted a wide range of *declarations, proclamations, recommendations, guidelines,* and *principles*. These statements, particularly when they are adopted unanimously or by consensus, represent important political and moral commitments by States that may influence their conduct of international relations" (http://www.ohchr.org/Documents/Publications/GuideMinorities1en.pdf, p. 7).
[5] E/CN.4/Sub.2/1982/2/Add.1, Annex v (1982).
[6] G.A. res. 3318 (XXIX), 29 U.N. GAOR Supp. (No. 31) at 146, U.N. Doc. A/9631 (1974).

Violence Against Women[7] or the Declaration on the Protection of All Persons from Enforced Disappearances,[8] which all passed methodically through the U.N. and often evolved later into conventions, the Declaration on Indigenous Peoples' Rights literally fought its way through the U.N. system, encountering continual and often fierce resistance from states during its more than thirty year life at the UN. In contrast to other human rights regimes, why did the indigenous rights movement need to fight so hard and so long to secure passage of a bare minimum standard on indigenous rights? Why is it that certain countries are so threatened by an emerging international indigenous rights consensus?

The international human rights consensus that grew up in the shadow of World War II was based exclusively on an individual rights understanding of human rights.[9] This body of human rights law did provide indigenous peoples with the human rights of equality and protection from discrimination within the state, including protection of their cultural and religious practices.[10] But, because the land and self-determination rights that indigenous peoples often sought were collective in nature, the existing body of human rights law and discourse, designed around the liberal conception of the universality of individual rights, largely excluded indigenous rights as articulated by indigenous peoples. Furthermore, although self-determination is the one group right that was originally included in the international human rights consensus, indigenous peoples' self-

---

[7] G.A. res. 48/104, 48 U.N. GAOR Supp. (No. 49) at 217, U.N. Doc. A/48/49 (1993).
[8] G.A. res. 47/133, 47 U.N. GAOR Supp. (No. 49) at 207, U.N. Doc. A/47/49 (1992).
[9] Donnelly, Jack (1998) *Universal Human Rights in Theory and Practice.* Ithaca, NY: Cornell University Press; Lauren, Paul Gordon (1996) *The Evolution of International Human Rights: Visions Seen.* Philadelphia: University of Pennsylvania Press.
[10] Anaya, S. James (2004) *Indigenous Peoples in International Law.* New York: Oxford University Press.

69

determination was specifically and deliberately excluded from the decolonization regime by the "saltwater" or "blue water" thesis, which asserted that only overseas colonial territories were eligible for decolonization and self-determination.[11] The UN Declaration on Indigenous Rights not only sought better protections for the individual rights of Indigenous peoples, it also established indigenous peoples' collective rights and rights to land and self-determination.[12]

I argue that the process for an indigenous rights declaration was so arduous because the self-determination and collective rights principles central to indigenous global politics pose deep challenges to the constitution of the Westphalian, or modern, states system and to liberal world order. For in order to achieve this set of bare minimum international standards on indigenous rights, indigenous global politics needed to forge two enormous and fundamental changes in the international system—changes which were fiercely resisted by states. First, in order to meet the self-determination and self-governance needs of indigenous peoples, the international system and individual states needed to make allowances and political space for plural sovereignty arrangements within existing nation states. This is a direct challenge to the constitution of the Westphalian modern states system. Secondly, the international system and the international human rights consensus, which prior to the passage of the DRIP was strictly oriented around the rights of the individual, needed to recognize both the individual and collective rights of Indigenous peoples. The addition of broad collective rights to the

---

[11] Thornberry, P. (2002) *Indigenous Peoples and Human Rights*. Manchester, NH: Juris Publishing.
[12] Cohen, Cynthia Price (1998) *Human Rights of Indigenous Peoples*. Ardsley, NY:Transnational Publishers.

international human rights consensus constituted a major shift in the human rights discourse away from its strictly liberal, individual-rights construction.

Through a case study of the birth and development of the Declaration on the Rights of Indigenous Peoples, I demonstrate in this chapter how indigenous global politics constituted itself in such a way that it challenged the existing international system in these two fundamental ways. I will also show how states resisted the development of collective rights for indigenous peoples and, more significantly, how they fiercely resisted the expansion of self-determination rights for indigenous peoples, features that directly and respectively challenge the individualist foundations of liberal world order and its expression in human rights law, and the singularity of territorial sovereignty which is foundational to the modern states system.

The emergence and development of the Declaration remains largely undocumented in the scholarly literature, so this case study is based on original archival and field research in Geneva, New York and other locations in North America and relies on three sources of data. First, I utilize United Nations documents, which are found in the collection of doCIP, the Documentation Centre for Indigenous Peoples, located in Geneva. Through this archive, I acquired the full set of documents associated with the development and passage of the Declaration on the Rights of Indigenous Peoples, from 1977 through 2007. I supplement these UN documents with a set of interviews with key individuals involved in the Declaration process, and my direct observations of UN meetings and Indigenous Caucus meetings in both New York and Geneva. I was able to gain access to Indigenous Caucus meetings and other international indigenous activity

71

only because I am an indigenous person who holds a leadership position in a Native American NGO in St. Paul, Minnesota. As a non-indigenous person or as an academic, this access would have been denied. Because there have been individuals in the past who have infiltrated the Indigenous Caucus on behalf of states in order to disrupt the process, the Indigenous Caucus and other transnational indigenous meetings are typically closed to outsiders. Indigenous individuals active in the international system are often reluctant to speak to academics or others who may or may not have their best interests in mind. Because maintaining consensus and solidarity has been so critical to the success of the indigenous rights movement at the UN, the Indigenous Caucus and individuals associated with the movement do not easily trust outsiders. I had to be introduced to members of the international indigenous rights movement by someone from the inside the movement who trusted me, and then I also had to build and maintain trust with individuals in my own right.[13]

Through my research, I have identified and named four distinct life-stages of the Declaration on the Rights of Indigenous Peoples:

1) Precursors and Preparation: Up to 1984

2) Drafting Stage: 1984-1994

3) Elaboration Stage: 1995-2006

4) Passage and Implementation Stage: 2007 forward

---

[13] In order to maintain this level of trust, I have removed identifying information from almost all of my interviews and transcripts. With only a few exceptions, the indigenous activists that I have interviewed will remain anonymous. Many identities could be easily ascertained by the inclusion of specific dates and locations of interviews, and so I typically cite anonymous interviews only by an interviewee number, which I have assigned, and by the year of the interview, although I will cite the location and date of interviews where doing so would not divulge the identities of the individuals who gave the interview. All transcripts of both named and anonymous interviews are on file with the author.

Through each of these phases, indigenous global politics constituted itself as a challenge to the international system, rather than as a typical transnational advocacy network.[14] Indigenous global politics has, since its inception, been subtly revolutionary in international politics in two specific ways. First, it has conducted international relations in a new way, in accordance with indigenous cultures and worldviews. Second, it has set out, from its very inception, to move beyond the state-centered, individual rights focus of the existing international system. State resistance to this subtle revolution was manifested most often in issues of definition, participation and scope—particularly the peoples/populations debate, collective rights versus individual rights, and a persistent state concern over self-determination. It was this dynamic of international change which explains the long and arduous fight in the U.N. for Indigenous rights.

1) **Precursors and Preparation: Laying the Groundwork (Up to 1984)**

There were several major events which preceded and laid critical thematic groundwork for the first draft of the Declaration of the Rights of Indigenous Peoples. These are: the first transnational indigenous peoples' conference in 1977, a follow up conference in 1981, the Cobo Study, and the initial sessions of the Working Group on Indigenous Populations, through the United Nations Sub-Commission on Prevention of Discrimination and Protection of Minorities.

Through these events, five themes emerged which constituted indigenous global politics as a challenge to the existing international order, specifically in the areas of

---

[14] Keck and Sikkink (1998).

collective rights and self-determination. First, the global indigenous rights movement sought solidarity by grounding itself in diverse indigenous cultural and spiritual practices and taking strong consensus positions. Second, the existing laws of states dealing with equality of citizens and the anti-discrimination provisions of international human rights standards were deemed insufficient to protect indigenous peoples. Third, land rights, including the possibility of communal land ownership, are central to indigenous peoples' struggles. Fourth, self-determination is a critical issue for Indigenous peoples, which states resist. Finally, the primary strategy of indigenous peoples was to utilize moral persuasion with states through the international human rights system.

1977 NGO Conference in Geneva

Indigenous global politics was born in Geneva in 1977. The International NGO Conference on Discrimination Against Indigenous Populations in the Americas was held in Geneva 20-23 September 1977. It was at this conference where the framework for indigenous global politics was laid. First the way that indigenous global politics would function was established, and the targets of this transnational movement were also identified and illuminated, thus constituting indigenous global politics as a challenge to the existing international system. The Conference, which at this point included only indigenous groups from the Western Hemisphere, was sponsored by the U.N. Sub-Committee on Racism, Racial Discrimination, Apartheid, and Decolonization of the Special Committee on Human Rights which was part of the Economic and Social Council. The conference was organized primarily by the International Indian Treaty

74

Council, the American Indian Law Resource Center, and the World Peace Council.[15]

Over 100 indigenous delegates attended, along with 60 NGOs and international

organizations and forty UN member states.

Mr. Theo Van Boven from the Division on Human Rights of the United Nations,

addressed the insufficiency of existing international human rights standards for

indigenous peoples in his welcoming remarks at the Opening Plenary session:

> From the start it was evident that indeed many aspects of the problems
> confronting Indigenous populations could not be approached from the
> point of view of racial discrimination alone, since also complex ethnic,
> social, cultural, linguistic and religious aspects and fundamentally
> different world views were very much involved.[16]

The Social and Cultural Commission of the 1977 Conference reported that

indigenous peoples are not only victims of specific acts of injustice but are also victims

of the worldview dominant in the states which have attempted to assimilate indigenous

peoples. The report acknowledges that "it is the human right of all peoples to develop

and transmit their own culture."[17] The Legal Commission also stated that legal

discrimination against indigenous peoples takes place when they are forced to participate

in legal structures and systems, which are "detrimental to their interests." Thus,

assimilation, integration and incorporation of indigenous peoples into state legal systems

are forms of discrimination.[18]

---

[15] International Indian Treaty Council (IITC). 1977. *The Geneva Conference: International NGO Conference on Discrimination Against Indigenous Populations In the Americas.* New York: International Indian Treaty Council. The International Treaty Council was founded in 1974 by Jimmie Durham and members of the American Indian Movement, including Bill Means, Russell Means and Vernon Bellecourt. IITC gained ECOSOC status in 1977.
[16] IITC, 1977, p. 3.
[17] IITC, 1977, p. 18.
[18] IITC, 1977, p. 21.

Furthermore, while many states have strongly advocated for a reliance on the Universal Declaration of Human Rights, the Universal Declaration on Human Rights only covers rights of the individual and specifically excludes collective rights to land and culture, which are crucial to the survival of indigenous peoples as peoples.[19]

One of the first major issues the indigenous representatives wanted to discuss was land. Jose Mendoza Acosta, Representacion de Autoridad y Pueblo Indigena de Panama, addressed the states regarding the importance of indigenous lands:

> Representatives of all nations of the world, remember one thing and do not forget it. We will not give up our territories. We are not going to abandon them. We are going to defend our territories through all possible means because that territory, recognized as a nation or not, has been ours and will continue to be ours.[20]

The Economic Commission Report of the conference also articulated the importance of land, noting in particular the spiritual tie between indigenous peoples and the land:

> For Indigenous peoples of the Americas, land is sacred. The mother earth provides the sustenance of all life. The land must be respected, carefully used, and meticulously restored. The concept of land being sacred is the basis of native religions and societies.[21]

The conference Legal Commission resolved that "the land question is fundamental to the attainment of the goals of the Indigenous peoples"[22] and, as an indigenous activist told me, "It's all about land. Everything else emanates from that."[23] Furthermore, since in

---

[19] Anonymous interview with indigenous rights activist #2, 2007.

[20] IITC, 1977, p. 6.

[21] IITC, 1977, p. 14.

[22] IITC, 1977, p. 19.

[23] Interview with indigenous activist #4, 2007.

many cases, indigenous peoples prefer to own their land communally, that is a right which should be nationally and internationally protected.

Indigenous delegates from all regions also argued for self-determination and for their recognition as nations. Most demanded that states recognize indigenous organizations and enter into meaningful negotiations while both the Six Nations and the Lakota Nation made their case for immediate recognition as states under international law. States raised two legal issues regarding self-determination. First, Indigenous self-determination appears to conflict with the territorial integrity principle of the UN Charter and other international instruments. Second, the international right of peoples to self-determination "has never been authoritatively defined."[24] So, beginning at this first conference in 1977, states resisted indigenous self-determination on the grounds of state territorial integrity and began to invoke definitional lines of argumentation.

During this conference, indigenous peoples elaborated a document which represented the broad consensus among Indigenous groups from the Western Hemisphere, the Draft Declaration of Principles for the Defense of the Indigenous Nations and Peoples of the Western Hemisphere ("The 1977 Declaration of Principles")[25] (Appendix 1). The 1977 Declaration of Principles was the first attempt to articulate an international rights standard for indigenous peoples which could be used as moral leverage with states in an attempt to adjust state behavior. The 1977 Declaration of Principles, which the indigenous delegates wrote and presented to states, consisted of a Preamble and thirteen paragraphs.

---

[24] IITC, 1977, p. 19.
[25] IITC, 1977, p. 25-26.

When asked about how the Declaration of Principles was written and who did the drafting, an activist who participated in the 1977 Indigenous Caucus told me that:

> It was a combination. What we did was have various caucuses on different issues like land, another maybe on education—all the issues that we were dealing with socially—we sort of divided to see what impact, how we could impact and begin to deal with those social issues. So each group brought out specific issues that were eventually contained in the Declaration of Principles—so it was really a combination. So different writers from each group presented their issues in the plenary. In the plenary sessions, each group presented different issues and then a team of writers which included NGOs who were not indigenous, indigenous NGOs of which there were very few at the time. ...But there were a lot of writers and it was a combination and, of course, we had to keep drafting, each session.[26]

The five-phrase Preamble makes the case that the exclusive individual rights focus of the international human rights system is inherently discriminatory against indigenous peoples because it imposes conditions which deny or destroy indigenous cultures. The Preamble specifies the need for including indigenous collective rights in the international consensus by noting that,

> The Universal Declaration of Human Rights and related international covenants have the individual as their primary concern, and
> Recognizing that individuals are the foundation of cultures, societies and nations, and
> Whereas, it is a fundamental right of any individual to practice and perpetuate the cultures, societies and nations into which they are born, and
> Recognizing that conditions are imposed upon peoples that suppress, deny or destroy the culture, societies or nations in which they believe they are members..."

The thirteen paragraphs in the body of the Declaration of Principles make various points which all advocate that the international system must recognize and support the

---

[26] Anonymous interview with indigenous activist (#7) who participated in 1977 conference, 2008. Transcript on file with the author.

nationhood status (with or without statehood status) of indigenous peoples. There are three dominant themes which emerge from these thirteen paragraphs, all of which insert indigenous peoples as subjects into international law, in a nascent articulation of the self-determination principle. The three themes in the Declaration of Principles are: 1) nationhood, 2) land, territories, treaties and resources, and 3) self-determination.

Paragraph one in the Declaration of Principles explicitly calls for the international recognition of indigenous nationhood while paragraph two adds that indigenous groups that do not meet the international territorial, governmental and populations requirements for nationhood shall still be recognized as subjects of international law, "provided they are identifiable groups having bonds of language, heritage, tradition, or other common identity."[27]

Several more paragraphs in the Declaration of Principles deal with land, territories, treaties and resources. Paragraph eight invalidates the Doctrine of Discovery, a principle of international law which enabled European colonization of the rest of the world over the course of several centuries[28] and which remains valid law in many settler states, "No state shall claim or retain, by right of discovery or otherwise, the territories of an Indigenous nation or group, except such lands as may have been lawfully acquired by valid treaty or other cessation freely made." Paragraphs five and six deal with treaties, declaring that indigenous nation treaties must be accorded the same international rights

---

[27] IITC, 1977, p. 25

[28] See Steven T. Newcomb. 2008. *Pagans in the Promised Land: Decoding the Doctrine of Christian Discovery.* Golden, CO: Fulcrum, for an analysis of how the Doctrine of Discovery enabled European colonization of the Americas.

and respect as other international treaties, while paragraph nine declares that land claims and treaty disputes must be settled in a fair and just manner.

Paragraphs four, seven, ten and twelve all address the self-determination concerns of indigenous peoples, declaring unequivocally that "all actions on the part of the state which derogate from the Indigenous nations' or groups' right to exercise self-determination shall be the proper concern of existing international bodies."[29] In addition, "Indigenous nations shall be accorded such degree of independence as they may desire in accordance with international law."[30] In other words, indigenous nations may choose from a spectrum of autonomy which ranges from establishing themselves as independent states on one end, to total integration with nation states on the other end, with variations of degrees of autonomy in between. It is important to note that the possibility of the independence of indigenous nations, i.e. secession, was included as a possibility for indigenous nations. Paragraphs ten and twelve address issues related to self-determination of indigenous nations, including the preservation of national and cultural integrity as well as environmental and resource protection of indigenous nations. The exclusive right of indigenous nations to determine their own membership free of state interference, another element of self-determination, is also mentioned: "No state...shall take actions that interfere with the sovereign power of an Indigenous nation or group to determine its own membership."[31]

The 1977 conference was, up until that point, the "broadest, united representation of the Indigenous nations and peoples that has ever gathered at any international

---

[29] IITC, 1977, p. 25.
[30] *Ibid.*
[31] IITC, 1977, p. 26.

80

conference."[32] But that was not its primary significance. The Draft Declaration of Principles which emerged from this conference "could be characterized as the fundamental political document of the international Indigenous movement"[33] and it would later provide the backbone of the Draft Declaration process in the Working Group on Indigenous Populations. This conference also represented the beginning of an important shift in international relations, forged by indigenous global politics. With the Declaration of Principles, the transnational indigenous rights movement shifted the international conversation on indigenous peoples from one focused solely on discrimination against indigenous individuals toward a conversation also based in the rights of indigenous nations to self-determination, an international conversation which would necessarily and inevitably lead toward discussions of group rights and plural sovereignty arrangements. Romesh Chandra, the conference chairman, recognized this shift, in his closing statement to the conference:

> I think there are some words in this document which it is worthwhile learning fast for all of us non-governmental organizations who have learned so much. The first word is nation. Indigenous peoples, Indigenous nations and peoples.
> We began this conference with a conference of discrimination against Indigenous peoples, right? We end the conference with a clear-cut declaration in solidarity with Indigenous nations and peoples.
> Thank you for giving us that word. Thank you for giving us another word, which is in this resolution. It's a shorter word. The word, land. This is the key. It's a key word. Our land, our beautiful land, our mother earth. This land belongs to us. No one can take it from us. ...
> One other word I want to speak of is a word which we have put into this resolution. Self-determination. ...Self-determination means in this document and for us a simple fact: people have the right to decide its own destiny, of what it wants, to do with its own wealth, with its own land, its

---

[32] Closing Statement by Romesh Chandra, Chairman, NGO Subcommittee on Racism, Racial Discrimination, Apartheid and Decolonization, and Chairman of the conference. IITC, 1977, p. 30.
[33] Dunbar-Ortiz, 2006, p. 67.

own life. …Self-determination is what we ask for and what we stand for for the Indigenous peoples and nations.[34]

Because of the enormity of the changes being forged by the indigenous rights movement and the inherent conflict with states that was developing, indigenous activists immediately sensed the need to unite in solidarity and common cause if they were to achieve success. The behavior of the indigenous delegates at the 1977 conference thus also represented an early expression of indigenous peoples' transnational solidarity and drive for consensus positions vis-à-vis states, and they "developed a strong sense of unity and common cause."[35] Since this was the first conference which brought indigenous delegates from diverse places together for nearly the fist time, one would not expect there to be a strong consensus among them. Further, international relations theory teaches us that such events are likely to be characterized by discussions of the diversity of interests that individual groups bring to the meeting. But, by contrast, this conference demonstrated how such a diversity of individual indigenous groups could come together in strong consensus positions. There were two issues which emerged immediately among the indigenous delegations, which met in caucus[36] ahead of the full conference with governments and NGOs. These issues needed resolution prior to the actual conference in order for indigenous groups to present a stronger and more unified position to state

---

[34] IITC, 1977, p. 31.

[35] IITC, 1977, p. 1.

[36] Meetings of the indigenous delegates in caucus is also documented by Roxanne Dunbar-Ortiz, a participant in these early meetings, in her article "The First Decade of Indigenous Peoples at the United Nations" in *Peace & Change* 31:1, 2006, p. 58-74. The author has also witnessed meetings of the Indigenous Caucus in Geneva, New York and Minneapolis in 2007 and 2008.

governments, the UN system and NGOs. The resolution of these issues helped pave the way for indigenous transnational solidarity and consensus building.

The first issue to come up was self-identity, or what should the indigenous groups call themselves in the conglomerate? IITC Board Member Bill Means tells the story:

> The first part is what do we call ourselves?
> Some people said "Well I'm a Mayan." Other people said "I'm a Catchwa." They didn't want to certainly be identified by the nation state they came from--the whole hemisphere agreed on that. Well, what do we call ourselves? Indigenous people? Do we call ourselves Mestizo? Do we call ourselves Indians? And finally one of the elders from South America, an organization called CISA, Indian Council of South America, but the Spanish acronym was CISA.
> He got up and said "If Indian was a name under which we were oppressed, then Indian will be the name under which we will rise." That settled that argument. So we identified as Indian, and, believe me, this was a difficult decision, especially for Latin America because to call someone *Indio* in Spanish, more so in those days but, even today, is a very derogatory term, and so this coming – emanating from South America where there is so much discrimination, as much or more than America, that it had particular significance; and so that was the beginning.[37]

While the terminology used by the transnational indigenous rights movement would later change from "Indian" to "indigenous peoples" in order to draw in groups from outside the Western Hemisphere, the method used by the movement to resolve the issue laid the groundwork for how future issues would be resolved within the movement. The movement met in caucus ahead of any meeting with states and/or NGOs in order to resolve internal disagreements and build solidarity and present stronger consensus positions in the larger meetings.

---

[37] Interview with Bill Means, 17 January 2008.

IITC's Bill Means continues the story by talking about the resolution of the second major issue among indigenous groups—who would speak first at the upcoming conference:

> Another phenomena happened on who would speak first, that was the next item on the agenda. So, of course, the Houdenousaunee, the Six Nations, they said 'Well, we sent Deskaheh here in …the era of the League of Nations,' which was housed in Geneva. 'Therefore as a continuation reminder, we should go first.'
> Us Lakotas, we said, 'Well, we've got a strong treaty and this mandate of the Treaty Council to put forth the issue of treaties, and because of that we should go first because treaties represent the legal foundation of nation to nation.'
> The Central Americans said that their civilization, Mayan civilization, is the oldest recorded history in this part of the world. South Americans said, 'We represent millions, we're not just one million, we're not just two million, we're many millions, and so we should go first.'
> Then a great thing happened. Phil Deere, who is a Muskogee Creek, and board member, and one of the founders of Treaty Council, got up when it came his turn to speak, and said, 'Many years ago before we had electricity we had fire-keepers, people who kept the flint and the stone. It was their responsibility to start the fire. Before they prepared the fire, they would get all the wood and the kindling and everything together, and then they would get around in a circle, and each one then would start from a different point around that kindling using their flint and stone to make the spark. Nobody really knew who made the first spark that created the fire. They all were given credit as fire keepers for starting the fire. Today we are starting a fire in the United Nations, it doesn't matter who goes first.' That ended that argument.[38]

These stories demonstrate how the indigenous rights movement, even at its very first transnational meeting, was able to forge unity and solidarity within the movement. As Jose Mendoza Acosta, Representacion de Autoridad y Pueblo Indigena de Panama, expressed, "we are very confident that we, the Indigenous Populations, are united and we feel united because we are confident that each Indian is a brother ready to stand by us at

---

[38] *Ibid.*

all times."[39] These two stories also demonstrate how the movement invoked indigenous worldviews and an indigenous model of conflict resolution in order to enhance its unity and solidarity. Even though indigenous peoples are extremely diverse and come from all corners of the Earth, one strong commonality among them is a particular style of consensus-building conflict resolution. As Maori lawyer and activist Moana Jackson expressed:

> There are a number of similarities in what I would call an indigenous worldview. There are similarities of perceptions about the Earth as mother, the importance of *whakapapa*, or relationships. And in the workings of an organization like the UN, the genuine and agreed commitment to seek consensus.[40]

For many indigenous peoples, conflict resolution typically occurs through open discussion of issues (which can often get quite heated) but where all viewpoints are heard and then consensus positions are reached through discussion and persuasion rather than majority vote. Often, the most effective persuasion is done by elders who rise to tell a story. Often contained in the story is a metaphor which then convinces the group of the best course of action. While consensus does not necessarily mean unanimity and individuals remain free to defect, this model of conflict resolution tends to lead to stronger solidarity and unity among indigenous peoples.

The search for unifying indigenous consensus positions continued throughout the conference. The IITC conference report notes that "nightly meetings were held during which consensus was reached concerning the content and structure of the next days (sic)

---

[39] IITC, 1977, p. 6.
[40] Interview by author with Moana Jackson, Maori attorney, law professor and global indigenous activist. March 2008, Wellington, Aotearoa/New Zealand.

work."[41] An indigenous delegate from the 1977 conference explains how the traditional model of consensus works in his North American Native community:

> The whole idea of consensus is that all viewpoints are heard and if there's a disagreement then we have to deal with the particular aspects, points of that disagreement and not just make some kind of blanket decision. As Indian people we do that, have consensus or try to go by consensus. I've been to meetings as a young person where the elders appoint—and the English word they use is critic—after people have their say then this person we call critic, has the right to limit the debate and then to ask people or a council of chiefs depending on the situation, a number of people, a smaller number of people I should say agree on how to go forward. Usually it's not even a vote, it's just a smaller group of elders—in our ways.[42]

Indigenous representatives began another struggle at the 1977 conference which required a significant alteration in the methods and procedures of international politics, specifically the insertion of indigenous culture and spirituality into official conference proceedings. The day before the conference opened, the Mayor of Geneva was presented with a special invitation wampum by the Iroquois Chiefs in a special ceremony.[43] In the closing conference ceremony, Larry Redshirt of the Lakota Treaty Council, addressed the cultural and spiritual significance of the Lakota Pipe and why he had brought it into this international political conference:

> We've explained already what the Pipe meant and why we come here with it. We explained that this Pipe is a symbol of peace and as such we have offered it to many of our brother nations. We have even offered it to the United States of America, and they have accepted. We made agreements in good faith and blessed it with this Pipe and their Bible. When we were sent here on behalf of myself, my brothers, relatives, from the Lakota Nation, they told us to bring the Pipe. ...As we come with this Pipe, also we come with the Treaty, the 1868 Treaty. ..As we talked among ourselves

---

[41] IITC, 1977, p. 1.
[42] Anonymous interview by author with indigenous activist, (#1) 2007. Transcript on file with the author.
[43] IITC, 1977, p. 3.

we said this is just a beginning, and the process of understanding had just begun. In due time, this Pipe we will offer to the world. ...Together, our leaders, our chiefs, our governments will smoke with leaders of the world, with the United Nations. This morning we prayed and smoked it among ourselves, and the Indians of the nations know what it means, what it represents. ...We'll pray with it...and I am sure the Creator will hear us. I can already feel his presence among us.[44]

Indigenous participants in the 1977 conference have testified to the importance of cultural and spiritual grounding in achieving the solidarity found in the global indigenous rights movement. Although it required modification of UN standing rules and procedures, and, as Bill Means expressed, "sometimes at the UN they don't know how to react, but other times, they feel good about it. It's just that they're taught, all taught to keep that separate and we're taught that it can't be separated."[45] Another activist stated unequivocally that "a spiritual foundation laid the groundwork" for global indigenous solidarity. He said, "At a lot of these meetings, I've participated in a lot of ceremonies around the world where indigenous peoples have come together in that way and I think that's strengthened us and made the movement a little bit different than other movements."[46] Another activist stated that this tradition in indigenous global politics began at the 1977 conference and that this "phenomenon introduced by indigenous people is a recognition of culture at least in terms of reminding ourselves where we come from."[47]

It was also reported by indigenous activists that although indigenous peoples share a common history of oppression and dispossession, it is the taking and holding of a

---

[44] IITC, 1977, p. 32.

[45] Interview by author with IITC's Bill Means, January 2008, Minneapolis, MN.

[46] Anonymous interview by author with indigenous activist (#6), 2007. Transcript on file with the author.

[47] Anonymous interview by author with indigenous activist (#4) 2007. Transcript on file with the author.

87

strong position that helps keep consensus and unity within the indigenous groups: "A hard position attracts consensus, a soft position drives it away. Changes can come later."[48] For this reason, there was a tradition beginning in 1977 of "presenting your ideal situation—your strongest position—you have to maintain that. Otherwise the other side will never move off their position."[49] In 1977, this took the form of including the right to independence for indigenous nations, including the right of secession, among the principles for which indigenous delegates argued. Over time, the "realities of the UN system" convinced the indigenous delegates to place "lesser emphasis on independence."[50]

1981 NGO Conference in Geneva

In September 1981, the Sub-Committee on Racism and Racial Discrimination organized a follow-up conference in Geneva focused on indigenous peoples' issues, particularly the issue of land. This time, there were more than 300 delegates, observers and guests present. Many more indigenous organizations, from more parts of the world, participated in this conference than at the 1977 conference, which had focused exclusively on the indigenous peoples of the Western Hemisphere. This conference, which is described as "giving new confidence and support"[51] to the global indigenous rights struggle, was much bigger and broader than the 1977 conference in terms of

---

[48] Anonymous interview by author with indigenous activist (#7) 2007. Transcript on file with the author.
[49] Interview by author with IITC's Bill Means, St Paul, MN, September 2008.
[50] *Ibid.*
[51] International NGO Conference on Indigenous Peoples and the Land, organized by the Sub-Commission on Racism, Racial Discrimination, Apartheid and Decolonisation of the Special NGO Committee on Human Rights (Geneva), 15-18 September 1981, Geneva, Switzerland. Final Report, 1981, p. 5. This Report is available from doCIP, Avenue de Trembley 14 – CH 1209 Genève.

indigenous representation, since the 1977 conference had focused exclusively on indigenous peoples of the Western Hemisphere. In 1981, 130 indigenous representatives from North America, Central America, South America, Australia, and New Zealand[52] participated in order "to call the attention of the international community to the desperate conditions in which they live and to their struggle to survive as nations and communities."[53] Fewer governments participated in the 1981 conference than in the 1977 conference, largely due to a government boycott of the conference initiated by the U.S. Reagan administration which viewed the global indigenous rights movement as tied to global communism within the Cold War atmosphere that pervaded international politics of the time.[54] This had not been an issue in 1977 because the Carter administration had a stated commitment to international human rights. Because of the US-led boycott, only a handful of Western countries attended and participated in the 1981 conference, namely Denmark, France, Norway, and The Netherlands.[55] Despite the Western boycott, fifteen Latin American, Asian and African governments participated in the conference along with several national liberation organizations, like the Palestinian Liberation Organization, and more than 50 international NGOs.[56]

Participants in the 1981 NGO Conference echoed the same themes which emerged from the 1977 conference, but also expanded upon them in important ways which pushed for fundamental change in the very international system through which

---

[52] NGO Conference Report, 1981, p. 44-47.

[53] NGO Conference Report, 1981, p. 10.

[54] Dunbar-Ortiz, 2006, p. 68.

[55] While Dunbar-Ortiz , 2006, reports that Norway was the only Western country participating in the conference, the Conference Report of the 1981 NGO Conference shows Denmark, France, The Netherlands and Norway as participants, p. 47.

[56] 1981 NGO Conference Report, p. 47-48.

they were working. As in 1977, indigenous groups met in caucus prior to the conference, as well as during the conference, in order to reach consensus positions which would give them stronger and more unified positions vis-à-vis states during the conference.[57] The Final Conference report notes that the success of the Conference was "particularly due to the very thorough preparations prior to the conference on the part of Indigenous peoples' organizations" who had produced more than 50 papers in advance of the conference.[58] As they had in 1977, indigenous peoples pushed for and achieved a change in UN rules, which allowed them to open and close the meeting on a spiritual basis, with an indigenous prayer ceremony.[59]

In addition to addressing the issue of the insufficiency of existing laws to protect indigenous peoples, participants at this conference directly claimed that the Anglo-American bias in international law was contributing to the plight of the world's indigenous peoples. They thus advocated for change in the international system. The Final Conference Report notes that,

> It was recommended that these definitions be expanded so as to include Indigenous notions of law and fundamental rights such as communal ownership of land.

---

[57] Many early records of Indigenous Caucus meetings do not exist for several reasons. First, there were often not careful notes taken during these meetings. Second, the Indigenous Caucus did not have language translation services available at this time, so the Caucus was constantly pre-occupied with correctly translating conversations and documents into Spanish and English. Third, there was a suspicious fire at the doCIP document depository in Geneva in 1982 which destroyed many early records of the international activities of the Indigenous rights movement. The author has conducted 11 interviews with individuals who were involved with the global Indigenous rights movement since its inception and each interviewee testified to the existence and the strategic importance of the Indigenous Caucus. Transcripts of these interviews are on file with the author.

[58] 1981 NGO Conference Report, p. 6.

[59] The 1981 NGO Conference Report lists this as an "Invocation" on p. 8, but interviewees have stated that all international meetings of Indigenous peoples since 1977 have always been opened and closed with an Indigenous prayer. The United Nations has bent its standing rules to accommodate the demands of Indigenous peoples on this point. Indigenous peoples' meetings remain the only exception to this UN rule against public prayers and ceremonies.

Several suggestions were put forward to improve the status of Indigenous peoples under international law. These included representation in the United Nations, mandatory jurisdiction over Indigenous questions by the International Court of Justice, United Nations supervision of negotiations between Indigenous peoples and the governments concerned, and the international recognition of the validity of treaties and agreements concluded or accepted by Indigenous peoples.[60]

Building upon the earlier articulations of the importance of land and self-determination for indigenous peoples, it was at the 1981 conference that the global indigenous rights movement first "affirmed that land rights and self-determination are inseparably connected"[61] and then articulated the connection between land and self-determination and the desperate situation of the world's indigenous peoples. Indigenous participants made the case that "the root cause of this crisis is the denial of the right to their land"[62] and it is "the constant grabbing of more of their land and the denial of self-determination that is destroying their traditional value systems and the very fabric of their societies."[63] Indigenous delegates further argued that "if the Indigenous peoples were accorded the genuine exercise of their right to self-determination, they would be able to live in their lands and feed their people in accordance with their own traditions, technology and culture."[64] One Maori activist told me: "From the very beginning there was absolute unity on the need for the recognition of the right of self-determination as the baseline from which all other minimum standards would flow."[65] Furthermore, the national governments and the international system must accommodate the possibility of

---

[60] *Ibid.*, p. 14.

[61] *Ibid.*, p. 13.

[62] *Ibid.*, p. 10.

[63] *Ibid.*, p. 6.

[64] *Ibid.*, p. 14-15.

[65] Interview by author with Moana Jackson, Maori attorney, law professor and global Indigenous activist. March 2008, Wellington, Aotearoa/New Zealand.

indigenous communal land ownership if indigenous peoples feel that communal ownership of their lands is necessary. The delegates asserted that "indigenous nations and peoples have the complete right to determine their own land tenures."[66]

Finally, the moral persuasion strategy of the global indigenous rights movement was extended. The indigenous participants recognized the need to engage in several simultaneous levels of struggle to secure rights for indigenous peoples. The strategy of the indigenous rights movement from 1981 onward was to be a two level moral persuasion game: the international level, which would be focused at the United Nations, and the national level of each state. The Final Conference Report, which was unanimously supported by the conference participants, recommended to the Commission on Human Rights that a Working Group on Indigenous Populations be established,[67] in part to develop international standards for relationships between states and Indigenous peoples. Once these international standards and possibly a convention were developed and included in the international human rights consensus, then the Indigenous rights movement would hold each state morally accountable to the standards.

In sum, the 1981 NGO Conference solidified the themes of Indigenous global politics, which first emerged at the 1977 conference. It also crystallized and extended these themes in several important ways: 1) international awareness of indigenous issues increased and the indigenous rights movement broadened its participation from the Western Hemisphere to the global level; 2) land rights and self-determination were linked together and asserted to be the solution to the problems of indigenous peoples; 3)

---

[66] *Ibid.*, 15.
[67] *Ibid.*, p. 11.

the accommodation of collective land rights for indigenous peoples was articulated as a necessity; and 4) the recommendation to establish a Working Group on Indigenous Populations to elaborate international standards on indigenous peoples' rights.

The Cobo Study

In 1970, the United Nations Sub-Commission on the Prevention of Discrimination and Protection of Minorities recommended that a complete study of the problem of discrimination against indigenous populations be undertaken.[68] It was also charged with making suggestions about national and international measures, which should be taken to eliminate such discrimination. This study was named the "Study of the Problem of Discrimination against Indigenous Populations" and a Sub-Commission member, Ambassador José Martinez Cobo of Ecuador, was selected as its Special Rapporteur.[69] The study was completed more than a decade later, in 1982, and the final twenty-chapter report, which was the most voluminous document ever produced by the United Nations, was issued in two parts in 1982 and 1983.[70] While the Cobo study was an official UN undertaking, the process it followed meant that the end report more strongly represented the views of the indigenous participants in the reporting process than it did those of the UN Member states. The Special Rapporteur focused attention on the situation of indigenous peoples in several dozen countries. In the investigation, the UN study team

---

[68] United Nations. Sub-Commission on Prevention of Discrimination and Protection of Minorities. Resolution 4B (XXIII). 26 August 1970.

[69] United Nations. Sub-Commission on Prevention of Discrimination and Protection of Minorities. Resolution 8 (XXIV). 18 August 1971.

[70] Each of the twenty chapters is an individual U.N. document, but the full report was issued in a consolidated form in both English and Spanish in 1986 as E/CN.4/Sub.2/1986/7 and Add.1-3.

met with the indigenous groups first, then offered the governments of these countries the opportunity to clarify and/or correct information and to offer their perspectives. Governments were generally slow to respond, if they responded at all. The last chapter of the report (Chapter XXI), published in 1987, serves as an accessible and comprehensive summary of the conclusions, proposals and recommendations of the full report.[71]

The summary of the Study Report presents two major conclusions from the study which lent credence to claims made by indigenous participants at both the 1977 and 1981 international conferences:

1) The principles in existing international human rights standards are not being adequately applied in all countries where indigenous peoples are impacted.

2) "It is also clear that the provisions contained in the instruments in question are not wholly adequate for the recognition and protection of the specific rights of Indigenous populations."[72]

The report summary specifically identifies many areas where existing international standards pertaining to equality and non-discrimination are not adequately applied to indigenous peoples, including health, housing, education, language, culture, employment, religion, and administration of justice. At the same time, the report summary also articulates the two main areas where the existing international standards failed to recognize and respect the realities of indigenous peoples: land and political rights.

---

[71] Cobo, José Martínez. *Study of the Problem of Discrimination Against Indigenous Populations, Volume V: Conclusions, Proposals and Recommendations.* New York: United Nations, 1987. E/CN.4/Sub.2/1986/7/Add.4.

[72] *Ibid.*, p. 45.

Land

The Cobo report represented the first official acknowledgement within the UN system of a special relationship which exists between indigenous peoples and land, which existing national and international norms and laws did not accommodate:

> It is essential to know and understand the deeply spiritual special relationship between Indigenous peoples and their land as basic to their existence as such and to all their beliefs, customs, traditions and culture. For such peoples, land is not merely a possession and a means of production. The entire relationship between the spiritual life of Indigenous peoples and Mother Earth, and their land, has a great many deep-seated implications. Their land is not a commodity which can be acquired, but a material element to be enjoyed freely.[73]

The report further made explicit the connection between land, religion and cultural heritage for indigenous peoples: "(Indigenous peoples) have the right to the natural cultural heritage contained in the territory and freely to determine the use to be made of it."[74] While there was nothing in the international system which specifically excluded indigenous individuals from owning land, there was nothing in the existing international system to adequately protect Indigenous forms of land tenure:

> No proper or really effective guarantees exist regarding the right of Indigenous populations to the land which they and their forefathers have worked from time immemorial, the forms of land tenure, the use of the resources traditionally generated, or the resources which that land contains.[75]

The Cobo report also makes special note of the struggles of many indigenous peoples to maintain communal or group rights to land in the face of state efforts to individualize

---

[73] *Ibid.*, p. 16.
[74] *Ibid.*
[75] *Ibid.*

95

land into private ownership.[76] Finally, the report also acknowledged the centrality of land

to indigenous peoples: "The recognition and protection of land rights is the basis of all

indigenous movements and claims today."[77]

Political Rights

The Cobo Report articulates the complexity of indigenous political rights:

> In the case of Indigenous peoples, the effective exercise of political rights
> is conditioned by a large number of complex circumstances which
> transcend the abstract, formal recognition proclaimed in international
> instruments, in the constitutions and other fundamental legislation of the
> various countries, and in the agreements, conventions and treaties
> concluded between such countries and Indigenous communities and
> peoples as contracting nations.[78]

While active discrimination is decreasing, it is the *de facto* state of indigenous political

rights that remains problematic.[79] Because indigenous peoples have "their own national

identity based on historical realities" and "the natural and original right to live freely on

their own territories" "respect for the forms of autonomy called for by Indigenous

peoples is the necessary condition for guaranteeing and ensuring these rights."[80]

Indigenous peoples' self-determination, therefore, is a "basic pre-condition" to the

enjoyment of indigenous peoples' fundamental rights and preservation of ethnic

heritage.[81]

---

[76] *Ibid.*
[77] *Ibid.*, p. 17.
[78] *Ibid.*, p. 20.
[79] *Ibid.*
[80] *Ibid.*
[81] *Ibid.*

The Cobo report acknowledged that self-determination has many aspects, but must also include political factors. "Internal" self-determination within a nation state means that "a people or group possessing a definite territory may be autonomous in the sense of possessing a separate and distinct administrative structure and judicial system, determined by and intrinsic to that people or group."[82]

In order to adequately protect indigenous peoples' rights to land and self-determination, the Cobo Study recommended that the Sub-Commission prepare a "declaration of the rights and freedoms of Indigenous populations."[83] On 7 May 1982, the United Nations Economic and Security Council in Resolution 1982/34, "believing that special attention should be given to appropriate avenues of recourse at the national, regional and international levels in order to advance the promotion and protection of the human rights and fundamental freedoms of Indigenous populations"[84] and in light of the conclusions of the Cobo Study, authorized the establishment of an annual working group on indigenous populations. The mandate of the working group was two-fold: to review developments pertaining to the human rights and fundamental freedoms of indigenous populations and "to give special attention to the evolution of standards concerning the rights of Indigenous populations."[85]

---

[82] *Ibid.*

[83] Cobo, p. 45.

[84] United Nations Economic and Security Council Resolution 1982/34. 7 May 1982.

[85] *Ibid.*

Working Group on Indigenous Populations (1982-1984)

The Working Group on Indigenous Populations (WGIP) was proposed by the Sub-Commission on Prevention of Discrimination and Protection of Minorities in its resolution 2 (XXXIV) of 1 September 1981, endorsed by the Commission on Human Rights on 10 March 1982 and authorized by resolution 1982/34 of the Economic and Social Council on 7 May 1982. The WGIP held its first meeting in 1982 in Geneva.

The Working Group was made up five members of the Sub-Commission who are appointed by the Chairman of the Sub-Commission. Representatives from UN member states and also from indigenous peoples were also encouraged to participate. The WGIP was to meet annually for five working days prior to the annual sessions of the Sub-Commission. At the first meeting of the WGIP in 1982 in Geneva, the group stated that, although it was mandated to review developments regarding indigenous peoples' rights the Working Group should not become a "chamber of complaints," but its first priority was to articulate international standards on Indigenous rights.[86] Discussions centered both on definitional issues and standards. The primary areas of concern were identified as: a) the right to life, to physical integrity, and to security of indigenous populations, b) the right to self-determination, c) the right to freedom of religion and traditional religious practices, d) the right to land and natural resources, e) civil and political rights, f) the right to education, and g) other rights.[87]

---

[86] UN Commission on Human Rights, Sub-Commission on Prevention of Discrimination and Protection of Minorities. Thirty-Fifth Session. 25 August 1982. Study of the Problem of Discrimination Against Indigenous Populations. *Report of the Working Group on Indigenous Populations on its First Session.* E/CN.4/Sub.2/1982/33, p. 22.

[87] *Ibid.*, pp. 16-21.

Participants at the first WGIP session included twelve states: Australia, New Zealand, Canada, the United States, Argentina, Brazil, Nicaragua, Panama, India, Morocco, Yemen, and Sweden, along with the Palestinian Liberation Organization. There were three indigenous NGOs with ECOSOC consultative status participating: the International Indian Treaty Council (IITC), the World Council of Indigenous Peoples (WCIP) and the Indian Law Resource Center (ILRC). In addition, a number of indigenous nations and confederations of Indigenous nations from the United States, Canada, South America and Australia participated, including the Houdenousaunee, the Six Nations Iroquois Confederacy, the Oglala Lakota, Grand Council Treaty No. 9, Grand Council of the Mikmaq Nation, South American Indian Council (CISA), and the National Federation of Fund Councils.[88] Participation by states, NGOS and indigenous nations and organizations grew steadily in successive meetings of the Working Group in 1983 and 1984.

The dynamics of the first three sessions of the WGIP reflected the shift in international discourse which had occurred through indigenous global politics and also illustrated the threat that states began to feel as changes were emerging in the human rights consensus and the territorial sovereign state system. Indigenous global politics had begun conducting international relations in a new way and for a new set of purposes, which the states now felt to be a direct threat to the established system.

First, the WGIP agreed on the principles that would guide its work, principles which would differ in some remarkable ways from all other UN meetings. As mentioned above, there was broad agreement that the WGIP should not become a "chamber of

[88] *Ibid.*, pp. 3-4.

complaints," but that it should review developments in indigenous rights as part of the work toward the articulation of international standards.[89] In addition, the WGIP determined that it should be open and accessible to indigenous peoples, whether or not their organizations held official ECOSOC consultative status.[90] This was a major departure from UN standing rules and procedures. Furthermore, there would be a voluntary fund set up in order to assist indigenous peoples to attend WGIP meetings in the future. And, as in the 1977 and 1981 conferences, indigenous participants insisted on opening and closing the WGIP meetings with indigenous prayers and ceremonies in direct opposition to standing UN rules and procedures.[91]

Second, the indigenous groups presented their unified argument that existing international human rights standards, which were based on rights of the individual and the equality of individuals, are inadequate to protect indigenous peoples. Furthermore, the integrationist approach of states and the international system, which had encouraged or forced indigenous people to assimilate into settler societies, had led to the desperate situation of indigenous peoples. Therefore, there was a twofold need: 1) to revise the integrationist ILO No. 107, which was the only existing international standard at the time regarding indigenous peoples, and 2) a need to develop a new international standard on indigenous rights which would focus on three priorities: self-determination, land and

---

[89] *Ibid.*, p. 22.

[90] *Ibid.*

[91] There is no mention of this in the official WGIP report; however, several interviewees have described the Pipe ceremony which opened the first session of the WGIP. Transcripts of these anonymous interviews are on file with the author. Audrea Meuhlebach also mentions the importance of indigenous spiritual practices in the WGIP in her article, "'Making Place' at the United Nations: Indigenous Cultural Politics at the U.N. Working Group on Indigenous Populations" *Cultural Anthropology* 16(3): 426.

natural resources, and respect for treaties and international agreements.[92] Governments

recommended that the WGIP examine all existing standards and come up with a new

draft declaration and, at a later stage, possibly one or more conventions.[93] In 1982 at the

first WGIP meeting, the Indian Law Resource Center presented a document, "The

Principles for Guiding the Deliberations of the Working Group"[94] which closely

resembled the Draft Declaration of Principles that was produced by the participants of the

1977 Geneva Conference. It contained statements that asserted indigenous peoples'

rights to land and natural resources and self-determination. It also invalidated any

version of the Doctrine of Discovery which has been relied on by states to deprive

indigenous peoples of their land, natural resources and self-determination without their

"free, prior and informed consent."[95] The document articulated that indigenous peoples'

treaties and other agreements with states must be protected. It also argued that

indigenous peoples were eligible for the same protection of their individual rights as all

other human beings as articulated in the Universal Declaration on Human Rights.

Governments began to argue against indigenous autonomy, land rights and self-

determination in earnest in 1984, taking positions that such "controversial issues go to the

heart of the sovereignty and national integrity of United Nations member states."[96] In an

effort to assuage the fears of some states that these moves necessarily threatened state

sovereignty and national integrity, Canada stated that it had recently inscribed indigenous

---

[92] *Report of the Working Group on Indigenous Populations on its First Session.* E/CN.4/Sub.2/1982/33.
[93] *Ibid.,* p. 7.
[94] WGIP82/AME/2.
[95] *Ibid.*
[96] *Report of the Working Group on Indigenous Populations on its Third Session,* E/CN.4/Sub.2/1984/20, p. 8.

treaty rights into its constitution and had successfully negotiated a major land claim settlement, all without destroying Canada's territorial integrity.[97] This position is ironic given Canada's final vote against the Declaration on the grounds that it threatened Canada's national integrity, but it should be noted that, at that time, Canada was a supporter of the indigenous movement; its resistance to the Declaration came later as Canada was confronted with the realization that the accommodations it had already made were insufficient, as will be elaborated in Chapter 6, since they remained rooted in colonial discourses.

Third, the question of the definition of indigenous peoples was discussed. Several definitions of indigenous peoples were mentioned during this first meeting of the Working Group, with discussion centered largely on three possible models: the working definition used by the Cobo Study, the definition used by the World Council of Indigenous Peoples, and a proposal made by the Indian Law Resource Center. The main problem identified with the existing definitions was that indigenous peoples themselves had not been involved in their formulation.[98] It was decided that indigenous peoples must be involved in formulating the definition which would be used by the WGIP and that the matter should remain under discussion. States argued for clarity, especially in the scope, of the definition of "indigenous populations."[99] Initial definition guidelines included: the existence of different culture, self-identification, and such objective elements as historical continuity or separate institutions than the surrounding state.[100] At the second meeting of

---

[97] *Ibid.*, p. 11.
[98] E/CN.4/Sub.2/1982/33, p. 8.
[99] *Ibid.*, p. 9.
[100] *Ibid.*

102

the WGIP in 1983, it was decided that the WGIP would rely on the U.N. earlier Cobo

Study definition as a working definition and that indigenous peoples must participate in

their self-definition, that the definition not rely on race as that would violate the principle

of non-discrimination and that the indigenous peoples must not be confused with ethnic

minorities.[101] The Cobo definition reads:

> Indigenous communities, peoples and nations are those which, having a
> historical continuity with pre-invasion and pre-colonial societies that
> developed on their territories, consider themselves distinct from other
> sectors of the societies now prevailing in those territories, or parts of them.
> They form at present non-dominant sectors of societies and are determined
> to preserve, develop and transmit to future generations their ancestral
> territories, and their ethnic identity, as the basis of their continued
> existence as peoples, in accordance with their own cultural patterns, social
> institutions and legal systems.[102]

A particular gap in language usage also emerged at the first meeting of the WGIP

which indicated a significant difference in positioning between states and indigenous

peoples which would characterize the WGIP throughout its existence. States and the UN

system consistently used the term "indigenous populations" while indigenous groups

referred to themselves as indigenous "peoples." By using the term "peoples" rather than

populations, the indigenous representatives were asserting their right to self-

determination, which under the UN Charter is a right inherent to all peoples, while the

states preferred to use the term "populations" to indicate that indigenous peoples were not

inherently entitled to self-determination in the same way that "peoples" are.

"Populations" is a term which would continue the international status quo while

---

[101] *Report of the Working Group on Indigenous Populations on its Second Session.* E/CN.4/Sub.2/1983/22, p. 22.
[102] E/CN.4/Sub.2/1983/21/Add.8, para. 379.

103

"peoples" would de-legitimize the "salt water" or "blue water" thesis which had limited

the twentieth century decolonization regime to overseas colonies.[103] At the 1984 session,

this issue was explicitly addressed. Indigenous speakers argued that the WGIP use the

term "peoples" rather than "populations" to indicate the inherent right of self-

determination.[104] States moved quickly to dispute this position, arguing that self-

determination "in an external sovereignty sense did not apply in international law to

enclave populations within non-colonial States."[105] UN staff also indicated that the use of

the tern "peoples" would "create problems in international law."[106] It has been reported

that the United States in particular wanted to avoid the use of the word "peoples" in the

Working Group and would do anything to avoid it, coming up with all sorts of variations

including "persons of indigenous descent" and "persons of indigenous nations."[107] In

general, the states preferred to rely on definitions which would limit the scope of

indigenous rights and would keep the rights focused on individuals rather than

collectivities ("persons" versus "peoples"), while the indigenous delegates favored more

expansive definitions, relying largely on self-identification.

2) **Drafting Stage: Articulating Indigenous Rights (1985-1994)**

The workings and mission of indigenous global politics were well established by

1984, and it was at the fourth session of the Working Group on Indigenous Populations in

---

[103] This strategy was explained in an anonymous interview with an indigenous activist, 2008. Transcript on file with the author.

[104] E/CN.4/Sub.2/AC.4/1984/NGO/2.

[105] E/CN.4/Sub.2/1984/20, p. 13.

[106] *Ibid.*, p. 18.

[107] Anonymous interview with indigenous activist, 2007. Transcript on file with the author.

1985 that the WGIP determined that the "time had come to begin the preparation of a draft" set of official standards on the rights of indigenous peoples.[108] Participants from states, indigenous organizations and other NGOs "indicated general agreement with this drafting mandate and the need for and expectation of the preparation of new standards and norms on Indigenous rights."[109] Indigenous participants expressed a hope that "precise international standards would also bring into line national legislation and its prompt implementation."[110] One government observer noted that by pursuing a declaration, which would be sent to the General Assembly for adoption, could be just as or even more important than a convention. "A declaration on the basic principles of Indigenous rights could eventually become binding upon all members of the international community, like the Universal Declaration of Human Rights, while a convention would be binding only upon the States which choose to ratify it."[111]

Throughout the Drafting Phase, the indigenous rights movement continued to function in accordance with the five themes which had emerged in the earlier period. It maintained its unity and solidarity by grounding itself in diverse cultural and spiritual practices. The standards which were articulated during this phase were intended to be used as a tool of moral persuasion with and against states. Most importantly, the set of standards (the Declaration) which emerged from this process centered on collective rights and indigenous self-determination, a focus which challenged the very foundations of the existing international order and set up a long and difficult fight with states.

---

[108] *Report of the Working Group on Indigenous Populations on its Fourth Session*, E/CN.4/Sub.2/1985/22, p. 14.
[109] *Ibid.*
[110] *Ibid.*
[111] *Ibid.*, p. 19.

There were two draft texts submitted to the Working Group for consideration as starting points toward elaborating a Declaration. The first text was a Declaration of Principles adopted at the Fourth General Assembly of the World Council of Indigenous Peoples in Panama, September 1984.[112] The World Council of Indigenous Peoples (WCIP) had been founded in the 1970s by the National Indian Brotherhood of Canada, the National Congress of American Indians and the Nordic Saami Council. It had gained ECOSOC status in 1977.[113] For simplicity, I will refer to this first draft as the World Council of Indigenous Peoples, or "WCIP Draft." The second text presented to the Working Group was a Draft Declaration of Principles jointly proposed by the Indian Law Resource Center, Four Directions Council, National Aboriginal and Islander Legal Service, National Indian Youth Council, Inuit Circumpolar Conference, and the International Indian Treaty Council.[114] I will refer to this text as the "Indigenous Organizations Draft." These two draft texts, which resemble one another and earlier declarations of principles in some crucial ways, also differed in some important respects. While the basic rights and principles expressed in each draft are identical, the order and emphasis each principle receives varies by the draft. In general, the Indigenous Organizations Draft employs a more sophisticated legal, UN style, reflecting the international and UN experience and expertise many of these organizations had already gained by this time.

---

[112] E/CN.4/Sub.2/1985/22, Annex III. Also appears as E/CN.4/Sub.2/AC.4/1985/WP.4 and Corr. 1.
[113] Dunbar-Ortiz, 2006, p. 64.
[114] E/CN.4/Sub.2/1985/22 Annex IV. Also appears as E/CN.4/Sub. 2/AC.4/1985/WP.4/Add.4.

The WCIP Draft consists of 17 principles which are clearly stated at the end of the text as "the minimum standards which states shall respect and implement."[115] The Indigenous Organizations Draft contains 20 principles and opens with a statement that indigenous peoples are equal to all other human beings in their rights to life and right to be free from oppression and discrimination. Both texts place self-determination as the top priority—it is listed as Principle 1 in the WCIP Draft and Principle 2 in the Indigenous Organizations Draft (following the assertion of the full humanity of Indigenous peoples)—and the verbiage used in both drafts is similar, although with one difference which is small but of crucial importance: "All Indigenous peoples have the right *of* self-determination"[116] in the WGIP Draft, and "All Indigenous nations and peoples have the right *to* self-determination" in the Indigenous Organizations Draft[117] (emphasis added.) This difference between "of" and "to" is significant in international law, but it is a difference that the indigenous participants apparently did not notice or appreciate at this juncture, but it is a distinction which would later work to their detriment.

Both drafts also then proclaim the importance of land rights and natural resources rights. As the WCIP Draft states, "All States within which an Indigenous people lives shall recognize the population, territory and institutions of the Indigenous people."[118] The Indigenous Organizations Draft, in two statements, claims that states must respect the

[115] E/CN.4/Sub.2/1985/22, Annex III.
[116] WGIP Draft, E/CN.4/Sub.2/1985/22, Annex III, para. 1.
[117] Indigenous Organizations Draft, E/CN.4/Sub.2/1985/22 Annex IV, para 2.
[118] WGIP Draft, E/CN.4/Sub.2/1985/22, Annex III, para. 2.

jurisdiction of indigenous territory and makes a very strong statement regarding land and

resources rights in Principle 4:

> Indigenous nations and peoples are entitled to the permanent control and enjoyment of their aboriginal ancestral-historical territories. This includes surface and subsurface rights, inland and coastal waters, renewable and nonrenewable resources, and the economics based on these resources.[119]

The WCIP Draft devotes six more paragraphs to land and natural resources issues,

four paragraphs to culture, language, religion and educational rights, and five paragraphs

to other political rights issues such as participation in the State and respect for treaties

and other agreements. The Indigenous Organizations Draft includes all of these rights

and adds several more important rights to their draft text. First, the Indigenous

Organizations Draft proclaims that "Indigenous nations and peoples are subjects of

international law."[120] Second, this draft text includes the possibility of compensation for

lost lands as an option where return of land is not possible, whereas the WCIP Draft only

stated that "lands and resources shall be returned."[121] The Indigenous Organizations Draft

also included one paragraph which stated that disputes between indigenous peoples and

their surrounding states should be adjudicated by an international, rather than a domestic,

authority and another paragraph that reserved the right of indigenous nations to "engage

in self-defence against State actions"[122] as a part of the right to self-determination.

The Indigenous Organizations Draft also included another crucial component, one

which delegitimized the foundation of a number of states and a legal principle still

---

[119] Indigenous Organizations Draft, E/CN.4/Sub.2/1985/22 Annex IV, para 4.
[120] Indigenous Organizations Draft, E/CN.4/Sub.2/1985/22 Annex IV, para 15.
[121] WGIP Draft, E/CN.4/Sub.2/1985/22, Annex III, para. 9.
[122] Indigenous Organizations Draft, E/CN.4/Sub.2/1985/22 Annex IV, para 18.

present in international law and politics. This Draft included a statement which
invalidated all doctrines of discovery or conquest: "Discovery, conquest, settlement or a
theory of *terra nullius* and unilateral action are never legitimate bases for states to claim
or retain the territories of Indigenous nations or peoples."[123] The Indigenous
Organizations Draft then closed with another statement which acknowledged that
indigenous peoples have the same human rights and fundamental freedoms as all other
peoples and shall not be subject to discrimination.

States reacted swiftly and immediately to the strong indigenous claims to self-
determination, land and natural resources rights present in both of these drafts. One state
member of the Working Group stated that self-determination does not grant the right to
independence because the UN international definition of "peoples" remained unclear.[124]
Another government observer expressed "concern over proposals relating to the right of
self-determination…which would imply a right of secession."[125] He also made the claim
that, since they were not states, indigenous peoples were not in fact subjects of
international law. The UN-appointed Working Group responded to these two drafts by
creating a first set of seven draft principles,[126] which I will refer to as the "1985 Working
Group Draft Principles" (shown as Appendix 2). These seven principles acknowledged
that indigenous peoples had the same fundamental rights and freedoms as reflected in
existing international instruments and acknowledged that indigenous peoples enjoyed
individual and certain collective rights. The 1985 Working Group Draft Principles

---

[123] Indigenous Organizations Draft, E/CN.4/Sub.2/1985/22 Annex IV, para 6.
[124] E/CN.4/Sub.2/1985/22, p. 15.
[125] *Ibid.*, p, 19.
[126] Working Group on Indigenous Populations Draft Principles (preliminary wording).
E/CN.4/Sub.2/1985/22, Annex II.

indicated that the UN-appointed members of the Working Group which has drafted the principles were beginning to accept that indigenous rights must include collective rights, but it also indicted resistance on land rights and self-determination. The 1985 Working Group Draft stated that indigenous peoples had the "collective right to exist and to be protected against genocide", the right to "religious traditions and practices", education, language, and cultural identity, but there was absolutely no mention of land rights or self-determination in this version. Governments and indigenous organizations were invited to submit comments and suggestions on this draft "point of departure" prepared by the Working Group.

Prior to the next regular Working Group meeting in Geneva in 1987, a frustrated Indigenous Caucus merged the two 1984 draft documents prepared by indigenous organizations into a single consensus document which it presented back to the Working Group at its 1987 session. This new document was again called a Declaration of Principles.[127] I will refer to this document as the 1987 Declaration of Principles. This document "had obtained consensus among the participants of the 1987 (Indigenous) Preparatory meeting, including Indigenous leaders and representatives who had not been present at the 1985 session."[128] The Indigenous Caucus presented this document to the WGIP for its consideration as a basis for the Draft Declaration on Indigenous Peoples' Rights in place of the Working Group's set of principles that it had drafted at the last 1985 session.

---

[127] Declaration of Principles adopted by the Indigenous Peoples Preparatory Meeting, held at Geneva 27-31 July 1987. E/CN.4/Sub.2/1987/22, Annex V.
[128] E/CN.4/Sub.2/1987/22, p. 14.

This new set of 22 principles more closely resembles the 1984 Indigenous Organizations Draft in its style, tone and content. It opens with an assertion of the equal humanity of indigenous peoples, followed by assertions of what I will call the "hard rights" of self-determination and land rights and then articulations of various "soft rights" of individuals and collectives. I chose to break down rights into "hard" and "soft" categories at this point in the analysis in order to indicate not only that one set was more difficult to deal with in a practical sense within the Working Group setting, but also to get at the critical nuance of these rights in an international relations context. The "hard" rights strike at some important fundamentals of the existing international system of states: land, territory, sovereignty and self-determination. Because indigenous groups were presenting and pushing for certain re-articulations of these concepts, I term them "hard" rights in order to indicate both difficulty in negotiation but also to expose their perceived threat to the "hard core" of the international system, that is, state territorial sovereignty. "Soft" rights, such as rights to culture, language, education and religion, are merely extensions of existing human rights and do not challenge the existing international order in the same way as "hard" rights because states can make efforts to secure these rights with very little systemic change. While recognition and protection of these rights involves some change to thinking about the inclusion of collective rights in the international human rights consensus and the complementary of collective rights to individual rights, the changes required by states and the UN system to secure these rights is not as fundamental as the changes brought forward by the "hard" rights.

111

The first article in the 1987 Declaration of Principles asserts that indigenous peoples have the same rights to life and freedom from oppression as all other human beings—a statement that indisputably places this document squarely within the human rights framework of the UN. Article 2 then states that "all Indigenous nations and peoples have the right to self-determination" following the verbiage of the 1984 Indigenous Organizations Draft. The next five articles deal explicitly with the right to land and territory, including "the permanent control and enjoyment of their aboriginal ancestral-historical territories" in article 4. Article 6 invalidates any theory of discovery, conquest, settlement or *terra nullius*. Negotiated compensation is offered as an alternative to land return in article 7. Articles 11 through 21 deal with a variety of individual and collective rights such as education, culture, religion and travel.

When this 1987 Declaration of Principles was presented to the WGIP, states again voiced their objections. Canada argued that the principle of self-determination only applied to colonial or foreign occupation and not to "support secessionist or separatist moves within democratic and independent states."[129] Other states, led by India, re-asserted that the international definition of "peoples" entitled to the right of self-determination was "subject to different interpretations" and should not apply to "indigenous populations" or other minorities.[130] The governments did show strong support for the cultural, educational and religious rights of indigenous peoples since indigenous cultures "formed part of humankind's cultural heritage."[131] So, while collective rights of indigenous peoples to "softer areas" such as culture, education and

---

[129] E/CN.4/Sub.2/1987/22, p. 15.
[130] *Ibid.*, p. 16.
[131] *Ibid.*

religion did not pose a great deal of conflict in the WGIP, the "harder rights" to land and self-determination of indigenous peoples invoked the fiercest resistance from states. Given the substantial differences in content between the UN-drafted 1985 Working Group Draft Principles and the indigenous-drafted 1987 Declaration of Principles, and the desire of both the states and Indigenous organizations to focus discussion on specific proposals, the Working Group members agreed to ask Chair/Rapporteur Erica-Irene Daes to prepare a full draft text of a declaration on indigenous peoples' rights prior to the next session of the Working Group in 1988.

Ms. Daes presented her draft Universal Declaration on Indigenous Rights to the Working Group at its 1988 session. I will call this the First Daes Draft. She stated in the WGIP session that she considered this text "a very preliminary first draft" but that she had "tried to cover all the substantive issues brought to the attention of the Working Group"[132] using existing human rights instruments and the Cobo report, as well as oral and written proposals presented to the WGIP during its previous sessions.

There were several significant features of this First Daes Draft which showed some resolution to points of conflict which had existed between states and indigenous groups since discussions on international indigenous rights had begun in 1977. First was the usage of the term "indigenous peoples" rather than "indigenous populations." Although certain states still objected to the use of "peoples" in the text, one member of the Working Group[133] stated that "although the concept of 'peoples' had not been defined

---

[132] E/CN.4/Sub.2/1988/24, p. 17.

[133] Every attempt has been made to specify countries and individuals who made particular statements in the Working Group, however many such details are often not recoverable based on existing documentation. The Working Group reports often do not list specifics of which country or which individual on the Working

113

by the United Nations, State practice and other indications in national legislation showed that it could be used in the case of Indigenous peoples."[134]

Second, Ms. Daes noted that the text included both individual and collective rights "with a special emphasis on the latter as an inherent and essential element of Indigenous rights."[135] As another Working Group member noted as well, "collective rights should not be considered as contrary to already existing individual rights, but rather as complementary and supportive of those."[136] Again, some states objected to this but were reassured by members of the Working Group that an appropriate balance between individual and collective rights was being sought. One member noted that "the draft declaration should place emphasis on collective rights and ensure that the exercise of individual rights would not be used to jeopardize the rights of the community."[137] The complementarity of collective rights to individual rights was a particularly important victory for the indigenous representatives as they had been making their case for years that the recognition of individual rights alone was inadequate to protect indigenous societies and cultures. The tenacity, solidarity and persuasiveness of the Indigenous Caucus had resulted in this major success in the Working Group.

Group made a particular statement. The reports typically refer to "one state" or "a group of states" or "one member of the Working Group" rather than specify them by name. I have examined the numerous official statements submitted by governments and NGOs to doCIP, in order to decipher the source of statements, but in same cases, these details were not possible to reconstruct. In these instances, I have followed UN Working Group practice as executed in their reports and refer simply to "a state," "some states," and "a member of the Working Group." This practice reflects only a paucity of detailed information in the documentary record, and does not reflect any attempt on my part to hide identities.

[134] E/CN.4/Sub.2/1988/24, p. 20.
[135] *Ibid.*, p. 18.
[136] *Ibid.*, p. 20.
[137] *Ibid.*

Third, there was an affirmation of land and resources rights for indigenous peoples, although it was much weaker than the verbiage in the earlier texts which had been prepared by indigenous groups, indicating that the victory of collective rights inclusion was tempered by a continued resistance regarding land and self-determination. The First Daes Draft stated that indigenous peoples "had the right of ownership and possession of the lands" and "the right to special measures to ensure their control over surface resources"[138] but it left out subsurface rights, did not protect communal land ownership and did not condemn doctrines of discovery, conquest or *terra nullius*. Governments continued to voice their concerns that the draft text needed to address all the differing factual and legal situations of indigenous land tenure throughout the world. Governments also stated their continued desire to keep the declaration text "realistic and acceptable to all the parties involved to the greatest extent possible."[139] States were also concerned about the extent to which such a declaration would imply that they had certain duties toward indigenous peoples. In other words, states expressed concerns about the extent to which they might be expected to protect, guarantee or provide such rights for indigenous peoples.

Finally, the First Daes Draft did not include a definition of indigenous peoples as had been earlier requested by states. Ms. Daes decided to favor the position of the Indigenous Caucus and leave the issue of definition unarticulated in the draft text.

There were two striking features of the First Daes Draft which fell far short of indigenous peoples' expectations, specifically surrounding the issue of self-

---

[138] E/CN.4/Sub.2/1988/24, p. 24.
[139] *Ibid.*, p. 19.

determination. In the First Daes Draft, the order of the articles was reversed from the earlier indigenous texts. Placed at the top now were rights to culture, identity, religion, language and education while rights to land and resources came second. In Part V, articles 23 and 24 (out of a total of 28 articles) mention a right to "autonomy" and to "autonomous institutions." So, despite clear articulations of the importance of self-determination to indigenous peoples in their earlier draft texts and every year in Working Group discussions, Ms. Daes appears to have deliberately softened and reduced it in importance in her first draft text. The Indigenous Caucus made a statement that while they appreciated Ms. Daes' standard-setting activities, this draft did not adequately reflect indigenous peoples' "needs, concerns and aspirations"[140] because it did not include the right to self-determination and it did not fully address the collective right to lands and resources. The Indigenous Caucus position was that self-determination and land rights should be the fundamental principles of the draft declaration.

In the next session of the Working Group, Ms. Daes presented her first revision of the Draft Universal Declaration on the Rights of Indigenous Peoples, which I will refer to as the Revised Daes Draft.[141] Very few substantive changes appeared in this draft. The order of the articles remained the same as it was in the First Daes Draft, with "soft rights" to education, culture, language and religion placed ahead of "hard rights" to land and "autonomy." Although, there was now a nod to self-determination in the preamble, it was more exclusionary in character than inclusionary in terms of indigenous peoples. The Preamble phrase reads: "nothing in this declaration may be used as a justification for

---

[140] *Ibid.*, p. 21.
[141] E/CN.4/Sub.2/1990/42, Annex II.

116

denying to any people, which otherwise satisfies the criteria generally established by human rights instruments and international law, its right to self-determination."[142] In essence, if a people already qualified for self-determination under existing international instruments, they may not be denied it. So, this text was merely restating the international status quo, not recognizing any extension of self-determination rights to indigenous peoples.

When I asked an indigenous participant of the WGIP about the reticence of Ms. Daes to include self-determination as a right of indigenous peoples and to place it prominently in the draft text, he responded:

> What I always remember was (Ms. Daes') gavel. Because anytime we would bring specific points that differed from her original declaration and we also kept hammering on those two themes of treaties and self-determination. We also introduced the term of sovereignty which to her at the time—she could almost get self-determination because it's in the UN Charter and we used that reference. But when we started talking about sovereignty, then we were relegated to the position of being ethnic minorities. Or...she would use the term that the Charter said, that one country cannot interfere with the internal affairs of another country. So these were the arguments against us.[143]

As this activist expressed, the Working Group itself (which was comprised of government representatives and UN staff), with Ms. Daes as its chair, was interested in maintaining the international status quo or at least minimizing change to the international order. Although there was wide acceptance that indigenous peoples' were not being adequately protected under existing international instruments, the Working Group resisted the fundamental changes which indigenous peoples argued were necessary,

---

[142] *Ibid.*
[143] Anonymous interview by author with indigenous activist (#6). 2008.

especially in the areas of self-determination and land rights. Resistance at this juncture centered around the draft text, what would be included, excluded and placed in positions of prominence. Arguments continued over issues of indigenous definition as well as the "peoples/populations" debate. Several governments, particularly the United States, New Zealand and Australia, voiced continued concern over the use of the term "peoples" and the implication this term carries in international law in rights of secession. These states wanted a clear articulation of indigenous self-determination as strictly limited to internal interpretations and to exclude the possibility of a right to secession. The United States in particular also continued to express concern over the inclusion of collective rights.[144] Indigenous representatives, on the other hand, continued to assert the importance of two elements in the text of the declaration: self-determination and collective rights. As anthropologist Andrea Muehlebach wrote in an article on the dynamics of the Working Group, there was a "striking unity of the Indigenous arguments in the hundreds of Indigenous interventions made before the WGIP."[145] Muehlenbach attributes this unified indigenous position to several factors: a common history of oppression, the work of the global Indigenous Caucus, and, most importantly, a discourse of global indigeneity founded on the centrality of self-determination, which emerged out of the UN process itself. At this point, however, the Indigenous arguments met fierce resistance from both states and the UN system over self-determination, land rights, and to a lesser extent, collective rights.

---

[144] E/CN.4/Sub.2/1989/36, p. 18.
[145] Andrea Meuhlebach, "'Making Place' at the United Nations: Indigenous Cultural Politics at the U.N. Working Group on Indigenous Populations", *Cultural Anthropology* 16(3):415-448, 2001, p. 421.

Given the seeming impasse between states and the UN on the one hand and indigenous groups on the other hand, Ms. Daes recommended to the 1990 session of the Working Group that three drafting groups be established in order to accelerate work on the draft text of the declaration. The three groups, which were each open to all Working Group participants, including state representatives, UN staff, and indigenous representatives, were charged with elaborating the Revised Daes Draft, based upon the consensus decision-making model advocated by the indigenous representatives.[146] Drafting Group I, which was chaired by Miguel Alfonso Martinez, was to consider land and resources rights, Drafting Group II, chaired by Danilo Turk, was entrusted with political rights and autonomy and Drafting Group III, chaired by Erica-Irene Daes, considered all other rights.[147] These three groups met during the first week of the Working Group session in 1990, followed by full plenary sessions during the second week where they presented their recommendations for revisions to the Revised Daes Draft.

Drafting Group I on land and resources made a number of changes to the text which enhanced the collective land and resources rights of indigenous peoples. Drafting Group II recommended that a new paragraph should come at the very beginning of the operative part of the declaration which would read: "Indigenous peoples have the right to self-determination"[148] in order to represent the fundamental importance of this issue. Drafting Group III made a few non-substantive changes in the wording of several articles.

---

[146]E/CN.2/Sub.2/1990/42, p. 14.

[147]*Ibid.*, p. 4.

[148] Report of the informal drafting groups established to consider the first revised text of the draft Universal Declaration on Indigenous Rights, E/CN.4/Sub.2/AC.4/1990/7/Add.1.

Some governments continued to strongly object to the use of certain terminology, specifically the terms "territories," "peoples," and "self-determination"[149] as implying that indigenous peoples had a right of secession as was the case for former colonial territories. Governments also expressed continued concern over the reference to collective rights, especially whether the rights were actually collective per se or whether they were a collection of individual rights.[150]

A member of the Working Group observed that:

> The time has now come to give some fresh thought to the concept of self-determination. …Legal concepts undergo a constant process of evolution, and that it is the responsibility of the Working Group to help shape the development of those concepts which are of relevance to the continued survival and flourishing of the world's Indigenous peoples.[151]

In other words, there was now public acknowledgment that the process had reached a point where a new conception of self-determination could be emerging which would apply to indigenous peoples. The Working Group drew upon a recent statement that Professor S. James Anaya made at a conference in Moscow that same year in order to help elaborate this emerging and evolving conception of indigenous self-determination:

> In that statement, it had been pointed out that the concept of self-determination would only in rare instances imply the right to independent statehood; rather, an Indigenous non-statist conception of self-determination implies substantive rights to the economic, political and social means for Indigenous modes of life, and procedural rights to shape the decisions affecting those modes of life, all of which will vary with the contemporary circumstances of particular Indigenous peoples around the world. …This conception of self-determination would, like many other

---

[149] *Ibid.*, p. 23.
[150] *Ibid.*, p. 24.
[151] *Ibid.*, p. 25.

international human rights standards, condition but in no way deny the principle of territorial integrity.[152]

This emerging indigenous conception of self-determination that was developing out of the Working Group process would alter, yet support, state territorial integrity. While the understanding of self-determination found in the existing international order was based on territorial sovereignty, the indigenous use of the term was somewhat different. This difference required clarification, and indigenous organizations hoped that such clarification would allay the fears of some governments about the implications of the declaration.

At the ninth session of the WGIP in 1991, Chairperson Daes presented a further revised draft declaration working paper[153] based upon the draft proposals of the three drafting groups at the 1990 WGIP session, as well as comments she received throughout the year from governments, indigenous organizations, international organizations and others. This revised draft, which I will refer to as the First Reading Draft,[154] was arduously discussed paragraph by paragraph in the Working Group. This draft text now had a preamble and 30 operative paragraphs. In accordance with indigenous groups' requests and the recommendation of the prior drafting group, the first operative paragraph read unequivocally:

> Indigenous peoples have the right to self-determination, in accordance with international law. By virtue of this right, they freely determine their relationship with the States in which they live, in a spirit of coexistence

---

[152] E/CN.4/Sub.2/1990/42, p. 25-26 referencing S. James Anaya, "The Capacity of International Law to Advance Ethnic or Nationality Rights Claims", statement delivered at the Conference of USSR-USA Scholars' Dialogue on Human Rights and the Future, held at Moscow, 19-21 June 1990.
[153] E/CN.4/Sub.2/1991/36.
[154] E/CN.4/Sub.2/1991/40 Annex II.

with other citizens, and freely pursue their economic, social, cultural and spiritual development in conditions of freedom and dignity.[155]

Next came a series of operative paragraphs relating to the equal rights of indigenous peoples to all other peoples and then three paragraphs that explicitly articulated the "collective and individual rights" of indigenous peoples to existence, to maintain their distinct cultures, and the freedom to be protected from genocide. The "soft rights" to education, language, culture and religion appeared in the middle paragraphs, followed by a series of paragraphs on land rights. Indigenous peoples had the right to "maintain their distinctive and profound relationship with their lands, territories and resources" and had the "collective and individual right to own, control and use the lands and territories they have traditionally occupied or otherwise used." Land restitution was called for, although compensation was indicated where restitution was not possible. This text included "the right to participate fully at the State level" while also maintaining the "collective right to autonomy in matters relating to their own internal and local affairs" and the "right to decide upon the structures of their autonomous institutions." Also included was the "right to maintain and develop traditional contacts, relations and cooperation...across State boundaries." Fair and mutually acceptable dispute resolution with States was also included as a right. Finally, there was a statement that these were the "minimum standards" for indigenous peoples' survival and well-being.[156]

This draft text was strongly supportive of indigenous rights as articulated by indigenous peoples, largely based upon scant participation by governments in the drafting

---

[155] *Ibid.*
[156] *Ibid.*

122

groups at the previous session of the Working Group and the handful of comments and suggestions sent by governments to Ms. Daes during the year. So when this draft received its first reading during the 1991 session of the Working Group, it faced some familiar strong resistance from states. New Zealand argued that any new international instrument must be consistent with existing international standards. Brazil expressed concern over ambiguity within the text and also warned against adopting text which may be unacceptable to governments. Several governments indicated that a modification of self-determination would be necessary to make the text acceptable to states.

The issue of indigenous prayer and ceremony emerged during the WGIP in the early 1990s. Indigenous representatives had insisted, as they had in earlier international and UN meetings, that the WGIP sessions be opened and closed with an indigenous prayer and/or a ceremony. Chair Daes had allowed this practice since she took over the Chairperson position in 1984. During one session (either 1991 or 1992, according to the memory of indigenous delegates who were present[157]), Ms. Daes forbade the prayer. She was met with such an angry reaction by the indigenous delegates present that she left the room. When she returned to the room, the indigenous delegates were just finishing their prayer. So the centrality of a spiritual and cultural foundation for unity and solidarity in the global indigenous rights movement was confirmed in the WGIP, even if in protest.

Following this first reading, a second reading draft was prepared for the tenth session of the Working Group in 1992. This text will be referred to as the Second Reading Draft.[158] Again, this draft text was subjected to an arduous paragraph by

---

[157] This story is told by several indigenous activists who were present at both the 1991 and 1992 meetings.
[158] E/CN.4/Sub.2/1992/33, Annex I.

123

paragraph reading. Yet again, the first operative paragraph underwent a change of text. It now read:

> Indigenous peoples have the right of self-determination, in accordance with international law by virtue of which they may freely determine their political status and institutions and freely pursue their economic, social and cultural development. An integral part of this is the right to autonomy and self-government.[159]

This revised text represented two particular and divergent moves. First, the paragraph reflected a return to the verbiage "right of self-determination" which indicated the inherency of this right for all peoples in accordance with existing international human rights conventions. As IITC's Bill Means articulated,

> We had not only our interpretation of self-determination, but we had to go into other documents in the UN system which talked about self-determination. And so we had to do our homework, and so that's how we began to emphasize the human rights aspect because human rights are inalienable and inherent. Once we turned that corner on human rights, we began to emphasize that more, the right of self-determination.[160]

The second notable move in this revised text on self-determination was its qualification as meaning "autonomy and self-government." This was in response to a number of government complaints that the earlier text on self-determination was in conflict with international law and undermined state sovereignty. New Zealand and Brazil in particular voiced concern over inconsistency of indigenous self-determination with other international standards.[161] Canada indicated that it was prepared to accept the principle of self-determination as long as it meant solely an internal self-determination and

---

[159] *Ibid.*

[160] Interview by author with Bill Means, September 2008, St. Paul, Minnesota.

[161] E/CN.4/Sub.2/1992/33, p. 13.

recognized the jurisdiction of existing states.[162] Australia also indicated that it could

support this emergent view of self-determination involving a special position for

indigenous peoples within the state, as long as it did not threaten territorial integrity.[163]

The United States noted, however, that the current text in paragraph one could possibly

undermine state sovereignty.[164] Guest scholar Douglas Sanders noted that the Working

Group was creating a double meaning of self-determination as an international rights

standard.[165] Australia noted that self-determination for indigenous peoples should be "an

aspirational concept which provided a firm basis for progressively increasing the

decision-making powers of Indigenous peoples."[166]

New paragraphs were also added regarding protection during armed conflict and a

prohibition on the forcible removal of indigenous peoples. No changes were made to the

passages on collective rights even though the United States continued to voice its

objection to the inclusion of any rights other than those that support non-discrimination

and equality of individuals.[167] Japan also noted that the inclusion of so many collective

rights was unprecedented in international instruments, and it was concerned about this.[168]

Governments continued to take exception with the use of certain terminology without

definition, such as "peoples" and "lands and territories." The United States, Canada,

New Zealand and Australia also expressed general concerns about the document's

compatibility with domestic law and whether it was a "balanced and realistic aspirational

---

[162] *Ibid.*, p. 17.
[163] *Ibid.*
[164] *Ibid.*
[165] *Ibid.*, p. 18.
[166] *Ibid.*, p. 17.
[167] *Ibid.*, p. 14.
[168] *Ibid.*, p. 20.

text."[169] Indigenous groups, on the other hand, recognized that they would likely lose all input into the process once the text moved beyond the Working Group[170] and back into the UN Sub-Commission where only member states could change and make decisions regarding the text. Therefore, the Indigenous Caucus aimed to create a document which was as strong as possible, as it would likely be weakened later by UN member states.

At the 11th session of the Working Group in 1993, agreement was reached on a final text which was to be sent to the Sub-Commission on Prevention of Discrimination and Protection of Minorities for approval. This text, the Draft Declaration on the Rights of Indigenous Peoples as agreed upon by the Members of the Working Group at its Eleventh Session[171] closely resembled the Second Reading Draft from 1992. While there were some cosmetic changes like renaming the "operative paragraphs" as "articles", the only major substantive change concerned self-determination. The article on self-determination was moved down from first to third, behind a new Article 1 which mentioned specifically the UN Charter and the Universal Declaration of Human Rights and a new Article 2 which articulated the equality of indigenous individuals with all other individuals and their equal right to be free from discrimination. The addition of these two articles was a direct result of concerns expressed by certain governments, most notably the United States, Canada, New Zealand and Australia regarding the consistency of this declaration with existing international instruments.[172] With these two articles as preliminaries which attempted to balance indigenous self-determination within the

---

[169] *Ibid.*, p. 13.
[170] Anonymous interview by author with indigenous activist, 2007. Transcript on file with the author.
[171] E/CN.4/Sub.2/1993/29, Annex I.
[172] Anonymous interview by author with indigenous activist, 2007. Transcript on file with the author.

context of equality of all citizens, the text of Article 3 now read: "Indigenous peoples have the right of self-determination. By virtue of that right they freely determine their political status and freely pursue their economic, social and cultural development." No specific clarification was now offered about indigenous self-determination meaning autonomy or self-government. It was already implied in the preceding articles that this version of self-determination fully respected the territorial integrity of sovereign states as established in the UN Charter. At the same time, the use of the term "right *of* self-determination" rather than "the right *to* self-determination" retained the meaning of inherency desired by indigenous peoples. Chairperson Daes further advocated for drawing a distinction between

> "external" self-determination, by which peoples liberated themselves from imposed alien rule, and "internal" self-determination, by which collective groups of Indigenous peoples sought to preserve and develop their cultural and territorial identity within the political order of the State in which they lived.[173]

Even with these clarifications, Canada, New Zealand and Chile still withheld support for indigenous self-determination.[174]

The United States also remained opposed to the collective rights provisions in the declaration which went "far beyond the limited collective rights recognized in international law."[175] Canada raised concerns that the final draft was unclear about the issue of land rights. Did indigenous land rights mean all traditional lands and territories?

---

[173] E/CN.4/Sub.2/1993/29, p. 16.
[174] *Ibid.*, p. 15.
[175] *Ibid.*, p. 18.

This would be problematic for states like Canada, and so it proposed some sort of a "reasonable limits" clause on land rights.[176]

Despite these remaining concerns and reservations by states, the Working Group on Indigenous Populations celebrated the fact that, after 11 years, it had achieved a final consensus text, which was sent to the Sub-Commission for consideration in 1994. The Sub-Commission on Prevention of Discrimination and Protection of Minorities in resolution 1994/45 adopted the Draft Declaration on the Rights of Indigenous Peoples (Appendix 3) on 26 August 1994. It then also created a new inter-sessional working group on the Draft Declaration on the Rights of Indigenous Peoples (WGDD) in order to move the declaration process into its next phase, elaboration.[177]

3) Elaboration Phase: The Fight for Change (1995 – 2006)

The highly volatile and often hostile elaboration phase of the Declaration on the Rights of Indigenous Peoples began in 1995 with the first meeting of the inter-sessional working group (WGDD). The WGDD was mandated by the Human Rights Commission to elaborate the Draft Declaration for adoption by the General Assembly before the end of the International Decade on the World's Indigenous Peoples in 2004. The first meeting of the WGDD was attended by 61 governments and 64 Indigenous and non-Indigenous NGOs, so the participation by both NGOs and governments grew substantially since the WGIP meetings, which had active participation by only a handful of governments. Apparently the circulation of the 1994 Draft Declaration to all UN

---

[176] *Ibid.*
[177] Human Rights Council Resolution 1995/32 of 3 March 1995.

member states had sparked more government interest in the indigenous rights process. It is important to note that, in contrast to the WGIP meetings, the WGDD was officially comprised only of governments and UN organizations; indigenous representatives were technically only "observers" not participants. As was the custom by this point, the indigenous representatives again requested that a short ceremony be held at the opening session of the inter-sessional working group (WGDD).[178]

During the first session of the WGDD, the indigenous representatives stood strongly unified. Their position was that the Draft Declaration text adopted by the Sub-Commission in 1994 represented their minimum standard for protection of indigenous peoples. They would accept no limits or qualifications on that text as to do so would legitimize the violations of the rights of indigenous peoples.[179]

Governments, however, raised a series of concerns and advocated for "clarification", "streamlining" and "consistency" with existing international instruments and relied on the primary tactic of "creatively using language to obscure rather than resolve some of the underlying issues."[180] Some states, especially the United States, argued that indigenous peoples were already adequately protected under existing human rights standards and that additional collective rights were not necessary and could be problematic to the principles of equality and universality of human rights. The United States, New Zealand and Australia all advocated that there should not be any special rights which adhered to indigenous peoples but other governments (Canada and the

---

[178] E/CN.4/1996/84.

[179] Statement by the International Indian Treaty Council at the Open-Ended Inter-Sessional Working Group on the Draft Declaration, Geneva, 20 November 1995.

[180] Interview by author with indigenous activist, 2007. Transcript on file with the author.

Netherlands) did not object to the inclusion of collective rights "as long as their contents were clear and they were compatible with international law."[181] Some governments, notably the United States and Australia, stated that the Draft Declaration should be viewed as an aspirational document and not an articulation of existing rights. Other governments requested clarification of certain terminology, especially "peoples", "indigenous peoples", and "self-determination". The most time, however, was spent on discussions of self-determination.

Much debate surrounded the meaning of "self-determination" as used in the Draft Declaration. Many governments argued that the Draft Declaration unacceptably moved the meaning of self-determination beyond its historical context of decolonization, while indigenous representatives made the case that international law should not be frozen in time so that it prohibits a progression of the principle.[182] Governments were most concerned about the implications for state territorial integrity and unity, although a few governments (Colombia, Bolivia, and Venezuela) indicated that a balance could be struck between self-determination for indigenous peoples and the unity and territorial integrity of states. Indigenous representatives argued forcefully that any limitation or qualification of Article 3 on self-determination would be discriminatory since it would imply that indigenous peoples did not enjoy the same inherent right to self-determination as all other "colonized" peoples do.

At the second meeting of the WGDD in 1996, a dramatic conflict arose between the indigenous representatives on the one hand and the states and UN on the

---

[181] E/CN.4/1996/84, p. 12.
[182] E/CN.4/1996/84, p.10.

130

other. The session opened with a statement from the Indigenous Caucus which called for the immediate "adoption of the Draft Declaration on the Rights of Indigenous Peoples in its current text, as approved by the WGIP and the Sub-Commission, in its entirety and with no changes, amendments, or deletions as a minimum standard protecting, promoting and recognizing the rights of Indigenous peoples."[183] The Chairman/Rapporteur Mr. José Urrutia then proposed that the WGDD begin a re-examination of the Draft Declaration article-by-article. This proposal was rejected outright by the Indigenous Caucus, standing by their position that the Sub-Commission text already represented more than 10 years of article-by-article work, and it comprised a minimum standard of indigenous rights. The Indigenous Caucus, in a consensus statement read by Moana Jackson,[184] then requested that there be open debate on the Draft Declaration as a whole with the full participation of indigenous representatives in order to bring a "sense of dignity to the proceedings." The Indigenous Caucus stated that "the need for a cooperative approach is crucial to building consensus" and if indigenous peoples were merely observers in the process, "then many have no desire to subject themselves to such a low standard of recognition." The rules of the WGDD were flawed, they said, and violated "the spirit of cooperation and consensus that should guide this process." Chairman/Rapporteur Urrutia reacted with indifference to the requests by the Indigenous Caucus and did not accept any amendment to the inter-sessional working group rules or procedures. The indigenous representatives then staged a "walkout in protest of the agenda and the lack of response to

---

[183] This handwritten statement dated 25 October 1996, issued by the International Indian Treaty Council on behalf of the Indigenous Caucus, is on file with doCIP in Geneva.
[184] Statement by the Indigenous Caucus, October 25, 1996.

their collective proposals for change."[185] The indigenous representatives wanted to defend the Draft Declaration in its entirety, not discuss articles one-by-one. They viewed this as another tactic by governments to alter and diminish the text.[186]

The Chair then agreed to allow a general debate on the Draft Declaration to be added to the WGDD agenda and so many indigenous representatives returned to the plenary session so that they could defend the Draft Declaration against amendments, especially on Article 3 concerning self-determination. The indigenous representatives were still gravely disappointed that they held only "observer" status even though they were allowed to make statements for the record. Some indigenous delegates from Australia, New Zealand and North America went home and never returned to the UN because the "observer" status did not allow for full and equal participation. As Moana Jackson stated, "because of the implacable opposition of states to self-determination, the Maori delegation that year withdrew from the process."[187] Other indigenous representatives stayed on, yet, according to the Indigenous Caucus, all indigenous peoples' remained united in their commitment to defend the current Draft Declaration[188] and to the principle that the decision of a group to stay or leave was a reflection of that group's inherent self-determination.[189]

This walkout protest was a success for the indigenous rights movement in two important ways.[190] First, it succeeded in gaining a partial change in the agenda, even if

---

[185] Press Release: Indigenous Peoples' Caucus Calls for Change to UN Rules, 28 October 1996.
[186] Anonymous interview by author with indigenous activist, 2007. Transcript on file with the author.
[187] Interview by author with Moana Jackson, Wellington, Aotearoa/New Zealand, 11 March 2008.
[188] Press Release: Indigenous Peoples' Caucus Calls for Change to UN Rules, 28 October 1996
[189] Statement by Indigenous People's Caucus, 25 October 1996.
[190] These successes were articulated by an indigenous activist in interview with the author, 2007.

the participation of indigenous peoples in the WGDD remained incomplete. Second, it helped sort out which governments supported indigenous peoples and which ones were attempting to use rules to limit genuine partnership. The governments which supported the return of indigenous representatives to the plenary were: Canada, Denmark, Sweden, Finland, Norway, Mexico, Chile, Bolivia South Africa and Venezuela. However, Brazil and Argentina requested that the session continue with a discussion of individual articles, a proposal which was supported by the United States, China, Colombia, Australia, and New Zealand.[191]

A general debate on the Draft Declaration was held followed by a discussion of the articles, organized into twelve thematic clusters. In general, there was the least amount of concern about or resistance to the articles that dealt with "softer" rights such as education, language, religion and culture, although certain states like the United States, still regularly voiced their opposition to the inclusion of collective rights. The United States remained concerned that collective rights violated the spirit of citizen equality, non-discrimination and rights of the individual. They asked that these areas be clarified. Government opposition grew as discussion moved into the articles that dealt with lands, resources, territories, treaties and cross-border activities. Canada and Brazil joined the United States in their opposition to such articles, although they usually articulated this opposition in terms of "needing clarification" on the articles in question. The final cluster discussed were the articles dealing with self-determination. At this point, the United States voiced complete opposition. Canada also voiced its "concerns" about these

---

[191] Working Group on the Draft Declaration, Organization of Work (Participation), E/CN.4/1996/WG.15/CRP.7.

articles. During the discussion of each cluster of articles, indigenous representatives strongly and tenaciously made almost the same statement each time: the Indigenous Caucus supports immediate adoption of the existing Sub-Commission text without changes or amendments.

At the next WGDD meeting in 1997, the Chair/Rapporteur again decided to hold general debate before moving to a specific discussion of articles. The WGDD also decided that the group would operate on a consensus decision-making basis.[192] At this meeting, two articles were adopted by consensus of the WGDD without changes or amendments: Article 43, which guaranteed equal rights to male and female indigenous individuals, and Article 5, which stated that every indigenous individual has the right to a nationality, defined as citizenship in a state.[193] Discussion was held on eleven other articles and substantial changes to the text were proposed by Australia, New Zealand, Canada, Brazil, France, Japan, and the United States.

No further articles were adopted in the WGDD for the next seven years. Year after year in the WGDD, general debate was held, but there was a stalemate. Indigenous peoples argued for immediate adoption of the Sub-Commission text and considered it a victory that there was no qualification of "peoples" or of the right to self-determination.[194] States (especially the United States, Canada, New Zealand and Australia) attempted to make amendments and alterations to the text, particularly in the areas of land rights and self-determination. These proposed changes almost always took the form of

---

[192] Interview by author with Andrea Carmen, Executive Director, International Indian Treaty Council, Mille Lacs Nation, 24 September 2007.
[193] E/CN.4/1998/106.
[194] Interview with Andrea Carmen, 24 September 2007.

clarifications, or enhancements of issues of definition. Indigenous groups held strongly

to their support of the original Sub-Commission text while governments attempted to

change, alter, weaken and "clarify" the text, especially in regard to land and self-

determination rights. Discussions were held and changes in text were proposed each

year, but there was only minimal progress and no consensus.

At the 1999 session of the WGDD, the United States made a statement which

summarized its position on the Draft Declaration. The U.S. had difficulties with: a)

turning indigenous peoples' aspirations into "rights", b) the unlimited scope that a lack of

defining "indigenous peoples" provided, c) a lack of taking local realities into account, d)

providing autonomy in international law to all indigenous groups everywhere, and e) the

inclusion of collective rights. Canada, Australia and New Zealand each expressed

support for the Draft Declaration in principle but chided the indigenous groups for not

engaging in "full and constructive dialogue."[195]

At the 2000 WGDD session, a long discussion was held which made some

progress on the issue of self-determination and its evolving nature in international law.

Indigenous organizations tried to make the point that self-determination was not a static

concept locked in the decolonization era but was continually evolving and that most

governments were not viewing self-determination in this way. A number of governments

(New Zealand, Canada, Venezuela, Norway, Finland, France, Spain, Ecuador, Russian

Federation, and Denmark) recognized that self-determination had both internal and

external aspects, but the international consensus had not yet recognized self-

determination this way. Canada spoke up on this point and stated how it "accepted a

---

[195] *Ibid.*, p. 7.

135

right to self-determination for Indigenous peoples which respected the political, constitutional and territorial integrity of democratic States."[196] In 2001, an indigenous co-chair for the meeting was appointed in order to facilitate dialogue but the issue of indigenous participation remained as indigenous representatives were still not involved in agenda setting, or the drafting and adoption of reports. Also that year, the possibility of voting on articles, rather than a pure consensus model, was also discussed as a way to expedite the process.[197]

In 2002, Mexico and Guatemala announced that they both supported the version of the Draft Declaration adopted by the Sub-Commission. That same year, indigenous representatives demanded that they be invited as observers to all private meetings being held between states to discuss the text of the Draft Declaration and the Indigenous Caucus continued to express its desire to fully participate in the plenary WGDD sessions.[198]

Beginning in 2001, the Indigenous Caucus stated that it could consider changes to the text as long as the core principles and the integrity of the original text was maintained. This "cracked the egg" and there was no going back to the original hard-line indigenous position on pure and unwavering support for the Sub-Commission text, according to Andrea Carmen, Executive Director of the International Indian Treaty Council.[199]

---

[196] E/CN.4/2000/84., p. 8.
[197] E/CN.4/2001/85.
[198] E/CN.4/2002/98.
[199] Interview by author with Andrea Carmen, 24 September 2007.

On the first day of the 2004 session of the WGDD, New Zealand, supported by

Denmark, Finland, Iceland, Norway, Sweden and Switzerland, introduced an amended

text for the Draft Declaration.[200] The Indigenous Caucus argued that this text introduced

a number of changes that weakened the rights of indigenous peoples, especially in the

area of land rights, and so they opposed this text in favor of the original Sub-Commission

text.[201] The Chair and many states, however, decided to use the new amended text as the

basis for WGDD discussion for the next two weeks.

On November 29, 2004, the first day of the third week of the 2004 WGDD

session, six indigenous delegates[202] began a hunger strike and spiritual fast "to call the

world's attention to the continued attempts by some states, as well as the UN process

itself, to weaken and undermine the Draft Declaration developed in the UN Working

Group on Indigenous Populations and adopted by the UN Sub-commission."[203] The

hunger strike called for the Sub-commission text to be sent back to the Human Rights

Commission with the message that no consensus had emerged in the WGDD process in

ten years. They rejected attempts to represent any new amended text as a consensus

document. They also protested that "a handful of States" had "the opportunity to weaken

the human rights of Indigenous Peoples" and they insisted that the process must include

the voices of Indigenous peoples themselves.[204] The process that had been implemented

---

[200] E/CN.4/2004/WG.15/CRP.1.
[201] E/CN.4/2005/89.
[202] Adelard Blackman (Buffalo River Dene Nation, Canada), Andrea Carmen (Yaqui Nation, Arizona, USA), Alexis Tiouka (Kalina, French Guyana), Charmaine White Face (Oglala Tetuwan, Sioux Nation Territory, North America), Danny Illie (Traditional Independent Seminole Nation of Florida, United States), Saul Vincente (Zapoteca, Mexico).
[203] Press Release: Hunger Strike by Indigenous Peoples' Representatives at the United Nations, 29 November 2004.
[204] Press Release, 29 November 2004.

137

in the WGDD, they argued, encouraged "openly discriminatory proposals for changes by States which weaken the Declaration, but does not allow us to defend the position of the vast majority of Indigenous Peoples of the world by calling for adoption of the text approved by the Subcommission."[205] The mandate of the WGDD had ended and there was no consensus text.

The hunger strike ended on 2 December 2004 after a meeting of the hunger strikers with the UN High Commissioner on Human Rights and the Vice President of the UN Commission on Human Rights resulted in an important turning point in the process. The High Commissioner promised that no document which differed from the Sub-Commission text would be adopted by the Human Rights Commission if it was not produced by a consensus of indigenous peoples.[206] In response, the WGDD Chair/Rapporteur decided to ask four groups of facilitators to consult with all participants on proposed changes of language. The Human Rights Commission also extended the mandate of the WGDD by one year.

During 2005, the government of Mexico held a workshop intended to discuss, in an informal manner, the major outstanding issues of self-determination, lands, territories and resources. Indigenous experts had also held a meeting during the year and noted that the Indigenous Caucus was ready to provisionally adopt many articles. In the 2005 meeting of the WGDD, Chair/Rapporteur Luis-Enrique Chavez indicated that there was a

---

[205] Open Letter to the President of the UN Commission on Human Rights, from 130 indigenous nations and organizations, 15 March 2005.
[206] Interview by author with Andrea Carmen, 24 September 2007.

need to show progress to the Commission on Human Rights,[207] and therefore, in the spirit of moving forward, he presented a Chairman's proposal[208] on all articles which had been previously discussed. He proclaimed that this text was "as close to the original text as possible, while including proposed amendments where they seemed to be required."[209] I will refer to this text as the Chairman's Proposal.

Even though many states expressed disagreement with the text of the Chairman's Proposal on self-determination, lands and resources and collective rights, this was the last meeting of the WGDD and a consensus on a text was needed. The United States, Australia and New Zealand submitted a proposal on 13 December 2005 intended to weaken Article 3 on self-determination by restricting the meaning of indigenous self-determination to self-management, but this wording was rejected by indigenous representatives and their small group of allied states (especially Mexico and Guatemala.) Some changes were made to the Chairman's text, most notably the addition of Article 45 which added protections for state territorial integrity, some changes to Article 30 regarding land rights and Articles 32 and 34 on collective rights, all intended to provide additional protections to state sovereignty vis-à-vis indigenous peoples' self-determination. The Chairman's Proposal was presented to the Human Rights Council in June 2006 as a final compromise text even though language in the areas of self-determination and land rights could not be agreed upon. The United States, Canada, New Zealand, Australia and the Russian Federation still objected to the key provisions on land

---

[207] The Human Rights Commission was being dissolved and replaced with a new body called the Human Rights Council.

[208] Revised Chairman's Summary and Proposal, E/CN.4/2005/WG.15/2

[209] E/CN.4/2006/79, p. 4.

and self-determination.[210] The majority of states, indigenous organizations and international organizations did voice support for this compromise text.[211]

4) Passage and Implementation Stage: Forging Change (2007 forward)

The Human Rights Council passed the Declaration on the Rights of Indigenous Peoples on 29 June 2006[212] and forwarded it to the General Assembly for adoption by the end of 2006. The Human Rights Council resolution was adopted by a vote of 30 votes for, 2 against and 12 abstentions. Of the states which had posed the majority of opposition to the Declaration in the WGDD, only four were voting members of the Human Rights Council at the time. Brazil voted in favor, Canada and the Russian Federation voted against, and Argentina abstained.

On 20 December 2006, a non-action resolution was put forward by a group of African states (led by Namibia) to defer action on the Declaration in the General Assembly arguing that, since the African countries had not been involved in the working groups, more time was needed for further consultation.[213] Although African countries have had longstanding issues with how to define "indigenous peoples", it has also been widely charged by indigenous groups that the African Group was being manipulated behind the scenes by the United States and Canada.[214] Amnesty International issued a

---

[210] Anonymous interview by author with indigenous activist, 2008.
[211] UN Doc A/59/258 (2004).
[212] UN Human Rights Council Resolution 2006/2.
[213] UN Doc A/61/448 (2006).
[214] The author heard this accusation numerous times in interviews and during attendance at meetings of the Indigenous Caucus in Geneva.

statement on 6 June 2007[215] which accused the Canadian government of being "obstructionist and exploitative in it efforts to block discussion" on the Declaration. Amnesty International also contended that Canada had been encouraging states in Africa, Latin America and Asia to oppose the Declaration. While there is little hard evidence of such manipulation, the frequency with which it is voiced by indigenous activists testifies to the depth of suspicion that had built up over the years against the US and Canadian governments.

Between January and August 2007, a group of states which were supporting the Declaration (led by Mexico, along with Peru, Guatemala and Fiji) worked with the African Group on a 'package' proposal of amendments[216] to resolve the impasse without re-opening negotiations on the Declaration itself. The Mexican delegation was of the opinion that if negotiations on the text of the Declaration were re-opened, it would fail.[217] At the request of the African Group, indigenous representatives were excluded from all discussions, even as observers.

On 31 August, the African Group along with Mexico, Guatemala and Peru, presented the Indigenous Caucus with yet another new draft of the Declaration (Appendix 4).[218] The African Group package, which proposed nine proposals (five deletions and four additions) to change text in the Declaration, maintained about 95% of the original language of the Declaration and kept the following provisions intact: self-determination,

---

[215] Press report by Canada Press, Ottawa. Source:
http://ca.news.yahoo.com/s/capress/070606/national/cda_un_native_rights.
[216] GRULAC/African Group Package.
[217] Statement by Enrique Javier Ochoa Martinez, First Secretary, Humanitarian and Social Issues, Permanent Mission of Mexico to the United Nations at a Progress Report on the Declaration on the Rights of Indigenous Peoples, 12 April 2007, Church Center at the UN, New York.
[218] African Group Package, United Nations Declaration on the Rights of Indigenous Peoples, 30 August 2007.

treaties, lands, territories and resources.[219] The major changes put forward by the African

Group involved enhanced protections for state sovereignty and territorial integrity, most

notably in Article 46. The African Group also reported that, although a few states had

indicated their intent to oppose the Declaration, they felt they had sufficient votes to pass

the Declaration.[220] The African Group also told the Indigenous Caucus that they would

block any additional amendments.[221]

Beginning on Saturday 1 September 2007, urgent faxes and emails went out from

the Indigenous Caucus to indigenous nations and organizations around the world asking

for consultation on the proposed amendments made by the African Group. The regional

coordinators of the Indigenous Caucus collected responses until noon on Tuesday 4

September 2007. Clearly, there was no time for the Indigenous Caucus to seek

consensus. Les Malezer, Chair of the Indigenous Caucus, stated that "these urgent

consultations will determine whether or not we can live with the amendments, and the

Declaration is adopted OR whether we cannot accept the agreed version and the

Declaration will not be adopted."[222]

While some indigenous organizations opposed the amendments and some elected

to simply "not support" yet "not oppose" the African Group amendments,[223] the

---

[219] Urgent Request and Update Relating to Final UN Action on the Declaration on the Rights of Indigenous Peoples issued by Les Malezar and Mililani Trask, Pacific Regional Coordinators on the Draft Declaration on the Rights of Indigenous Peoples, 2 September 2007.
[220] *Ibid*. The states voicing opposition were Canada, Australia, New Zealand, the United States, the Russian Federation and Columbia.
[221] Anonymous interview by author with indigenous activist, 2007. Transcript on file with the author.
[222] Urgent Message – Indigenous Peoples – Global Consultation – Important Notice. Sent out by Les Malezer, Chairperson, Indigenous Peoples Caucus at the UN, 1 September 2007.
[223] Some indigenous organizations, like IITC, decided to not support yet also not oppose the amendments. IITC's Executive Director Andrea Carmen explained that while they supported the Sub-Commission text

Indigenous Caucus held a press conference on 6 September 2007 to endorse the amendments to the text of the Declaration.[224] Again, the indigenous representatives accused Canada of manipulating the African Group by trying to use aid as a tool and also accused Canada of recently pressuring the Kenyan ambassador to make a statement that Kenya had no indigenous peoples.[225] The Indigenous Caucus called for the adoption of the Declaration by the General Assembly of the UN the following week.

On 13 September 2007, Mr. Luis Enrique Chavez, Chair of the Working Group on the Draft Declaration introduced to the General Assembly, on behalf of Peru, draft revolution A/61/L.67, to adopt the Declaration on the Rights of Indigenous Peoples (Appendix 5).[226] This document was included in the official report of the sixty-first session of the Human Rights Council in 2006. Australia, New Zealand and the United States requested a recorded vote. There were 143 votes in favor, 11 abstentions and 4 votes against. The votes against were: Canada, New Zealand, Australia and the United States. The Abstentions were: Azerbaijan, Bangladesh, Bhutan, Burundi, Columbia, Georgia, Kenya, Nigeria, the Russian Federation, Samoa and Ukraine.[227]

The Indigenous Caucus celebrated the vote as a victory and expressed that it looked forward to the Declaration being implemented as international customary law. Les Malezer, Chair of the Indigenous Caucus, stated:

> The Declaration does not represent solely the viewpoint of the United Nations, nor does it represent solely the viewpoint of the Indigenous

---

and the Human Rights Council text, they would not oppose these amendments. She said, "It was either this or worse." Interview by author with Andrea Carmen, IITC, Mille Lacs Nation, 24 September 2007.

[224] Press Conference on Indigenous Rights Declaration, UN Department of Public Information, New York, 6 September 2007.

[225] *Ibid.*

[226] UN Doc A/61/L.67 (12 September 2007)

[227] UN Doc A/61/295 (2007).

Peoples. It is a Declaration which combines our views and interests and which sets the framework for the future. It is a tool for peace and justice, based upon mutual recognition and respect.[228]

The United States issued a statement that same day, articulating its position on the Declaration.[229] The U.S. noted that, since it had participated in negotiations in Geneva over the years, it was "fully aware of what participants intended in its drafting" and so it was in a position to "provide an understanding of the intent of participating states on the core issues." The U.S. stated that the Declaration "was an aspirational declaration with political and moral, rather than legal, force." The U.S. also rejected outright "any possibility that this document is or can become customary international law." It also expressed its opposition to reproducing the Article 1 common to both the ICCPR and the ICESCR, which states that "all peoples have the right of self-determination."[230]

What most indigenous peoples had not noticed was that the resolution which passed the General Assembly on 13 September 2007 had undergone a critical and unannounced change at the last minute. The text that was presented to the General Assembly included a text of the Declaration which had newly (but silently) altered Article 3 on self-determination:[231] "Indigenous peoples have the right *to* self-determination (emphasis added)" which differed significantly from the African Group text of Article 3 which read: "Indigenous peoples have the right *of* self-determination (emphasis added.)   As Maori lawyer and activist Moana Jackson explained:

---

[228] Press Release: United Nations General Assembly Adopts the United Nations Declaration on the Rights of Indigenous Peoples. Issued by the Indigenous Peoples' Caucus Regional Steering Committee, 13 September 2007.

[229] "Observations of the United States with respect to the Declaration on the Rights of Indigenous Peoples", 13 September 2007, available through doCIP.

[230] International Covenant on Civil and Political Rights and the International Covenant on Economic, Social and Cultural Rights.

[231] Tēnā rāwā atu koe (many thanks) to Moana Jackson who brought this issue to my attention.

144

In all other human rights conventions, the wording read that all peoples have the right of self-determination[232] and the word 'of' implies inherency, that as a human, self-determination is something of you, it's within your humanity. What this says is that indigenous peoples have the right 'to' self-determination so that transfers to something which you might one day be fully entitled or you might one day aspire to. And that prepositional change was deliberately engineered by the UN and by the states and in a deeply legal sense and a philosophical sense I think it changes and diminishes self-determination. It is not accorded to indigenous peoples as it is accorded to other peoples.[233]

This last minute, unannounced, subtle change to the text of the Declaration likely indicates that, even with the added protections for state sovereignty, the Declaration represented a change in the conception of self-determination which was still too revolutionary for certain states to accept.

Conclusion

As James Tully has said "the transnational Indigenous rights movement engages in a wider struggle *against* the structures of domination by working *through* the structures of domination and utilizing the tools of government to modify and transform it."[234] This is a very good characterization of what indigenous global politics is and what it aims to do.

As I have discussed in this chapter, the features of indigenous global politics grew out of a particular set of developments during the late 1970s and early 1980s which laid

---

[232] The UN charter includes the fundamental principle of self-determination, but Article 1 of both the International Covenant on Civil and Political Rights and the International Covenant on Economic, Social and Cultural Rights state that "All peoples have the right of self-determination."
[233] Interview by author with Moana Jackson, Maori rights lawyer and activist, Wellington, Aotearoa/New Zealand, 11 March 2008.
[234] Tully, James (2000). "The Struggles of Indigenous Peoples for and of Freedom." In D. Ivison, P. Patton and W. Sanders. *Political Theory and the Rights of Indigenous Peoples*. Cambridge: Cambridge University Press.

its critical groundwork and, after a long and arduous process, eventually led to the passage of the Declaration on the Rights of Indigenous Peoples. It was the passage of this document by the UN General Assembly which signified important, yet often unnoticed, global change. So why did the Declaration on Indigenous Rights take so long and why was it so threatening to states? The answer to both questions lies in the initial constitution of indigenous global politics and the important international change required in order to recognize indigenous peoples' rights. From its earliest beginnings indigenous global politics set out, not simply to enhance the rights of indigenous individuals, but also to carve out a space in international politics for the recognition and accommodation of indigenous land rights and self-determination, necessitating significant shifts in both collective rights and the meaning of self-determination. The passage of the Declaration by the UN General Assembly added two sets of collective rights to the international human rights consensus: "soft rights" which focused on indigenous culture, language, religion, etc., as well as the "hard rights" of land and self-determination. In addition, indigenous global politics forged another important change in international politics by performing international relations in a new way, an indigenous way and from an indigenous perspective. Much of the progress forged by indigenous global politics came about through solidarity, consensus, protest and pure tenacity, largely made possible by the new indigenous style of international relations.

In constituting itself around land rights and self-determination, indigenous global politics necessarily placed pressure on two hegemonic ideas which are both also extremely threatening to certain states and constituted the source of state resistance to the

Declaration: first, the Westphalian system of sovereign nation-states and, second, liberal constructions of the state and the international human rights consensus. Indigenous global politics sees the Westphalian system of sovereign independent nation-states as a construct that privileges Euro-centric societies over all other societies in the international sphere. Ultimately, the transnational indigenous rights movement seeks both a renouncement of all colonial doctrines in both international and domestic discourse, and a reconfiguration of the system of sovereign independent nation-states toward a more pluralistic conception. Indigenous global politics aims to alter the accepted meaning of self-determination away from a purely statist conception in order to recognize the nationhood of indigenous peoples, and decouple that nationhood status from statehood status.[235] Securing indigenous rights to land and self-determination through a less state-centric and more multi-faceted view of sovereignty thus offers a new and particular challenge to the hegemonic, though increasingly pressured, Westphalian international system.

The indigenous movement's push for indigenous self-determination also challenges the global norm toward liberal conceptions of governance. While some of the demands of the indigenous rights movement revolve around non-discrimination, poverty and the disadvantages that indigenous individuals around the world experience when compared to other citizens of their states, the demand for self-determination and its correlate, land rights, pushes the bounds of the liberal state to its outer limits and normatively challenges its hegemony. Indigenous global politics, then, is also pushing

---

[235] Paul Keal. 2003. *European Conquest and the Rights of Indigenous Peoples: The Moral Backwardness of International Society.* Cambridge: Cambridge University Press.

147

for a more pluralistic vision of state and society—a vision which continues to challenge

the fundamental structure of the international status quo.

Chapter 4

State Responses to the Emerging Indigenous Rights Regime: Compliance, Under-Compliance, Partial Compliance and "Over-Compliance"

As discussed in Chapters 2 and 3, an international discourse and regime of indigenous rights has emerged in recent decades. This regime does not merely represent a new norm emergence cycle[1] but rather, an extension of the cycle. As was elaborated in Chapters 2 and 3, the emerging indigenous rights regime does not only add new indigenous rights norms to the international human rights consensus; it challenges some fundamentals of the human rights system and the international system of Westphalian sovereign states. The emerging indigenous rights regime places political and moral demands on states, asking them to enact and implement constitutional, legislative, and/or domestic policy instruments to recognize and protect not only the rights of indigenous peoples as individual citizens but also as collectives with land rights and the right of self-determination. Given the major, if not subtly revolutionary, international challenges involved in the emerging indigenous rights regime, the high level of commitment required of states in that regime, and the non-binding nature of the indigenous rights regime, states could be expected to respond to this emerging regime in a diversity of ways and at a variety of levels. This chapter will address the issue of state response to the changes in international indigenous rights. How are states responding to the emerging indigenous rights discourse? What patterns are emerging in state compliance with international indigenous rights standards? Since the indigenous rights movement is

---

[1] Martha Finnemore and Kathryn Sikkink (1998). "International Norm Dynamics and Political Change." *International Organization* 52(4):887-917.

not a typical human rights movement, are there any unusual patterns of state compliance? If so, how can such patterns be explained?

This chapter will proceed in two major sections. The first section will present and analyze a data set on state compliance in indigenous rights to determine the dominant patterns of state compliance. Analysis of this data set will show five possible outcomes in indigenous rights compliance by states: compliance, non-compliance, under-compliance, partial compliance, and a new concept, which I am terming "over-compliance." I define an "over-compliant" state as one that paradoxically takes constitutional, legal and/or policy actions which recognize specific rights or a category of rights that go beyond that state's international human rights treaty obligations or its normative international commitments. In the second part of the chapter, I will seek a general explanation for state over-compliance in indigenous rights, which I will then elaborate and substantiate in subsequent chapters devoted to specific states.

State Compliance in Indigenous Rights

Table 4.1 displays a data set I have compiled on state compliance with international indigenous rights standards as of 31 December 2008. The data set is composed of fifty-three countries, which are considered by the International Work Group for Indigenous Affairs (IWGIA)[2] to be the countries with significant populations of indigenous peoples. Every year, the IWGIA produces a report entitled "The Indigenous

---

[2] The International Work Group for Indigenous Affairs (IWGIA) is an NGO located in Copenhagen, Denmark.

World." Data on the status of indigenous rights shown in Table 4.1 is drawn primarily from the IWGIA's reports in years 2006, 2007 and 2008.[3]

Table 4.1 presents the fifty-three countries by region, following the lead of the IWGIA's reports, so that regional trends can be readily identified. The first column, percentage of indigenous population, is drawn from the IWGIA annual reports. Where indigenous population figures (rather than percentages of population) were provided, the percentage of indigenous population was calculated as a percentage from the IWGIA's figure of indigenous population and the country population figures given by the 2008 CIA World Factbook.[4] A country's political system is shown as either Parliamentary, Presidential, Semi-Presidential or One-Party, as reported by the 2008 CIA World Factbook. Each country's legal system is also coded according to the information provided by the 2008 CIA World Factbook as either Common Law, Civil Law, or Mixed.

The next three columns in Table 4.1 are indicators of a country's ratification or accession status regarding three major human rights treaties: the International Convention on the Elimination of All Forms of Racial Discrimination (ICERD), the International Covenant on Civil and Political Rights (ICCPR) and the International Covenant on Economic, Social and Cultural Rights (ICESCR). A country receives a check in the box if it has achieved ratification or accession on the convention in question. A country does not receive a check if it has signed the convention but there has not been ratification or

[3] IWGIA. 2006. *The Indigenous World 2006*. Copenhagen: IWGIA.; IWGIA. 2007. *The Indigenous World 2007*. Copenhagen: IWGIA.; IWGIA. 2008. *The Indigenous World 2008*. Copenhagen: IWGIA.
[4] Central Intelligence Agency. 2008. *The 2008 World Factbook*. Online edition: ww.cia.gov/library/publications/the-world-factbook/.

Table 4.1 **State Compliance with Indigenous Rights**

Country	% Indigenous Population	Political System	Legal System	ICERD	ICCPR	ICESCR	ILO No. 107	ILO No. 169	UN DRIP Vote	Status of Indigenous Rights in Country, as of 31 December 2008	Indigenous Rights Commitment	Constitutional, Legal & Policy Compliance	Indigenous Rights Compliance Level of Country
THE ARCTIC													
Greenland (Denmark)	88.00%	Parliamentary	Civil	☑	☑	☑	☐	☑	For	Self-governing within Danish realm. Negotiating more self-government since 2004.	High	High	Compliant
Norway	0.50%	Parliamentary	Civil	☑	☑	☑	☐	☑	For	Saami status recognized by constitutional amendment. Saami Parliament has consultation agreement with Norwegian Parliament. Government plan to map land rights. Land under pressure. Government will base new decisions on UN DRIP.	High	High	Compliant
Sweden	0.22%	Parliamentary	Civil	☑	☑	☑	☐	☐	For	Saami Parliament Act but Saami Parliament acts under Swedish Parliament. Recognizes reindeer herding areas, but no designated lands for Saami. Saami Parliament criticizes Sweden for lack of self-determination. Negotiations planned regarding a new land use model.	High	Medium	Partially Compliant
Finland	0.10%	Parliamentary	Civil	☑	☑	☑	☐	☐	For	Treats Saami as a minority, refuses special legislation for Saami. Focus of state is on equality of all. Finland sees itself as neutral in negotiations. Finnish government refuses to address Saami land rights.	High	Medium	Partially Compliant
Russian Federation	0.10%	Semi-Presidential	Civil	☑	☑	☑	☐	☐	Abstain	Russian constitution establishes cultural, political and territorial rights of Indigenous peoples. Land rights denied.	Low	Low	Non-Compliant
NORTH AMERICA													
Canada	2.50%	Parliamentary	Common	☑	☑	☑	☐	☐	Against	First Nations have reserves and self-governance. Self-governing Inuit territory of Nunavut established 1999. Land claims negotiations ongoing; many settled already. Many government programs and initiatives to reduce socioeconomic disparities. Land and resources rights for Indigenous peoples are limited. Canada recognizes cultural rights as collective rights.	Low	High	Over-Compliant
USA	1.40%	Presidential	Common	☑	☑	☐	☐	☐	Against	562 federally recognized Indigenous nations, many with treaty rights. American Indian law often subject to inconsistent rulings by US Supreme Court. Tribal sovereignty, but limited by plenary power of US Congress. US government trust status, so federal government hold land title in trust.	Low	Low	Non-Compliant

Table 4.1 State Compliance with Indigenous Rights (continued)

Country	% Indigenous Population	Political System	Legal System	ICERD	ICCPR	ICESCR	ILO No. 107	ILO No. 169	UN DRIP Vote	Status of Indigenous Rights in Country, as of 31 December 2008	Indigenous Rights Commitment	Constitutional, Legal & Policy Compliance	Indigenous Rights Compliance Level of Country
LATIN AMERICA													
Mexico	13.00%	Presidential	Civil	☑	☑	☑	☑	☑	For	Article 6 of amended Constitution declares Mexico a pluri-national country. 1996 San Andreas Accords included territorial and political rights for Indigenous peoples. In 2001 Mexican Congress passed Law on Indigenous Rights and Culture, but it did not integrate rights from the San Andreas Accords. Some states have recognized and are implementing portions of San Andreas Accords. Land conflicts and pockets of violence continue in Chiapas. Issues in Oaxaca over water and cultural rights, including reports of violent military repression. National policy against racism and discrimination. Many political constituencies resist Indigenous land rights in favor of status quo power structure and ethnic integration. Resource extraction licenses in Indigenous areas is an issue as these project threaten the Indigenous way of life in these areas.	High	Low	Under-Compliant
Guatemala	60.00%	Presidential	Civil	☑	☑	☑	☐	☑	For	Government held consultations with Indigenous communities over these licenses and then ignored the results, claiming that the consultations were not legally valid. Land registry office has produced regulations for the titling of communal Indigenous lands, but no system yet implemented.	High	Low	Under-Compliant
Nicaragua	5.00%	Presidential	Civil	☑	☑	☑	☐	☐	For	1987 Constitution recognizes collective rights of Indigenous communities. Some recent legislation to improve regional autonomy. Autonomous education system is recognized. Ideas for restructuring government along two lines: municipal and Indigenous, so the possibility exists that Indigenous governments could become administrators of territory. Indigenous rights advances are closely linked to the volatile political situation. Conflicts remain over Indigenous land ownership.	High	Medium	Partially Compliant
Panama	8.40%	Presidential	Civil	☑	☑	☑	☑	☐	For	Constitution recognizes collective right to autonomous Indigenous territories, although government has declined to recognize some communities. Recognizes Indigenous congresses as autonomous government entities. Some forced displacements without free prior and informed consent have been reported, especially related to hydroelectric power. Some reports of land incursions by local farmers which the government does not enforce. Reports of police repression in Indigenous communities.	High	Medium	Partially Compliant

153

Table 4.1   State Compliance with Indigenous Rights (continued)

Country	% Indigenous Population	Political System	Legal System	ICERD	ICCPR	ICESCR	ILO No. 107	ILO No. 169	UN DRIP Vote	Status of Indigenous Rights in Country, as of 31 December 2008	Indigenous Rights Commitment	Constitutional, Legal & Policy Compliance	Indigenous Rights Compliance Level of Country
Colombia	3.40%	Presidential	Civil	☑	☑	☑	☑	☑	Abstain	1991 Constitution recognizes ethnic and cultural diversity as well as recognizes Indigenous territories. Free Trade Agreement with US encourages privatization of Indigenous lands and resources. Conflicts over resource extraction on Indigenous territories. Issues over illegal land titles with Rural Statue. Many gains in Indigenous rights have been lost in recent years. Recent regulation that Indigenous must permanently occupy their land in order to retain it.	High	Medium	Partially Compliant
Venezuela	2.20%	Presidential	Civil	☑	☑	☑	☐	☑	For	1999 Constitution enshrines Indigenous rights and enhances Indigenous participation in national politics. Collective land titles have been issued to Indigenous communities. Ministry for Indigenous Peoples. Indigenous movement within country has shifted focus to implementing government's polices. Government passes laws to try to undermine Indigenous movement (e.g. Organic Law on Indigenous Peoples and Communities) in favor of increased participation by Indigenous peoples in state politics.	High	Medium	Partially Compliant
Suriname	10.00%	Presidential	Civil	☑	☑	☑	☐	☐	For	In 2007, an Indigenous community won material damages over logging and mining through the Inter-American Court of Human Rights. Indigenous people of the interior hold "entitlements" while the government holds title to the land. Interior peoples have held self-rule but government is increasingly encroaching on interior in search of forest resources.	High	Low	Under-Compliant
Ecuador	25.00%	Presidential	Civil	☑	☑	☑	☑	☑	For	Constitutional recognition of pluricultural character of country. Lack of enforcement and enabling legislation for Indigenous rights. Issues over oil and mining.	High	Low	Under-Compliant
Peru	48%	Presidential	Civil	☑	☑	☑	☑	☑	For	Right to communal lands in 1979 Constitution, but recent government actions have eroded these right in favor of economic development. No enshrinement of Indigenous rights in Constitution. Law to return "unused and unoccupied" to the government to be released for development. Conflicts over mining. Indigenous consultation and bilingual education.	High	Low	Under-Compliant

154

Table 4.1 State Compliance with Indigenous Rights (continued)

Country	% Indigenous Population	Political System	Legal System	ICERD	ICCPR	ICESCR	ILO No. 107	ILO No. 169	UN DRIP Vote	Status of Indigenous Rights in Country, as of 31 December 2008	Indigenous Rights Commitment	Constitutional, Legal & Policy Compliance	Indigenous Rights Compliance Level of Country
Bolivia	62.00%	Presidential	Civil	☑	☑	☑	☑	☑	For	Indigenous hold land title under legal concept of Native Community Lands. UN DRIP ratified as law in country. New Constitution recognizes multinational state and pre-existence of Indigenous peoples. Indigenous peoples defined as nationalities with language and cultural rights. Indigenous languages are official languages along with Spanish. Community democracy is accepted as equal with elective democracy. New constitution has special chapter on Indigenous rights, including collective cultural rights, self-determination, collective ownership of territories, autonomous management of territories and exclusive use of natural resources in their territories.	High	Medium	Partially Compliant
Brazil	4.00%	Presidential	Civil	☑	☑	☑	☑	☑	For	Erosion of Indigenous rights in recent years as de Silva government refused to recognize Indigenous territories. Conflicts over development and hydroelectricity. Biofuel production is placing pressure on Indigenous land which is delaying demarcation. Efforts to increase social services and language preservation. Land evictions, sometimes violent, for purposes of resource extraction. No recognized Indigenous autonomy.	High	Low	Under-Compliant
Paraguay	1.70%	Presidential	Civil	☑	☑	☑	☑	☑	For	Few national policies for Indigenous peoples. Inter-American Court of Human Rights has intervened in cases related to food, water and medical care. State has offered compensation and emergency aid. Atmosphere of discrimination remains. Gap between recognition of rights and implementation.	High	Low	Under-Compliant
Argentina	3.00%	Presidential	Civil	☑	☑	☑	☑	☑	For	Development efforts are encroaching on Indigenous land, violating their collective rights. Indigenous peoples are pressured or coerced into renouncing their lands. Indigenous groups removed from their lands. Indigenous education initiatives not implemented. 2006 law intended to halt Indigenous evictions.	High	Low	Under-Compliant
Chile	5.00%	Presidential	Civil	☑	☑	☑	☐	☑	For	Police violence against Indigenous peoples. State charged with 'environmental racism.' Plans for including Indigenous language into the school curriculum. Conflicts over hydroelectric plants in a near Indigenous territories. Indigenous consultation fails to meet standards, so protest often results.	High	Medium	Partially Compliant

Table 4.1   **State Compliance with Indigenous Rights (continued)**

Country	% Indigenous Population	Political System	Legal System	ICERD	ICCPR	ICESCR	ILO No. 107	ILO No. 169	UN DRIP Vote	Status of Indigenous Rights in Country, as of 31 December 2008	Indigenous Rights Commitment	Constitutional, Legal & Policy Compliance	Indigenous Rights Compliance Level of Country
PACIFIC													
Australia	2.50%	Parliamentary	Common	☑	☑	☑	☐	☐	Against	Terra nullius doctrine overturned in 1980s. Policy of reconciliation in place since 1990s. Ministry for Reconciliation. Apology offered by new Rudd government in 2008. Some recognition of collective rights of Indigenous people and partial autonomy for Aboriginal communities, although government in 2007 conducted "Emergency Intervention" in Northern Territories.	Low	Medium	Over-Compliant
New Zealand	15.00%	Parliamentary	Common	☑	☑	☑	☐	☐	Against	Excels in language, cultural, educational rights. Treaty settlements process underway since 1990s; many settlements finalized. Maori is official language, alongside English. Extensive government programs to reduce socioeconomic disparities.	Low	High	Over-Compliant
ASIA													
Japan	0.10%	Parliamentary	Civil	☑	☑	☑	☐	☐	For	Ainu recognized as Indigenous in 2008. Discriminatory attitudes prevalent. Government does not recognize national minorities as Indigenous peoples. Five Year Plan for Ethnic Minorities to increase their socioeconomic status.	High	Low	Under-Compliant
China	8.47%	One-Party	Civil	☑	☐	☑	☐	☐	For	Some laws to protect Indigenous rights, especially related to language and culture. Little legislative progress on self-governance.	High	Low	Under-Compliant
Taiwan	2.10%	Semi-Presidential	Civil	☐	☐	☐	☐	☐	N/A		N/A		N/A
Philippines	10.00%	Presidential	Mixed	☑	☑	☑	☐	☐	For	Indigenous Peoples Rights Act passed in 1997 which calls for respect of Indigenous cultural rights as well as rights to lands and self-determination. Gaps in implementation especially related to land and resource development.	High	Medium	Partially Compliant
Indonesia	5.50%	Presidential	Civil	☑	☑	☑	☐	☐	For	Amendment to Constitution recognizes Indigenous peoples' rights, but the government denies the existence of Indigenous peoples in the country as almost all are Indigenous. New Foreign Investment Law does not recognize any Indigenous rights to land. UN CERD has made recommendations regarding Indigenous rights.	High	Low	Under-Compliant
Malaysia	12.00%	Parliamentary	Common	☐	☐	☐	☐	☐	For	British colonial laws recognizing customary land rights and customary law still exist, however the government widely ignores them. Recent court cases have recognized communal Indigenous rights to land.	High	Medium	Partially Compliant
Thailand	0.10%	Parliamentary	Civil	☑	☑	☑	☐	☐	For	Tribal peoples often considered security threat. Many still lack Thai citizenship. 2007 Constitution does not recognize Indigenous peoples. Forest protection laws in recent years have dispossessed Indigenous peoples of land.	High	Low	Under-Compliant

Table 4.1 State Compliance with Indigenous Rights (continued)

Country	% Indigenous Population	Political System	Legal System	ICERD	ICCPR	ICESCR	ILO No. 107	ILO No. 169	UN DRIP Vote	Status of Indigenous Rights in Country, as of 31 December 2008	Indigenous Rights Commitment	Constitutional, Legal & Policy Compliance	Indigenous Rights Compliance Level of Country
Cambodia	9.00%	Parliamentary	Civil	☑	☑	☑	☐	☐	For	2001 Land Law recognized collective Indigenous rights to land by offering communal land and titles, although implementation is very slow. 2002 Forestry Law also references Indigenous land rights. Indigenous peoples arrested for protesting development projects.	High	Low	Under-Compliant
Bangladesh	1.75%	Parliamentary	Common	☑	☑	☑	☑	☐	Abstain	No constitutional recognition of Indigenous peoples. Widespread persecution. Violent conflicts in Chittagong Hill Tracts. Peace Accord in 1997 recognized traditional governance and autonomy.	Low	Low	Non-Compliant
Nepal	37.00%	Parliamentary	Common	☑	☑	☑	☐	☑	For	Some Indigenous nationalities recognized by the government but many are not. Indigenous experience substantial discrimination. Indigenous struggle for self-determination in creating constitutional processes.	High	Low	Under-Compliant
India	8.40%	Parliamentary	Common	☑	☑	☑	☑	☐	For	461 'scheduled tribes' recognized by the government. Some areas recognize Indigenous rights to land and self-governance. Many Indigenous experience land violations, civil and political rights violations, displacement and false prosecution. Land confiscations for development purposes. Serious implementation gap in laws intended to protect Indigenous peoples.	High	Low	Under-Compliant
AFRICA													
Morocco	28.00%	Parliamentary	Civil	☑	☑	☑	☐	☐	Absent	Indigenous peoples under constant threat of assimilation. Constitution recognizes only Arab identity, although Indigenous language rights are partially recognized in law although not in Constitution.	Low	Low	Non-Compliant
Algeria	30.00%	Presidential	Civil/Islamic	☑	☑	☑	☐	☐	For	Constitution recognized Indigenous language but Indigenous people remain marginalized.	High	Low	Under-Compliant
Niger	8.30%	Semi-Presidential	Civil	☑	☑	☑	☐	☐	For	No laws protecting Indigenous peoples. Constitution recognizes cultural diversity, but does not implement Indigenous rights.	High	Low	Under-Compliant
Mali	10.00%	Presidential	Civil	☑	☑	☑	☐	☐	For	No national policy to protect Indigenous peoples.	High	Low	Under-Compliant
Ethiopia	15.00%	Parliamentary	Civil	☑	☑	☑	☐	☐	Absent	No legislation for Indigenous rights.	Low	Low	Non-Compliant
Kenya	25.00%	Presidential	Common/Islam	☑	☑	☑	☐	☐	Abstain	Land and resource tenure insecurity.	Low	Low	Non-Compliant
Tanzania	1.30%	Presidential	Common	☑	☑	☑	☐	☐	For	No national policy or legislation for Indigenous rights.	High	Low	Under-Compliant
Nigeria	0.01%	Presidential	Common	☑	☑	☑	☐	☐	Abstain	Violent police repression of Ogoni demonstration.	Low	Low	Non-Compliant
Uganda	0.03%	Presidential	Common	☑	☑	☑	☐	☐	Absent	No government recognition of Indigenous peoples. No constitutional protections.	Low	Low	Non-Compliant
Rwanda	0.40%	Presidential	Civil	☑	☑	☑	☐	☐	Absent	Indigenous peoples have been completely dispossessed of traditional lands. Discrimination widespread. Government fails to recognize Indigenous people and practices policies of assimilation.	Low	Low	Non-Compliant

Table 4.1   State Compliance with Indigenous Rights (continued)

Country	% Indigenous Population	Political System	Legal System	ICERD	ICCPR	ICESCR	ILO No. 107	ILO No. 169	UN DRIP Vote	Status of Indigenous Rights in Country, as of 31 December 2008	Indigenous Rights Commitment	Constitutional, Legal & Policy Compliance	Indigenous Rights Compliance Level of Country
Burundi	1.25%	Presidential	Civil	☑	☑	☑	☐	☐	Abstain	Indigenous peoples have been completely dispossessed of traditional lands. 2005 Constitution provides designated seats in National Assembly and Senate for Indigenous group. Government has initiated a land reform process.	Low	Low	Non-Compliant
Dem. Rep. of Congo	7.00%	Presidential	Civil	☑	☑	☑	☐	☐	For	Discrimination widespread. Systemic violations of Indigenous rights. No government recognition or protection of Indigenous lands.	High	Low	Under-Compliant
Rep. of Congo	10.00%	Presidential	Civil	☑	☑	☑	☐	☐	For	No constitutional or legislative protections for Indigenous peoples.	High	Low	Under-Compliant
Gabon	0.01%	Presidential	Civil	☑	☑	☑	☐	☐	For	In 2005, government recognized existence of Indigenous people in an Indigenous Peoples' Plan, which was part of a World Bank policy loan. A few projects focused on Indigenous communities are in the planning stages. Constitution recognizes existence of Indigenous peoples, however government does not recognize their full citizenship. Development plan exists for Indigenous peoples in both poverty reduction policy and oil pipeline project. Conflicts over land.	High	Medium	Partially Compliant
Cameroon	0.40%	Presidential	Civil	☑	☑	☑	☐	☐	For	No national policy or laws to protect Indigenous peoples.	High	Low	Under-Compliant
Angola	0.04%	Presidential	Civil	☐	☑	☑	☑	☐	For	No constitutional or national legislation to protect Indigenous peoples. An anti-poverty program has been initiated. No land rights.	High	Low	Under-Compliant
Namibia	8.00%	Presidential	Civil	☑	☑	☑	☐	☐	For	Government does not recognize any groups as Indigenous. No specified laws protecting Indigenous peoples.	High	Low	Under-Compliant
Botswana	3.00%	Presidential	Civil	☑	☑	☐	☐	☐	For	No constitutional recognition of Indigenous peoples, although redress for past discrimination is included.	High	Low	Under-Compliant
South Africa	1.00%	Presidential	Civil	☑	☑	☑	☐	☐	For	Government expresses strong support for Indigenous rights in the international arena. Major Supreme Court victory for land and resources rights in 2003. Various language and cultural preservation programs.	High	Medium	Partially Compliant

accession. All information on the human rights treaty status of countries comes from the

UN Human Rights Treaty Website.[5]

The next three columns deal directly with international indigenous rights

instruments, specifically ILO No. 107 ("ILO 107"),[6] ILO No. 169 ("ILO 169")[7] and the

United Nations Declaration on the Rights of Indigenous Peoples ("the Declaration", or

"DRIP").[8] A check in the column for ILO No. 107 indicates that the country had ratified

ILO 107 at one time. Since ratification of ILO No. 169 meant that a country's support

for ILO 107 was automatically denounced, there are a number of countries which show

on the ILO website as having denounced ILO 107. However, a country gets a check in

the ILO 107 box if they had ever ratified ILO 107. A check in the ILO No. 169 box

indicates that the country has ratified ILO No. 169. All ratification information on ILO

No. 107 and 169 comes from the ILO website.[9] The next column shows the General

Assembly voting status of countries on the Declaration on the Rights of Indigenous

Peoples. There are four categories of voting status for the Declaration: For, Against,

---

[5] http://treaties.un.org.

[6] *International Labor Organization (ILO) Convention No. 107 on Indigenous and Tribal Populations concerning Protection and Integration of Indigenous and Other Tribal and Semi-Tribal Populations in Independent Countries*, the first international treaty dealing with indigenous issues, was passed in 1957. Drafted and passed without indigenous participation, this convention was criticized later for its paternalistic tone. States which ratified ILO No. 107 pledged to "protect" indigenous populations against discrimination and other social ills and also committed the state to assist indigenous populations toward "progressive integration into the life of their respective countries."

[7] *ILO Convention No. 169, concerning Indigenous and Tribal Peoples in Independent Countries*, was passed in 1989. No. 169 represents a significant advance over the paternalistic tone of No. 107. It no longer presumes the eventual disappearance or assimilation of indigenous peoples as in No. 107. Rather, it includes provisions for some collective land rights and political self-determination.

[8] The United Nations Declaration on the Rights of Indigenous Peoples (DRIP, or "the Declaration") was passed by the United Nations General Assembly on 13 September 2007. As a U.N. Declaration, DRIP is not yet an international convention and is not considered to be international law, but it does represent a normative international consensus on the rights of indigenous peoples. It should be noted that the three states examined here—Australia, New Zealand and Canada—are among only 4 states which voted against the DRIP in the General Assembly.

[9] http://www.ilo.org.

Abstain and Absent. Voting status on the Declaration is taken from the UN General Assembly document on the Declaration.[10]

Following the DRIP vote column is a column which offers comments on each country's individual indigenous rights status, as of 31 December 2008, taken primarily from the IWGIA reports from 2006, 2007 and 2008. For unknown reasons, New Zealand was not included in the IWGIA report but, since the Maori population in New Zealand is 15-17%, which in this author's opinion makes it a substantial indigenous population, I have included it in the data set and compiled the data from a variety of sources.

The next three columns constitute a coding of indigenous rights compliance behavior by the state. The first of these columns indicates the level of a country's indigenous rights commitment. For coding purposes, this column relies on the ratification record indicated in the columns on ILO 169 and the DRIP vote. If a country ratified ILO 169 and/or voted "For" the DRIP on the floor of the General Assembly, that country is deemed to have a "High" level of indigenous rights commitment. If a country has not ratified ILO 169 and voted against the DRIP, or was absent for the vote, or abstained from the vote, that country is coded as having a "Low" level of indigenous rights commitment.

The next column is a coding of constitutional, legal and policy conduct concerning indigenous rights standards. For this column, there are three possible codes: 1) High (indicating both a constitutional/legal compliance and policy compliance), 2) Medium (indicating a high level of constitutional/legal compliance but a low level of

---

[10] United Nations. UN Department of Public Information. "General Assembly Adopts Declaration on the Rights of Indigenous Peoples." 13 September 2007. UN Document GA/10612.

policy implementation, indicating an implementation gap), and 3) Low, indicating a low level of both constitutional/legal compliance and policy implementation.

The last column is a coding of a country's indigenous rights compliance behavior. This coding was done by comparing the previous two columns, Indigenous Rights Commitment and Constitutional, Legal and Policy Conduct, according to the formula shown in Table 4.2.

Table 4.2 Formula for Compliance Coding

Indigenous Rights Commitment	Constitutional, Legal & Policy Conduct	Indigenous Rights Compliance
High	High	Compliant
Low	Low	Non-Compliant
High	Medium	Partially Compliant
High	Low	Under-Compliant
Low	Medium	Over-Compliant
Low	High	Over-Compliant

In other words, if a country has a high level of indigenous rights commitment and a high level of constitutional, legal and/or policy conduct, the country would be considered compliant. Following Raustiala and Slaughter's definition,[11] compliance occurs when a country's behavior matches the legal standard. On the other hand, a country which does not make any commitment to the international standard and also does

---

[11] Kal Raustiala and Anne-Marie Slaughter "International Law, International Relations and Compliance." In *Handbook of International Relations*, edited by T. Risse and B.A. Simmons W. Carlsnaes, 538-58. London: Sage, 2002, p. 539

not alter its behavior would be considered non-compliant. A high level of commitment and a low level of policy conduct indicate a country that is under-compliant in indigenous rights because it is demonstrating a level of compliance which is far below that country's indigenous rights commitments. A partially compliant country is one that has a high level of commitment but is gapping in implementation such that it earns a medium score for policy conduct.[12] A country is considered partially compliant rather than under-compliant if it has made certain constitutional, legal and policy changes in the direction of its positive indigenous rights commitments, but it has not fully achieved its level of commitment. Finally, the "over-compliant" countries are ones where there is a medium or high level of constitutional, legal and/or policy conduct but only a low level of commitment, indicating that constitutional, legal and policy compliance exceeds that country's level of indigenous rights commitment. "Over-compliance" is a pattern and a concept which has not yet been considered by international relations theory. My supposition is that international relations theory has not considered "over-compliance" since the assumption is that states find it easier to sign or vote for an international covenant than to implement actual policy, so "commitment" is generally assumed to exceed "conduct" if the two do not match. It is under-compliance and, more recently partial compliance, which has typically received attention in IR theory and in policy

---

[12] Partial compliance is a term and a concept brought forth by Darren Hawkins and Wade Jacoby in "Partial Compliance: A Comparison of the European and Inter-American Courts for Human Rights" (2008), an unpublished paper presented at the 2008 Annual Meeting of the American Political Science Association. Partial compliance is defined in this paper as the "middle ground" between compliance and noncompliance. Hawkins and Jacoby maintain that states can partially comply in a variety of ways including, but not limited to, ratification but not legislative implementation or implementing part of a treaty but not the entire treaty or even underfunding agencies to monitor compliance. I follow the lead of Hawkins and Jacoby in an attempt to break down the dichotomy of compliance and noncompliance in an effort to better understand compliance behavior.

practice. Yet, in some curious cases, "conduct" exceeds "commitment" which is a counter-intuitive behavior.

I define "over-compliance" in indigenous rights as a situation where: (1) a state recognizes indigenous land or self-determination rights beyond that state's technical legal obligations, or the state (2) recognizes a category of indigenous rights while opposing that same category of rights in international discourse. For example, if a state has signed the first indigenous rights convention, ILO No. 107, and behaves according to its provisions, then that state would be compliant. However, if a state has signed the more advanced ILO No. 169, but its behavior matches only the weaker standards of ILO No. 107, it would be considered under-compliant. But, if a state has signed ILO No. 107 yet shows reform behavior that brings it in line with the stronger standards of ILO No. 169, then that state would be considered "over-compliant." I place the term "over-compliance" in quotes to indicate that while these states have exhibited some behavior which goes beyond their formal legal and/or normative international commitments, they still fall far short of indigenous peoples' expectations and demands. The term "over-compliance" does not indicate or imply that such states are completely complying with, or exceeding, international indigenous rights standards as articulated in the United Nations Declaration on the Rights of Indigenous Peoples (DRIP)—they are not—only that these states are performing above the level that would be expected based upon their low international commitments in indigenous rights.

Because this is a qualitative study, the data in Table 4.1 have been analyzed with an eye toward detecting dominant trends in indigenous rights compliance and have not yet been subjected to a rigorous multi-variant analysis. The compliance results from

163

Table 4.1 are shown in Table 4.3. The data shows that only 3.8% of the countries in the

Table 4.1 data set are compliant with their indigenous rights commitments, 19.2% are

non-compliant, 23% are partially compliant, 48% are under-compliant and 6% are "over-

compliant," meaning that their constitutional, legal and policy conduct exceeds their level

of commitment.

Table 4.3 Indigenous Rights Compliance Rates by Compliance Level

Level of Compliance	Number of Countries Exhibiting this Level of Compliance	Percentage of Countries Exhibiting this Level of Compliance
Compliant	2	3.8%
Partially Compliant	12	23%
Under-Compliant	25	48%
Over-Compliant	3	6%
Non-Compliant	10	19.2%
	Total: 52 countries	

Regionally, some trends are apparent from the data in Table 4.1.[13] Of the five

countries in the Arctic region, two are compliant, two are partially compliant and one is

non-compliant. In North America, one is non-compliant and one is "over-compliant."

Latin America shows the highest rate of under-compliance as all fourteen countries in the

data set are either under-compliant or partially compliant. All the Latin American

countries have a high level of commitment but range in practice from low to medium

---

[13] Region has been found to be a determinant in state compliance behavior in Simmons (2000) and Lutz and Sikkink (2000).

levels of compliance conduct, so Latin American countries appear to have high aspirations in indigenous rights but a serious implementation gap. In the two Pacific countries shown in the data set, both are "over-compliant" with a low level of commitment but a medium to high level of policy practice. Of the eleven Asian countries in the data set, seven are under-compliant, one is non-compliant and two are partially compliant. Taiwan cannot be evaluated for compliance as it is not currently a member of the United Nations and therefore unable to cast votes in the General Assembly. Among Asian countries, there is a tendency toward a high level of commitment but also a widespread resistance to recognizing indigenous peoples within their borders. Asian countries tend to consider these peoples to be ethnic or national minorities, rather than indigenous. The nineteen countries of Africa have a mixed compliance record as well. The level of commitment varies substantially and, like Asia, there is a strong tendency to not recognize certain populations as indigenous. Like other developing regions, implementation of indigenous rights policies is quite low.

Given the novelty and the implications of the emerging indigenous rights regime, a high rate of under-compliance and relatively small rate of compliance is not surprising; however, the 6% rate of "over-compliance," especially in developed countries of North America and the Pacific, is worthy of further investigation. While other Westernized, developed countries in the Arctic region and North America display compliance, non-compliance, under-compliance or partial compliance in indigenous rights, why do some of these countries exhibit this puzzling pattern of "over-compliance"?

Explaining "Over-Compliance"

The theoretical approaches for explaining state compliance or non-compliance with international law, including human rights law, fall into three basic streams: 1) rationalist; 2) liberal, and 3) constructivist. I argue that none of the existing literature has offered an explanation of compliance which can sufficiently explain the observation of "over-compliance" uncovered in the data set on indigenous rights, although a constructivist explanation coupled with Hathaway's cost of commitment theory[14] holds particular promise. I will then examine the Table 4.1 data set for additional evidence which can refine the hypothesis for "over-compliance."

Theoretical Approaches

The rationalist strand of explanation for state compliance or non-compliance with international law is rule-based and claims that states, as rational actors, join and comply with international law regimes that meet their national interests. Numerous scholars have relied on this stream of thought, arguing that "nation-states obey international law when it serves their short or long term self-interest to do so" or that "nations employ cooperative strategies to pursue a complex, multifaceted long-run national interest, in which compliance with negotiated legal norms serves as a winning long-term strategy in a iterated 'prisoner's dilemma' game."[15]

---

[14] Oona Hathaway (2003). "The Cost of Commitment." *Stanford Law Review.* 55:1821-1862.

[15] Robert O. Keohane (1997). "International Relations and International Law: Two Optics." *Harvard Journal of International Law.* 38(2): 487-501.; Duncan Snidal (1985). "The Game Theory of International Politics," *World Politics* 38:226.; K.W. Abbott (1992). "Elements of a Joint Discipline, International Law and International Relations Theory: Building Bridges." *American Society of International Legal Practice.* 86: 167-168.; J. K. Setear (1996). "An Iterative Perspective on Treaties: A Synthesis of International Relations Theory and International Law." *Harvard International Law Journal.* 37:139, 142-147.

Rationalists argue that states are unitary actors who pursue their best interests, given constraints on their capacity and power. Compliance for rationalists involves a strict calculation of interests in light of the existing distribution of power[16] or a positive calculation of costs and benefits of ratification.[17] Using the rationalist approach, there is likely no reason that any state would comply with human rights law in regard to indigenous rights. First, states have much greater material and discursive power than do indigenous peoples. Second, if states view concessions to indigenous groups as a zero-sum game, then the state only stands to lose power and capacity by making any domestic changes which would recognize indigenous rights within the state. Therefore, a rationalist explanation completely fails to explain why states would even comply, much less over-comply, with human rights relating to indigenous peoples. The rationalist explanation can be invoked for explaining the tremendous amount of non-compliance and non-adherence to the indigenous rights discourse among the majority of states, especially powerful states, in the world.

Chayes and Chayes[18] and Downs, et. al.[19] offer rationalist explanations for state compliance. The Chayes, while not purely rationalist, take a rationalist-leaning, managerial approach, assuming that non-compliance is actually deviant behavior and arguing that non-compliance can be dealt with through more effective management, enhanced communication or technical assistance. Their emphasis is on persuasion rather

---

[16] Benedict Kinsgbury (1998). "The Concept of Compliance as a Function of Competing Conceptions of International Law." *Michigan Journal of International Law.* 19(2):345-375.

[17] Wade M. Cole (2005). "Sovereignty Relinquished? Explaining Commitment to the International Human Rights Covenents, 1966-1999." *American Sociological Review.* 70:472-495.

[18] Abram Chayes and Antonia Chayes, "On Compliance," *International Organization* 47, No. 2 (1993).

[19] George W. Downs, David Rocke, and Peter Barsoom, "Is the Good news About Compliance Good News About Cooperation?," in *International Institutions: An International Organization Reader,* ed. Lisa Martin and Beth A. Simmons (Cambridge, Mass.:MIT Press, 2001.)

than enforcement. Downs, et.al. agree that non-compliance is deviant, not expected, behavior, since states only sign on to and comply with international regimes that are not so different from what they would have otherwise done. Downs, et. al. also focus on better cooperation and changes in technology to enhance compliance with a focus on the collective benefits to be obtained.

These rationalist theories ultimately fail to explain the compliance, much less the "over-compliance" of certain states with human rights law pertaining to indigenous people. Their claim that states will only join treaty regimes that they deem to be in their best interest can account for why only a few (20) states have ratified ILO Convention No. 169 but cannot account for the large number of states which voted for the Declaration. On the whole, then, the theory does not offer a good explanation of indigenous rights compliance and no explanation whatsoever for why a state would be reluctant to ratify an international instrument whose standards it is already exceeding.

Liberal approaches to explaining state compliance with international law ease up on the rationalist assumption of states as unitary actors, allowing for a disaggregation of the state into various domestic components, each with individual interests. The interest of the state, then, is represented by an aggregation of all of these varied interests. One strand of liberal compliance theory claims that compliance involves conformity with norms which are made by a variety of actors, rather than a system of rules. Compliance is thus understood as an outcome of political interaction of the aggregated preferences of relevant actors.[20] This theory rests on the notion of rule-legitimacy, as elaborated by Franck.[21]

The other strand of liberal theory rests on regime type as a critical explanatory variable. Moravcsik[22] and Slaughter[23] both argue that compliance with international law depends on the liberal democratic character of the regime. Resting on the same logic as the Democratic Peace theory that democracies do not fight one another, this strand of compliance theory argues that because democracies tend to be more transparent and more open to citizen and NGO influence, liberal democracies comply with international law better than non-democracies.

If liberal theory is to explain state compliance and non-compliance with international human rights law pertaining to indigenous rights, then one could expect to see a much higher number of liberal democracies complying than non-democracies. In fact, this is the case. Australia, New Zealand and Canada are all liberal democracies with a strong record of compliance. Where the theory loses some of its explanatory power is that it accounts for neither the non-compliance of a liberal state like the United States with the international indigenous rights standards nor does it account for the compliance of a rather illiberal state like Colombia. Along with many other liberal states, the United States has not ratified ILO No. 169, but it has also not made any domestic constitutional or legislative reforms to address its discrimination of indigenous peoples under the ICCPR. As a liberal democracy that has participated in other aspects of the ICCPR, its

---

[20] Kingsbury 1998.

[21] Thomas M. Franck. 1995. *Fairness in International Law and Institutions.* New York: Clarendon.

[22] Andrew Moravscik, "Taking Preferences Seriously: A Liberal Theory of International Politics," *International Organization* 51, no. 4 (1997).

[23] Anne-Marie Slaughter, "International Law in a World of Liberal States," *European Journal of International Law* 6, no. 4 (1995).

lack of compliance with indigenous rights norms weakens these liberal theories. Furthermore, some of the ratifying countries for ILO No. 169 were Latin American countries. Many of these nations cannot be classified as clear liberal democracies and those that are certainly do not have a high quality of democracy, yet many of these states (e.g. Colombia) have made bone fide attempts to improve their relationship with indigenous people in order to comply with the international human rights norm. Clearly, then, this strand of compliance theory, while supplying some potential insight into explaining compliance, leaves open a number of important questions. Most damaging in terms of its explanatory power, neither strand of liberal theory can explain why a state would recognize any collective rights nor can liberal theory explain why a state would over-comply with its indigenous rights treaty obligations while attempting to block the emergence of an international normative standard on indigenous rights in the form of the Declaration.

Constructivist explanations for compliance take a process, not rule oriented, approach and "give central significance to the social construction of identities and meanings among actors in the international system"[24] so that interests and identities are inter-subjectively constructed. Through this inter-subjective process, law enables a society to self-constitute so that states and other relevant actors thus become what they imagine themselves to be. In other words, norms do not have a regulative function as they do in liberal explanations but have a constitutive function. Norms constitute the identities of actors and it is these identities which drive their behavior. Under this theory, "nations thus obey international rules not just because of sophisticated calculations about

---

[24] Kingsbury 1998, p. 358.

how compliance or noncompliance will affect their interests, but because a repeated habit of obedience remakes their interests so that they come to value rule compliance."[25]

Other normative theories of compliance emphasize the transnational legal processes that help constitute state identities. Finnemore and Sikkink, for example, argue that international norms emerge through the activity of transnational actors.[26] These norms become institutionalized international instruments which then help guide state behavior as a "norm cascade" develops. According to these normative models, ratification and compliance are a matter of the normative commitments of state actors as states become socialized to international norms.[27] As Simmons argues,[28] reputational concerns explain compliance patterns, meaning that states will comply with international commitments in order to maintain their positive reputations as law-abiding countries.

Koh[29] offers a thick constructivist explanation for why states obey international law. His explanation provides a comprehensive explanation for state compliance, and he also provides part of the theoretical footing for an explanation of some states' "over-compliance" with international human rights standards pertaining to indigenous people. Koh argues that nations obey international law due to a process of interaction, interpretation and internalization of international norms into domestic legal systems. This legal process, which is transnational in character, claims that nation-states, international organizations, multinational corporations, NGOs and private individuals interact in a variety of domestic and international arenas in order to make, interpret and

---

[25] Harold Koh, "Why Do Nations Obey International Law?," *Yale Law Review* 106, no. 8 (1997), p. 2634.
[26] Keck and Sikkink, 1998.
[27] David Bearce and Stacy Bondanella (2007). "Intergovernmental Organizations, Socialization, and Member-State Interest Convergence." *International Organization* 61 (4):703-733.
[28] Beth Simmons (2000). "International Law and State Behavior: Commitment and Compliance in International Monetary Affairs." *American Political Science Review* 94 (4):819-836.
[29] Koh (1997).

internalize international law. This "international legal process" is distinctive in that it is "transnational, normative, and constitutive" in character.[30] Thus, it is through this dynamic process of making, interpreting and complying with legal norms that all relevant actors' identities become inter-subjectively shaped and constituted by the norm.

I suggest that a constructivist explanation provides solid theoretical grounding for an explanation of "over-compliance." In constructivist logic, all relevant actors' identities come to be shaped by making, interpreting and complying with the norms that emerge from dynamic processes. For the indigenous rights movement, the explanation begins in the late 1960s-early 1970s when indigenous leaders in several countries began linking up trans-nationally in a common struggle for protection and recognition of their rights. However, as Keck and Sikkink[31] describe, Indigenous people had reached an impasse with their states, and so the trans-national Indigenous movement attempted to "boomerang" around the state and thus bring international pressure back upon it and thus gain the domestic reforms desired. During the same time period, states were actively engaged in a concerted international effort to advance human rights around the world. By framing their quest for rights into the human rights frame, the indigenous movement entered a dynamic transnational legal process.

By their interactions over time, both the indigenous movement and the states came to constitute themselves in certain ways. A new supranational identity called "indigenous people," or "indigeneity," emerged out of this process[32] and, at least among

---

[30] Koh (1998), p. 2626.
[31] Keck and Sikkink (1998).
[32] D. Ivison, P. Patton, et., al. (2000). "Introduction." *Political Theory and the Rights of Indigenous Peoples*. D. Ivison, P. Patton and W. Sanders, eds. Cambridge: Cambridge University Press.; R. Neizen (2003). *The Origins of Indigenism: Human Rights and the Politics of Identity*. Berkeley: University of

certain segments of indigenous peoples, formed a new global layer of identity to indigenous peoples' already complicated pattern of kinship, tribal, and national minority identities. Likewise, certain states gained an identity as a "strong supporter of international human rights." Furthermore, this interaction has begun to change the domestic political discourse in certain countries in two important ways. First, the domestic political discourse regarding indigenous people began to shift in certain states from a completely needs-based discourse to one that is increasingly rights-based.[33] This means that rather than seeing indigenous people as a disadvantaged multicultural minority needing further integration into the dominant liberal society, these certain states began acknowledging that indigenous people had a unique set of rights, especially regarding land and/or self-determination. Second, all three "over-compliant" nations have increasingly distanced themselves from the British Crown, and, during the last several decades, each has enacted significant constitutional and electoral reforms to solidify their own identities. Thus, in order to establish a national identity distinct from the British Crown and unique in the post-Cold War world of globalization, these countries needed to find and articulate an identity that was distinctly Australian, Canadian or New Zealander, which required coming to terms with their British colonial legacy. As Tully[34] argued, the emergence of the discourse of indigeneity entailed a similar discursive shift in the domestic constitutionalisms that had historically supported colonial domination.

California Press.; K.S. Coates (2004). *A Global History of Indigenous Peoples: Struggle and Survival.* Hampshire: Palgrave Macmillan.

[33] R. Maaka and A. Fleras (2002). "Engaging with Indigeneity: Tino Rangatiratanga in Aotearoa." *Political Theory and the Rights of Indigenous Peoples.* D. Ivison, P. Patton and W. Sanders. eds. Cambridge: Cambridge University Press, p. 235-276.

[34] James Tully (1995). *Strange Multiplicity: Constitutionalism in an Age of Diversity.* Cambridge: Cambridge University Press.

It is this dynamic interaction, coupled with Hathaway's cost of commitment theory[35] which I propose can explain why certain states "over-comply" with human rights standards regarding indigenous people. The international indigenous movement framed its struggle under the human rights discourse even though their most desired rights were not technically included in the discourse, and, at the same time, certain states made some domestic reforms in order to enhance their identity as good stewards of human rights and reconcile their colonial legacy. But, as Hathaway argues, domestic enforcement mechanisms and the cost of making an international commitment must be considered in any evaluation of the effect of international law on state behavior. Therefore, for treaties with low enforcement mechanisms (as is the case with most human rights treaties), states will take into account the costs that would be entailed by bringing their practices into compliance as well as the likelihood that those costs would be realized. The end result is that, as Hathaway observed, countries with better rights practices are more reluctant to commit to rights instruments while those with poor domestic enforcement mechanisms are less reluctant. So, in the larger international context of emerging international indigenous rights discourse and norms, certain settler states must reconcile their colonial legacy and their post-colonial self-image. In these states, however, the cost of fully committing to the emerging indigenous rights discourse would be extremely high, based upon domestic enforcement mechanisms. Therefore, these states do not sign or ratify indigenous rights instruments with which they may already be in compliance. States whose international identities were not constituted by their compliance with and advancement of human rights norms or who had no compelling desire to reconcile their

---

[35] Hathaway (2003).

174

colonial past (e.g. the United States, Latin America) did not make the same level of domestic reforms as other states which did develop these identities.

The constructivist component of my explanation of "over-compliance" can account for why a state which exhibits "over-compliant" behavior would simultaneously resist signing treaties or adopting norms which would commit the state to recognizing the full body of indigenous rights. Because a change in domestic political discourse involves reconciling the colonial past, there is an upper limit on indigenous rights recognition that these liberal states can tolerate, which is significantly short of the emerging international indigenous rights discourse. The constitutions of these liberal states are premised on the doctrines of individualism, equality and multiculturalism. These doctrines ultimately limit the possibility of fully recognizing indigenous peoples' claims within the existing constitutional order since indigenous collective land ownership and self-determination require a sovereignty-sharing and nation-to-nation relationship between the state and indigenous nations since liberalism would consider indigenous rights to be "special rights" for certain groups of people. So, even though these states are willing to make certain rights concessions to indigenous people, these concessions appear to be rooted in the state's identity as a good and socially just global citizen and the state's desire to be identified as distinct from its colonial past. A liberal state, however, remains constrained by the doctrines of liberalism. Thus, the possibility of a full nation-to-nation relationship between indigenous nations and states in a plurinational state, as articulated in the Declaration and the indigenous rights discourse, is excluded, or at least diminished, as a discursive possibility. Therefore, while dynamic interactive identities may compel states

175

to "over-comply" with their human rights obligations in indigenous rights, they are likewise limited by that same dynamic.

The cost of commitment component of my explanation, which predicts that countries with better practices are more reluctant to commit to international instruments due to their expected costs, can account for the demonstrated reluctance of three democracies with strong domestic Indigenous rights policies to commit to the indigenous rights discourse. According to Hathaway's theory, the internal costs of that commitment are simply too high. Hathaway's findings[36] however, suggest that the determinant of treaty ratification is democracy. Since the Table 4.1 data set shows a wide variety of indigenous rights compliance levels among liberal democracies with strong internal enforcement mechanisms, a further refinement of Hathaway's theory, specifically in an indigenous rights context, is warranted. In the next section, I will examine the Table 4.1 data set in more detail, seeking to further unpack additional domestic determinants of the cost of committing to the emerging international Indigenous rights discourse.

Data

The advancement of indigenous rights evinced in certain countries and not in others is sometimes explained as a matter of domestic demographic and political factors. Three arguments are typically offered to explain this phenomenon. First, it is said that these advancements are the result of a large indigenous population. Second, advancements in indigenous rights can be attributed to parliamentary or proportional representative domestic political systems, as are used in Australia, Canada and New

---

[36] Hathaway (2003).

176

Zealand.[37] Third, indigenous rights compliance is often attributed to a country's legal system.[38] Using the data set in Table 4.1, I conducted a comparison of indigenous rights compliance by percentage of indigenous population, followed by comparative analyses by political (presidential versus parliamentary) and legal (common versus civil law) systems. Several trends emerge from the data set which show that the three arguments typically offered for indigenous rights compliance either cannot be well supported by the data from Table 4.1, or else they offer only a partial explanation of "over-compliant" state behavior.

First, the argument that a high population of indigenous people in a country leads to higher levels of indigenous rights sounds plausible at first, but the argument fails when the data on indigenous rights compliance is analyzed. First, the data set does not show any significant difference in indigenous rights compliance rates between those countries with large and small percentages of indigenous population. As Table 4.4 shows, the percentage distribution of countries which are compliant, non-compliant, partially compliant, under-compliant and "over-compliant" is very similar whether the percentage of indigenous population is small (less than 10%) or large (greater than or equal to 10%.) Figure 4.1 shows the compliance percentage distribution of countries with small indigenous populations while Figure 4.2 shows the compliance percentage distribution in countries with large indigenous populations. As both Table 4.4 and Figures 4.1 and 4.2 demonstrate, the percentage of partially compliant countries is

---

[37] A. Lijphart, *Patterns of Democracy: Government Forms and Performance in Thirty-Six Countries* (New Haven, CT: Yale University Press, 1999). As Lijphart argued, minorities in parliamentary, proportional representative systems have better representation than they receive in presidential and single-member district plurality systems, as are found in countries like the United States and many countries in Latin America.

[38] A forthcoming book by Beth Simmons finds that reluctance to commit to human rights treaties is more frequent among common law countries than in civil law countries.

slightly larger in the countries with a small indigenous population while the percentage of under-compliant countries is slightly larger in countries with large indigenous populations, but these differences are small and the similarity in the distribution between large and small indigenous populations is striking. This finding suggests that the percentage of indigenous population is not a driving force in rights compliance.

Table 4.4 Distribution of Indigenous Rights Compliance by Percentage of Indigenous Population

Percentage of Indigenous Population	Level of Indigenous Rights Compliance	Number of Countries Demonstrating the Level of Compliance	Percentage
Less than 10%	*Compliant*	1	2.8
(35 countries)	*Partially Compliant*	9	25.7
	Under-Compliant	16	45.7
	Over-Compliant	2	6.0
	Non-Compliant	7	20.0
Equal to or Greater than 10%	*Compliant*	1	5.8
(17 countries)	*Partially Compliant*	3	17.6
	Under-Compliant	9	52.9
	Over-Compliant	1	6.0
	Non-Compliant	3	17.6

Figure 4.1 Compliance Distribution with Small Indigenous Population

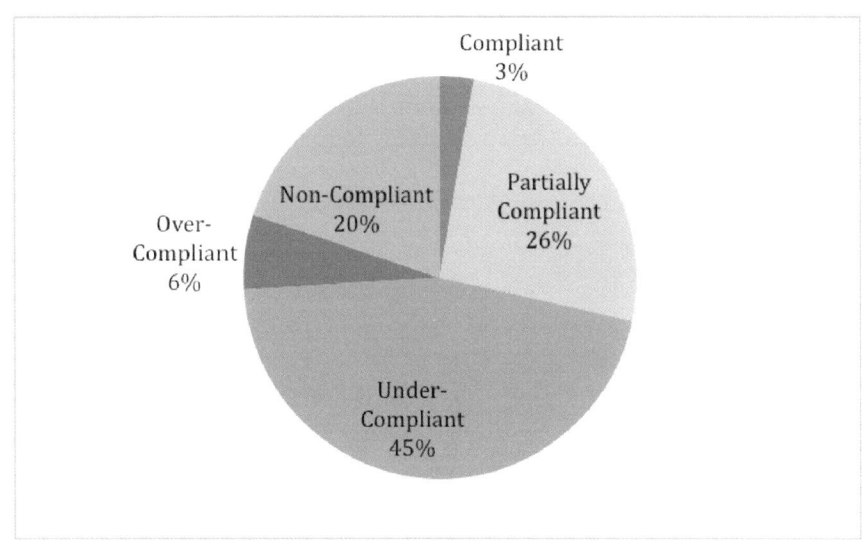

179

Figure 4.2 Compliance Distribution with Large Indigenous Population

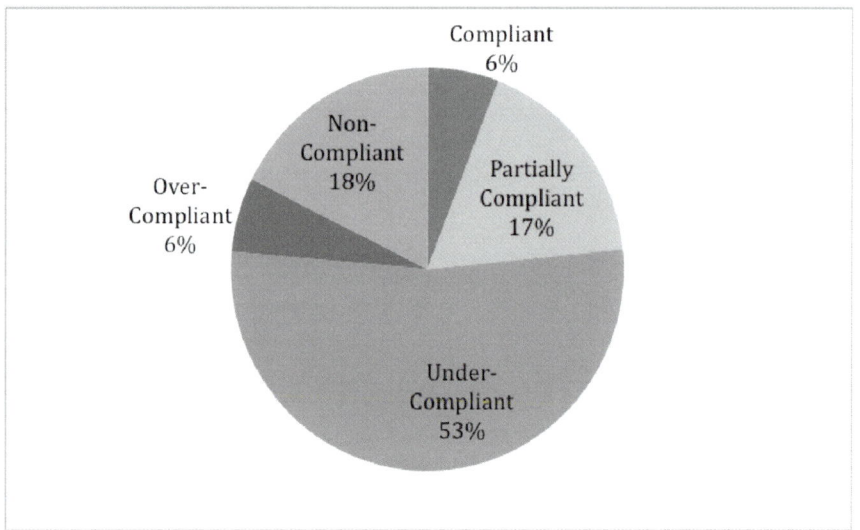

Second, a comparative analysis of indigenous rights compliance by political system suggests that a country's political system (presidential versus parliamentary) is a factor in both commitment to indigenous rights and the overall pattern of indigenous rights compliance. Table 4.5 shows that a presidential country is most likely to under-comply or partially comply, rather than to comply, with its indigenous rights commitments, indicating that presidential countries tend to make a higher level of indigenous rights commitment than do parliamentary countries. Indeed, Table 4.6 shows that the level of indigenous rights commitment in presidential regimes is significantly higher than in parliamentary systems, as almost 82% of presidential regimes have made a high level of indigenous rights commitment versus 62.5% of parliamentary countries which have made such a high commitment. There are no "over-compliant" countries among those with a presidential system.

Table 4.5   Distribution of Indigenous Rights Compliance by Political System

Political System	Level of Compliance	Number of Countries Demonstrating the Level of Compliance	Percentage
Presidential	*Compliant*	0	0
(33 countries)	*Partially Compliant*	9	27.3
	Under-Compliant	18	54.5
	Over-Compliant	0	0
	Non-Compliant	6	18.1
Parliamentary	*Compliant*	2	12.5
(16 countries)	*Partially Compliant*	3	18.75
	Under-Compliant	5	31.25
	Over-Compliant	3	18.75
	Non-Compliant	3	18.75

Table 4.6   Indigenous Rights Commitment by Political System

Political System	Level of Indigenous Rights Commitment	Number of Countries with this Level of Commitment	Percentage
Presidential	*High*	27	81.8
(33 countries)	*Low*	6	18.2
Parliamentary	*High*	10	62.5
(16 countries)	*Low*	6	37.5

Parliamentary countries are more evenly distributed in their compliance behavior than are presidential countries, so the compliance results are also far less conclusive than in presidential countries. Parliamentary countries are just as likely to comply with their indigenous rights commitments as to under-comply, and they are also just as likely to partially comply as to "over-comply." Their level of indigenous rights commitment is generally high (62.5% of parliamentary countries have a high level of commitment), but there is not such a high percentage of high commitment countries among parliamentary countries as there are among presidential regimes (62.5% for parliamentary versus 81.8% of presidential). Three parliamentary countries with a low level of commitment are "over-complying" with their indigenous rights commitments.

In sum, parliamentary countries have a tendency toward a lower level of indigenous rights commitment while presidential countries more often make a higher level of commitment. However, a higher level of commitment by presidential countries often means that they tend to come up short on compliance, with about 82% of presidential countries either partially complying or under-complying with their typically-high indigenous rights commitments. Parliamentary countries, on the other hand, tend to make a lower level of commitment, but they have more even compliance results. Roughly two-thirds of parliamentary countries make a high level of indigenous rights commitment. Two out of ten, or 20% of those parliamentary countries making a high commitment actually comply with those commitments, and eight out of ten such countries remain partially or under-compliant. 18.75% of all parliamentary countries are non-compliant, meaning that they have made low commitment to indigenous rights, and another 18.75% of parliamentary countries "over-comply" with their rights commitments. These results suggest that parliamentary countries tend to be a bit more restrained in their level of commitment to indigenous rights than are presidential regimes. They are also more likely to match or, even exceed, their level of commitment in their constitutional, legal and policy conduct. However, while "over-compliance" in indigenous rights has

182

occurred only in parliamentary systems, and there does appear to be some correlation between parliamentary regimes and lower levels of rights commitments, the data set shows that a parliamentary system is necessary but not sufficient as an explanation for, "over-compliance" in indigenous rights.

Third, there also appears to be a correlation between a country's legal system and its indigenous rights compliance. Table 4.7 displays the data on indigenous rights compliance in common law versus civil law countries. The data shows that the rates of under-compliance and partial compliance run much higher (56% and 26%, respectively) in civil law countries than in common law countries (25% and 8%). Rates of compliance are 5% in civil law countries versus 0% in common law systems while non-compliance runs at 13% on civil law countries and 42% in common law countries. As in the compliance analysis by political system, the only countries which are "over-compliant" fall entirely into one category, common law systems. This suggests an association between a common law system and over-compliance in indigenous rights, which represents a full 25% of common law countries in the data set.

Table 4.7 Distribution of Indigenous Rights Compliance by Legal System

Legal System	Level of Compliance	Number of Countries Demonstrating the Level of Compliance	Percentage
Common Law	*Compliant*	0	0%
(12 countries)	*Partially Compliant*	1	8%
	Under-Compliant	3	25%
	Over-Compliant	3	25%
	Non-Compliant	5	42%
Civil Law	*Compliant*	2	5%
(39 countries)	*Partially Compliant*	10	26%
	Under-Compliant	22	56%
	Over-Compliant	0	0%
	Non-Compliant	5	13%

Also like in the case of parliamentary versus presidential systems, much of the difference between compliance levels in common law and civil law countries is attributable to the level of indigenous rights commitment. Table 4.8 shows that the rate of high commitment among civil law countries is very high (87.1%) while common law countries tend to exhibit a lower level of commitment (66.6% are low commitment).

184

Table 4.8   Indigenous Rights Commitment by Legal System

Legal System	Level of Indigenous Rights Commitment	Number of Countries with this Level of Commitment	Percentage
Common	*High*	4	33.3%
(12 countries)	*Low*	8	66.6%
Civil	*High*	34	87.1%
(39 countries)	*Low*	5	12.9%

When political system and legal system are combined in the analysis, an even stronger relationship appears. As Table 4.9 displays, only parliamentary common law countries are over-compliant, and a full 44% of those countries with parliamentary common law systems demonstrate "over-compliance" in indigenous rights. As in prior analyses, "over-compliance" is associated with a comparatively low rate of indigenous rights commitment among parliamentary common law countries, as shown in Table 4.10.

Table 4.9   **Indigenous Rights Compliance by Political & Legal System**

Combined

Political and Legal System	Level of Compliance	Number of Countries Demonstrating the Level of Compliance	Percentage
Parliamentary Common Law	*Compliant*	0	0%
(7 countries)	*Partially Compliant*	1	14%
	Under-Compliant	2	28.5%
	Over-Compliant	3	43.8%
	Non-Compliant	1	14%
Parliamentary Civil Law	*Compliant*	2	22.2%
(9 countries)	*Partially Compliant*	2	22.2%
	Under-Compliant	3	33.3%
	Over-Compliant	0	0%
	Non-Compliant	2	22.2
Presidential Common Law	*Compliant*	0	0%
(9 countries)	*Partially Compliant*	2	22.2%
	Under-Compliant	3	33.3%
	Over-Compliant	0	0%
	Non-Compliant	4	44.4%
Presidential Civil Law	*Compliant*	0	0
(27 countries)	*Partially Compliant*	8	29.6%
	Under-Compliant	17	63%
	Over-Compliant	0	0%
	Non-Compliant	2	7%

186

Table 4.10   Indigenous Rights Commitment by Political & Legal System

Combined

Political and Legal System	Level of Commitment in Indigenous Rights	Number of Countries Demonstrating this Level of Commitment	Percentage
Parliamentary Common	High	3	42.8%
(7 countries)	Low	4	57.1%
Parliamentary Civil	High	7	77.7%
(9 countries)	Low	2	22.2%
Presidential Common	High	1	20%
(5 countries)	Low	4	80%
Presidential Civil	High	25	92.5%
(27 countries)	Low	2	7.4%

Given the low commitment to indigenous rights in parliamentary common law (57.1%) and presidential common law countries (80%), it appears that a common law country, whether a parliamentary or a presidential system, is less likely than a civil law country to make a high commitment in indigenous rights. In order to see if this reluctance among common law countries to make a high commitment is widespread among other human rights instruments or is unique to indigenous rights, one more analysis was conducted. Table 4.11 displays the percentage of the twelve common law countries which make high commitments (defined as signatory or ratification) in other human rights instruments, specifically the ICERD, the ICCPR and the ICESCR. The results range from an 83.33% to a 91.66% rate of high commitment among common law countries, indicating that common law countries do not have a general problem making

high levels of commitment to human rights instruments other than indigenous rights.

Table 4.11   Percentage of Twelve Common Law Countries Making High Commitments on Major Human Rights Instruments

Human Rights Instrument	Number of Common Law Countries Making High Commitments (i.e. signature or ratification)	Percentage
ICERD	11	91.66%
ICCPR	11	91.66%
ICESCR	10	83.33%

The twelve common law countries in the data set clearly have no problem making

high commitments to other major human rights instruments, so it does not appear that

common law alone is a determinant of a country's reluctance to commit to indigenous

rights. Therefore, while there is a strong correlation between common law and a

country's reluctance to make a high commitment to indigenous rights, and some

relationship between common law and "over-compliance" in indigenous rights, the

common law explanation is insufficient in itself to explain a pattern of "over-compliance"

in indigenous rights in certain countries.

To recap, the data set showed no noticeable relationship between percentage of

indigenous population and indigenous rights compliance. Also, both the political system

and legal system arguments have traction, as some association between common law

parliamentary systems and "over-compliance" with Indigenous rights was demonstrated.

Conclusion

In this chapter, I have examined state responses to the emerging international indigenous rights discourse and have identified four levels of state compliance with international standards: compliance, partial compliance, under-compliance and a new concept, which I have termed "over-compliance." "Over-compliance" occurs when a state's legal, constitutional or policy conduct regarding indigenous rights exceeds its level of commitment to international indigenous rights instruments.

Analysis of a data set on indigenous rights compliance shows that 71% of countries are partially or under-compliant with their indigenous rights commitments, 23% are compliant and 6% are "over-compliant." Compliance levels are highest in Europe, North America and the Pacific, although certain countries with medium to high legal, constitutional or policy conduct are reluctant to make a high commitment to indigenous rights and are considered "over-compliant."

"Over-compliance" is a concept that has thus far not been considered by international relations theory and deserves further examination. A brief review of the compliance literature reveals that rationalist and liberal theories fail to explain "over-compliance," however an explanation grounded in constructivist theory coupled with Hathaway's cost of commitment theory is offered as a possible explanation.

According to this explanation, "over-compliance" results when parliamentary common law settler states which identify as "strong supporters of human rights" get caught in a particular tension. These states must reconcile their colonial legacy and their post-colonial image within a larger context of emerging indigenous rights discourse. In a shifting international order, however, these same states are reluctant to commit to the

189

emerging indigenous rights standards because the cost of commitment is high, due to the domestic enforcement mechanisms present in those states and remnants of their colonial foundation. What is the remaining source of this high cost of commitment in these parliamentary common law settler countries? In the next two chapters, case studies of indigenous rights in two parliamentary common law settler countries, New Zealand and Canada, will seek further refinement of this high cost of commitment explanation for "over-compliance."

Chapter 5

Indigenous Rights in New Zealand

You can't be honourable in a fundamentally dishonourable process of dispossession.

--Moana Jackson, 2008

New Zealand is a country that takes its international reputation and its international human rights obligations very seriously. New Zealand has ratified numerous human rights instruments, including the ICERD, the ICCPR, and the Optional Protocol to the ICCPR. Upon ratification, these instruments have a significant impact on domestic New Zealand law. New Zealand has passed a number of domestic legislative acts to uphold its international human rights obligations to non-discrimination, including the Race Relations Act of 1971, the Human Rights Commission Act of 1977 and the New Zealand Bill of Rights Act of 1990.[1] New Zealand did ratify ILO No. 107, but not ILO No. 169,[2] so under its ratified instruments, New Zealand is obligated to respect the equality of the Māori as citizens of New Zealand and take positive steps to ensure non-discrimination of Māori. But, at the same time, New Zealand refused to ratify ILO No. 169 so it is not obligated under international human rights law to uphold indigenous land and self-determination rights. New Zealand also campaigned actively and voted against the Declaration on Indigenous Rights in the UN General Assembly, later issuing a statement that "provisions in the Declaration are fundamentally incompatible with New

---

[1] C.J.I. Magallanes. 1999. "International Human Rights and their Impact on Domestic Law in Indigenous Peoples Rights in Australia, Canada and New Zealand." *Indigenous Peoples' Rights in Australia, Canada and New Zealand.* P. Havemann, ed. Oxford: Oxford University Press.
[2] Allison Brysk. 2000. *From Tribal Village to Global Village: Indian Rights and International Relations in Latin America.* Stanford: Stanford University Press.

Zealand's constitutional and legal arrangements, the Treaty of Waitangi, and the principle of governing for the good of all our citizens."[3]

New Zealand is also known worldwide, and takes great pride in its reputation, as a beacon of hope for indigenous citizens. It has officially added Māori as an official language of New Zealand, including officially renaming the country Aotearoa/New Zealand, as Aotearoa is the Māori language word for the islands known in English as New Zealand. The government has mandated that all children learn some Māori language in school. It has renamed many place names from English back to their original Māori names. It has enacted extensive and expansive government programs to help reduce disparities and help "Māori achieve their full potential."[4] In fact, the disparities between Māori and non-Māori in New Zealand have been reduced to the smallest level anywhere in the world where indigenous peoples live in non-indigenous dominated societies. In short, New Zealand has demonstrated a remarkable commitment to Māori and has been recognized around the world for its efforts. Yet, at the same time, New Zealand is known among indigenous peoples as one of the 'gang of four' who vocally opposed and voted against the Declaration on Indigenous Rights in the UN General Assembly, and it has continually refused to consider ratification of ILO 169. Furthermore, activists for Māori self-determination find themselves perpetually at odds with the New Zealand government, even coming under arrest in some extreme cases for

---

[3] New Zealand Mission to the United Nations/ Te Mangai O Aotearoa. United Nations General Assembly, Declaration on the Rights of Indigenous Peoples. Explanation of Vote by New Zealand Permanent Representative H. E. Rosemary Banks. 13 September 2007.

[4] The main government agency charged with this mission is called Te Puni Kokiro, which translates as "Realising Māori Potential."

their advocacy of Māori rights and sovereignty.[5] New Zealand, therefore, is a paradox in indigenous rights compliance. It is far ahead of other settler societies in some ways and yet is one of the global leaders in resisting indigenous rights advancement. How can this paradox, this conjunction of overt opposition to the codification of indigenous peoples' rights and an "over-compliance" of practice in recognizing indigenous "rights" be explained?

Indigenous rights in New Zealand presents a paradox which defies the usual explanations of state compliance. Rationalists, who argue that states obey international law when it is in their best interest to do so, cannot account for the paradox of why New Zealand excels in some areas concerning indigenous peoples and then simultaneously resists the international rights standard. Liberals, who focus on state conformity with norms and equate compliance with liberal democracy, cannot explain why New Zealand, a liberal democratic country which is normally a world leader in human rights, actively resists the Declaration and indigenous rights. In the remainder of this chapter, I will explore the New Zealand case in light of the constructivist "cost of commitment" explanation presented in Chapter 4. This explanation argues that parliamentary common law countries which were founded on the Doctrine of Discovery are caught in a particular tension of reconciling their colonial legacy and their post-colonial image within the larger context of the emerging indigenous rights discourse. While the reliance on the Doctrine of Discovery in the New Zealand case is largely implicit, its presence nevertheless translates into a high cost for the "strong human rights supporter" of New Zealand to

---

[5] On 15 October 2007, 300 paramilitary police raided houses and arrested 17 Maori sovereignty activists under the Terrorism Suppression Act of 2002 (TSA), the first time that the Act was invoked in a search warrant. Ezra Black, "New Zealand's Police Accused of Repressing Indigenous Maori." *McGill Daily.* 25 October 2007.

commit to emerging indigenous rights standards because a full renouncement of the Doctrine of Discovery would challenge the foundation and the perceived legitimacy of the New Zealand state.

There are several important factors at play in the New Zealand case which I argue have led to its paradoxical indigenous rights behavior under a constructivist cost of commitment, factors which rationalist, liberal and common explanations also either miss or under-emphasize. First, an extremely vocal indigenous movement has been highly active in New Zealand since the 1970s and 1980s, a movement which is well connected to the international indigenous rights movement and invokes an international human rights framework for indigenous rights. Second, New Zealand has also come to demonstrate a high level of concern for its human rights reputation both overseas and in its own self-image. Third, the nation has a history of British colonialism, and, as I will argue, an implicit reliance on the Doctrine of Discovery. New Zealand, like some other Commonwealth countries, has become somewhat preoccupied with a search for its identity as it has increasingly separated from Britain in recent years. As it has become a more multiethnic society and, as trade has increased with its Asian and Pacific neighbors, its ties with Britain have weakened. In its attempt to carve out a new international identity, New Zealand as a whole has begun taking on Māori identity as part of national identity. All of these factors have converged to create an atmosphere of indigenous reconciliation in New Zealand, beginning in the 1970s. But, as I will argue in this chapter, the character of that reconciliation has pushed New Zealand in a direction in which it simultaneously opposes indigenous rights as articulated by the transnational indigenous rights movement while achieving a high level of indigenous "rights" in certain areas.

Reconciliation efforts in New Zealand have exposed a huge gap between two dominant Māori and Pākehā[6] understandings of the Treaty of Waitangi, and what the resulting governance structure of Aotearoa/New Zealand should look like. One understanding of indigenous reconciliation, which is often a Pākehā and New Zealand government position, is that the Treaty of Waitangi gave the Crown total sovereignty over New Zealand under one unified parliamentary government. I will refer to this as a "Doctrine of Discovery" understanding of the Treaty relationship, where the Crown assumes its cultural superiority and also presumes that, with the signing of the Treaty, Māori gave up, and it acquired, full and complete sovereignty. This vision of reconciliation and the Treaty requires settlement of past grievances so that the nation can move forward, unified and equal, under the "one law" of Crown sovereignty. The other, and contrasting, interpretation of the Treaty is what I will term the "Tino Rangatiratanga" understanding of the Treaty, which is one that preserves the Tino Rangatiratanga of Māori. Tino Rangatiratanga is a Maori term which best translates into 'sovereignty' although this is not a purely accurate translation. There are two versions of the Treaty of Waitangi, and Tino Rangatiratanga was reserved to Maori under the Maori language version of the Treaty. This interpretation pushes for a rearrangement of the Treaty relationship between Māori and Pākehā toward a plural sovereignty or multiple

---

[6] Pākehā is a Māori word which means the members of New Zealand's population which are not Māori. The word first referred to the settler population that had origins in the British Isles. The use of the term later expanded to refer to all settlers which were of European origin. Some New Zealanders still use the word in this context, however in its common contemporary usage it refers to all members of the population which are not Māori or Polynesian, therefore encompassing all other populations in New Zealand. It is thus more a term of political and/or social categorization, rather than strictly racial or ethnic.

sovereignty partnership in governance. I argue in this chapter that it is this gap between the two understandings of indigenous reconciliation and the Treaty relationship that ultimately accounts for indigenous rights over-compliance in New Zealand. I will examine how this gap has played out in recent years as discourses surrounding the Treaty of Waitangi have shifted and crystallized into these two understandings which are in direct tension with one another. I will demonstrate how New Zealand, as a strong supporter of human rights and a liberal democracy with effective domestic human rights enforcement mechanisms, emphasizes "soft rights" focus in indigenous rights yet remains firmly rooted in the Doctrine of Discovery understanding of the Treaty and reconciliation in order to avoid the high cost of commitment which would necessary under the Tino Rangatiratanga understanding, given indigenous demands for land and self-determination coupled with the strong domestic human rights enforcement mechanisms in New Zealand.

After providing some critical background on the Treaty of Waitangi, I will examine how the various conditions developed which have propelled New Zealand toward reconciliation efforts related to the Treaty, specifically an active domestic indigenous rights movement which invoked the international indigenous rights discourse, a reputation and self-image as a strong supporter of human rights, and a shifting national identity. These conditions propel New Zealand toward a particular understanding of reconciliation and the Treaty, the Doctrine of Discovery understanding. I will then look at two specific issues that illustrate the two reconciliation discourses at play in New Zealand and expose the gap between the two discourses. The "cost of commitment" of moving New Zealand, a "strong human rights supporter" closer to the indigenous, or

Tino Rangatiratanga understanding, is ultimately excluded in both instances as a discursive possibility. The Waitangi Tribunal and the Treaty Settlements process, and the 2004 Foreshore and Seabed legislation both demonstrate the limits of the Doctrine of Discovery understanding of reconciliation and the Treaty relationship. Each of these recent cases of indigenous rights controversies in New Zealand illustrates the two different and competing understandings of reconciliation and the Treaty at work in New Zealand, the gap that remains between them and, most illuminating, how New Zealand attempts to maneuver between them, thus 'over-complying' in certain rights areas in order to avoid a renegotiation and a restructuring of Crown sovereignty in Aotearoa New Zealand which would be required under a Tino Rangatiratanga understanding of reconciliation. I will close with a discussion of some of the most recent efforts to advance the Tino Rangatiratanga view of the Treaty relationship.

Conditions for Reconciliation in New Zealand

Unlike neighboring Australia, the relationship between the Māori and the Crown has never been defined by the *terra nullius,* or the "empty land" doctrine. Unlike in the United States, Doctrine of Discovery has not been explicitly relied upon in New Zealand's domestic jurisprudence as the basis of the nation's foundation. Rather, the British Crown signed a treaty with the Māori in 1840, the Treaty of Waitangi, which is considered the founding document of the state of New Zealand. This Treaty was not signed as a peace treaty, as there was no state of war between Māori and the English prior to the Treaty. Rather, this was a Treaty which was intended to peacefully found the new settler territory of New Zealand and establish a relationship of governance between Māori and the Crown.

When the Treaty was signed in 1840, there were two versions: the English language version and the Māori language version. These two versions of the Treaty differed in one critical respect, a difference which has remained salient throughout New Zealand's history. The English language version stated that the Crown was granted *full and complete sovereignty* over New Zealand while Māori were to receive full possession of their traditional lands. Māori were also to retain self-government over those lands.[7] The Māori language version, however, read that Māori retained *tino rangatiratanga*, which means chieftainship, or can best be translated as 'sovereignty'. The Māori have a different word, *rangatira*, which would have better reflected the English understanding of internal self-government over traditional lands, but this word was not utilized in the Māori language version. While there is a great deal of historical scholarship which delves into the differences between the English and Māori versions of the Treaty[8] and whether or not the English Crown attempted to trick Māori into signing the Treaty, it is not my intent to enter this historical debate. What is clear is that what was ceded to the Crown in the Māori version of the Treaty was something far less than the "full and complete sovereignty" expressed in the English version. Common law, which is the basis

---

[7] S. Wiessner. 2003. "Rights and Status of Indigenous Peoples: A Global Comparative and International Analysis." *International Law and Indigenous Peoples*. S.J. Anaya, ed. Burlington, VT: Rowman & Littlefield.

[8] For example Michael Belgrave, Merata Kawharu, and David Williams, eds. 2005. *Waitangi Revisited: Perspectives on the Treaty of Waitangi*. Oxford: Oxford University Press.; F.M. Brookfield. 2006. *Waitangi and Indigenous Rights: Revolution, Law and Legitimation*. Auckland, New Zealand: Auckland University Press.; I.H. Kawharu. 1989. *Waitangi: Maori and Pākehā Perspectives on the Treaty of Waitangi*. Auckland, New Zealand: Auckland University Press.; Claudia Orange. 1987. *The Treaty of Waitangi*. Wellington, NZ: Bridget Williams Books.; Matthew S. R Palmer. 2008. *The Treaty of Waitangi in New Zealand's Law and Constitution*. Wellington, New Zealand: Victoria University Press.

for New Zealand law, is very clear that when there is a dispute over translation, it is the indigenous language version of the Treaty that must be relied upon.[9] More important for analyzing the indigenous rights behavior of New Zealand, however, is the fact that these two translations of the Treaty do exist, and that they continue to represent two entirely different schools of thought on Treaty interpretation in contemporary New Zealand, continuing to frame the debate over indigenous rights, governance, and the relationship between Māori and the Crown.

General Hobson, the English General who had presented the Treaty of Waitangi to Māori leaders at Waitangi in 1840, immediately proclaimed, *"He iwi tahi tatou"* or "We are all one people now", in the earliest expression of what would become the Doctrine of Discovery understanding of the Treaty. In 1840, the essential reason that the British pursued a treaty was to "give legitimacy to the Crown to colonize the country."[10] While the British approached Māori with the Treaty rather than explicitly invoking the Doctrine of Discovery to settle the islands of New Zealand, I argue that the Doctrine of Discovery and its presumption of European cultural superiority has been and remains implicit in this understanding of the Treaty and indigenous rights in general. For the ink was barely dry on the Treaty before the British began taking Māori lands illegally.

---

[9] The source of this international law principle lies in the US Supreme Court case, *United States V. Winans*, 198 U.S. 371, 3801-81 [1905]. This case established the principle of the "canons of treaty construction." In this case, the US Supreme Court ruled that "by rule of interpretation of agreements and treaties with Indians, ambiguities occurring will be resolved from the standpoint of the Indians. Also Stephen L. Pevar. 2002. *The Rights of Indians and Tribes. Third Edition.* Carbondale, IL: Southern Illinois University Press, p. 50-51. In New Zealand, the Waitangi Tribunal has adopted the canons of treaty construction when interpretation of the Treaty of Waitangi is in doubt. See especially the Montunui Waitora Report, WAI 6. Waitangi Tribunal Reports, Wellington, New Zealand, March 1983. In Canada, two Supreme Court cases have supported this legal principle: *Nowegijick v. The Queen* [1983] 1 S.C.R. 29 and *Simon v. The Queen* [1985] 2 S.C.R. 29. These two cases together led to the Canadian Supreme Court's rule of treaty construction which stated that treaties must be interpreted liberally and fairly and most crucially, in line with how the Indians would have understood them.

[10] Mason Durie, speaking at "Finding Common Ground" Te Papa 2008 Treaty Debate Series, Te Papa National Museum of New Zealand, Wellington, New Zealand, 31 January 2008.

General Hobson, frustrated by what he viewed as the slow pace of Māori leaders'

acceptance of the Treaty on the South Island, on 21 May 1840--only three months after

the Treaty was first signed at Waitangi--completely cast it aside and, rather than continue

to seek Maori signatures on the South Island, explicitly and exclusively invoked the

Doctrine of Discovery to justify the taking of New Zealand's South Island for the British

Crown. Using the words, "on the grounds of discovery" Hobson proclaimed Crown

sovereignty over the whole of South Island.[11] In 1841, the colonial government again

presumed a Doctrine of Discovery when it passed the Land Claims Ordinance which

stated that lands not actually occupied by or used by Māori belonged to the Crown.

Crown land acquisition and settler encroachment of Māori land became commonplace in

subsequent decades. As more settlers arrived and English, and later Pākehā, power grew,

Māori became increasingly marginalized in their own country. The Treaty of Waitangi

was even declared a "simple nullity" in 1877 by Judge Prendergast in his ruling on a

major Māori land case.[12]

An Active Domestic Indigenous Movement Connected to the Global Indigenous
Rights Movement

Beginning in the 1970s, Māori political activism awoke with a vengeance, not

only domestically but also internationally, shifting the relationship between the Māori

---

[11] Evison, Harry C. 1990. *The Treaty of Waitangi and the Waitangi Tribunal: Fact or Fiction.*
Christchurch: Ngai Tahu Māori Trust Board.
[12] *Wi Parata v. Bishop of Wellington* [1877] 3 NZ Jur (NS) SC 72 at 78.

and the state of New Zealand from a needs-based one to a rights-based relationship.[13] The Māori of New Zealand have been powerful leaders in the international indigenous peoples' movement, maintaining an extensive network of international indigenous contacts, hosting numerous international conferences and taking a leadership role in the United Nations process which aimed to include indigenous rights in the international human rights regime. In fact, one of the first transnational indigenous peoples' meetings took place between representatives of the Māori and several Western Canadian First Nations.[14] Although some scholars consider Māori rights advances solely as domestic political victories,[15] the significant internationalization of the indigenous peoples' movement, coupled with New Zealand's strong commitment to international human rights, provides evidence for a more multi-faceted and nuanced explanation. As international linkages grew, so did Māori assertiveness. Since the international indigenous movement helped constitute indigenous identity and struggle for rights around the world,[16] the Māori, like other indigenous groups, began to bring home some of the language and protest techniques acquired at international forums for use in their domestic politics.[17] The New Zealand government seemed to be aware of international scrutiny and was increasingly wary of making any move to reduce Māori rights.[18] This interaction between the international and domestic realms resulted in significant changes to the

---

[13] R Maaka and A. Fleras. 2002. "Engaging with Indigeneity: Tino Rangatiratanga in Aotearoa." *Political Theory and the Rights of Indigenous Peoples.* Pp. 89-109 in D. Ivison, P. Patton, and W. Sanders, ed. Cambridge: Cambridge University Press.

[14] S. J. Anaya. 2004. *Indigenous Peoples in International Law.* New York: Oxford University Press.

[15] Magallanes, 1999; P. Havemann, ed. 2000. *Indigenous Peoples Rights in Australia, Canada and New Zealand.* Oxford: Oxford University Press.

[16] R. Niezen. 2003. *The Origins of Indigenism: Human Rights and the Politics of Identity.* Berkeley: University of California Press.

[17] Magallanes, 1999, p. 263.

[18] *Ibid.*

discourse surrounding the Treaty of Waitangi, particularly the relationship between Māori and the state of New Zealand. As the idea of self-determination evolved into a touchstone of indigenous politics around the world, the phrase "Tino Rangatiratanga" gained wide usage in Māori discourse and protest.

Beginning in the 1970s, and coincident with the rise of indigenous transnational activity, the Tino Rangatiratanga understanding of the Treaty of Waitangi, an understanding which centers around the idea of Māori-Pākehā partnership in sovereignty and governance, was increasingly asserted in domestic politics, producing not only an important shift in domestic political discourse regarding the foundational centrality of the Treaty in New Zealand, but it also marked an effort to remake the Treaty relationship between Māori and Pākehā into a new vision of sovereignty in New Zealand. The Te Papa National Museum of New Zealand, which opened in 1998 in the capital city of Wellington, was architecturally designed with a permanent exhibition of the Treaty of Waitangi, called "Signs of a Nation" at its center around which all other exhibitions circulate, clearly indicating the centrality the Treaty had come to represent in New Zealand political discourse by that time. During Waitangi Day celebrations and commemorations in February 2008, Massey University Professor and Treaty expert Mason Durie stated during Te Papa's Treaty Debate Series that "The Treaty is imbedded in the life of the nation," that "it is part of New Zealand's constitutional conventions" and that "the Treaty of Waitangi has come to equate with ...New Zealand values," and "that there is now a very high level of agreement that the Treaty of Waitangi ...signaled the emergence of New Zealand as a modern state."[19] Human Rights Commissioner Joris de

---

[19] Durie, 31 January 2008.

Bres also noted that the new national school curriculum launched in 2008 "acknowledges the principles of the Treaty of Waitangi and the bicultural foundations of Aotearoa New Zealand."[20] Te Papa's Chief Executive Seddon Bennington alluded to the rise of the Tino Rangatiratanga understanding of the Treaty and the possibility of rearranging New Zealand's sovereignty in his comments as moderator of the debate, stating that the Treaty "provides a platform for the future, a unique platform in this country, not just for Māori but for all New Zealanders."[21] Professor, Treaty expert and Treaty negotiator Matthew Palmer agreed, stating that, "there should be some ongoing relationship between the British Crown and Māori, hapu[22] and rangatira[23] concerning the exercise of public power," and that the Treaty should be inscribed in ordinary law so that it will "provide the basis for a healthy set of ongoing relationships between the Crown, Māori and other New Zealanders."[24] Mason Durie expressed this sentiment as representing what he called an "Aotearoa tradition" whereby Māori interact with the rest of New Zealand in a partnership, based "on the skills, knowledge, resources, and values that they can bring." In his words, "the yet-to-be realized promise of the Treaty of Waitangi is about the way in which we will prepare for the future, and the unique stamp we will place on New Zealand."[25]

---

[20] Joris de Bres, "Finding Common Ground" Te Papa 2008 Treaty Debate Series, Te Papa National Museum of New Zealand, Wellington, New Zealand, 7 February 2008.

[21] Seddon Bennington, "Finding Common Ground" Te Papa 2008 Treaty Debate Series, Te Papa National Museum of New Zealand, Wellington, New Zealand, 31 January 2008.

[22] A *hapu* is a Māori subtribe, made up of a group of extended families, or *whanua*. An *iwi* is a Māori tribe; several *hapu* make up an *iwi*. Traditionally, Māori governance occurred at the *hapu* level.

[23] *Rangatira* is the Māori word for chief or chiefs as the word is the same whether it is used in the singular or plural. It also means a chieftainship, or leadership position.

[24] Matthew Palmer, "Finding Common Ground" Te Papa 2008 Treaty Debate Series, Te Papa National Museum of New Zealand, Wellington, New Zealand, 31 January 2008.

[25] Durie, 31 January 2008.

Bone fide efforts to reconcile the Treaty with past behavior toward Māori began in 1975, the year the New Zealand Parliament passed the Treaty of Waitangi Act, which after 135 years, finally "accorded some effect to the Treaty."[26] The Act created the Waitangi Tribunal which was charged with investigating violations of the Treaty, reporting findings and making recommendations for governmental action. This is not simply a land claims settlement tribunal. Reports and recommendations range from monetary settlement for old land claims to return of disputed lands. Fishing claims have also featured heavily in Tribunal reports and recommendations. Although the Tribunal does not have direct enforcement powers, its recommendations impact the actions of all three branches of the New Zealand government.[27] As further evidence of the domestic impact of the international indigenous movement, the Tribunal often references indigenous activities and developments in other countries, especially in treaty interpretation.[28] There are also numerous references in Tribunal reports to the importance of upholding indigenous self-determination under international law.[29]

During the 1980s, a series of decisions was handed down by various New Zealand courts recognizing and upholding Māori fishing rights as part of their self-determination status, as articulated in the Treaty of Waitangi. The jurisprudence in these decisions relied extensively on similar indigenous rights jurisprudence in Canada, Australia and the United States.[30] So, international developments in indigenous rights had an impact on New Zealand jurisprudence as well.

---

[26] Wiessner, 2003, p. 271.
[27] Wiessner, 2003.
[28] Magallanes, 1999.
[29] *Ibid.*, p. 260.
[30] Magallanes, 1999.

All of these major domestic advancements toward indigenous reconciliation go well beyond New Zealand's technical obligation of compliance with its ratified human rights instruments. New Zealand has enacted laws and policies which recognize collective indigenous rights beyond its technical obligations.

Global Human Rights Steward

One discourse which has emerged in recent decades is a focus on New Zealand's emerging identity as a racially harmonious society based on fairness, tolerance and respect for universal human rights, especially as viewed by other countries and the international community. As stated in a 2006 Human Rights Commission submission regarding a revised national school curriculum, "In New Zealand, human rights underlie our expectations about life, education, health, work, personal security, equal opportunity and fair treatment, our ability to have a say and our system of government."[31] This "global human rights steward" identity for New Zealand manifests itself in numerous ways.

The *New Zealand Handbook on International Human Rights*, published in 2003 by the Ministry of Foreign Affairs extols the virtuous history of New Zealand as a global advocate and leading steward of international human rights. In the Forward, Prime Minster Helen Clark states that "our human rights record is one from which we can take great satisfaction and encouragement."[32] As the Handbook explains, New Zealand has always been a world leader in international human rights. In the drafting process for the

---

[31] New Zealand Human Rights Commission/*Te Kahui Tika Tangata*. The New Zealand Draft Curriculum for Consultation 2006: Human Rights Issues. Wellington: Human Rights Commission, October 2006.
[32] New Zealand Government. Ministry of Foreign Affairs and Trade. *New Zealand Handbook on International Human Rights*. Wellington: Ministry of Foreign Affairs and Trade. 2003.

United Nations Charter in 1944, New Zealand was one of a handful of outspoken states which called for stronger language on international human rights, and in a joint New Zealand-Australian statement which was issued in 1944, New Zealand took exception to the narrow vision of human rights offered by the US and the UK. New Zealand took a more progressive position on human rights, arguing that human rights should have a stronger place in the UN Charter. New Zealand also played an important leadership role in the 1948 deliberations over the Universal Declaration of Human Rights. The *Human Rights Handbook* also highlights the strong position New Zealand takes against discrimination. It also has several sections which extol the high standing and visible participation of New Zealand in contemporary human rights issues areas like women's rights, children's rights and refugees.[33]

Another Ministry of Foreign Affairs document states clearly and unequivocally that "human rights considerations are central to the Government's foreign policy" based upon the "**fundamental values and aspirations** that underpin our society (emphasis original)."[34] The same document also asserts that New Zealand has "a strong commitment to upholding the universality and indivisibility of human rights"[35] and that the Government places a "high priority on human rights."[36]

A 2004 report by the New Zealand Human Rights Commission found that "New Zealand meets international human rights standards in many respects, and often surpasses

---

[33] *Ibid.*

[34] New Zealand. Ministry of Foreign Affairs and Trade. Inquiry into the Role of Human Rights in Foreign Policy: Submission by the Ministry of Foreign Affairs and Trade. August 2000, p.1.

[35] *Ibid.*, p. 3.

[36] *Ibid.*, p. 5.

them"[37] because "New Zealanders place a high value on harmonious race relations"[38] and also on "fairness (and this is often expressed colloquially in terms of a 'fair go') and have a well developed tradition of tolerance and flexibility."[39]   This report also noted the pride which New Zealanders should feel since New Zealand was instrumental in the development of international human rights law itself.[40]

Interviews with Māori activists and New Zealand government officials during 2008 also attest to the importance of New Zealand's identity as a "good steward of international human rights," particularly where indigenous peoples are concerned. These interviews reveal how Māori activists connected with the international indigenous rights movement attempt to leverage the New Zealand government by utilizing a strategy of shaming the nation in the area of indigenous rights. Dr. John Tamahori, Chief Policy Advisor for the Te Puni Kokiri agency of the New Zealand government, discussed how Māori who are connected to the international indigenous movement attempt to gain leverage with the New Zealand government:

> (Māori who are active in international indigenous rights) are the most vigorous critics of their own government. ..So, they have earned their spurs by being critics of the New Zealand government; (they) demonize them overseas in all indigenous forums.[41]

As reported by Māori activists, the shaming strategy is not just criticism but is a deliberate attempt to expose the hidden racism and colonial mentality existing right under

---

[37] New Zealand Government. Human Rights Commission/Tu Kahui Tika Tangata. *Human Rights in New Zealand Today: New Zealand Action Plan for Human Rights.* Auckland: Human Rights Commission, 2004, p. 10.
[38] *Ibid.*, p. 15.
[39] *Ibid.*, p. 47.
[40] *Ibid.*, p. 6
[41] Interview with Dr. John Tamahori, Chief Advisor, Policy, *Te Puni Kokiri* (Realising Māori Potential), Wellington, New Zealand, 3 March 2008.

the surface of this emerging "good human rights steward" national identity. Exposing these stains on New Zealand's self-image is meant to change indigenous rights policies. One Māori activist said that, "we are very happy to have that support from the United Nations because it validates our position and it supports our rights that we always believed were valid, and it shames the government."[42]

Although many interviewees indicated that the results of these shaming campaigns often fall short of what is hoped, the various responses they have received from government when they have utilized the shaming strategy does indicate that the government is extremely sensitive when its human rights self-image is attacked. Typically, the government gets extremely defensive, sometimes trying to discredit the very same UN human rights apparatus that it extols so eloquently in other contexts. One activist described the actions of the New Zealand government in recent indigenous rights issues:

> We had the UN's Special Rapporteur on indigenous issues come and visit, issue a report, government dished it, said he was a low level bureaucrat in the UN system. We had the UN Committee on the Convention on the Elimination of Racial Discrimination write a report on New Zealand and question the Foreshore and Seabed Act and tell them that they really need more consultation and they dished the CERD. They just dismissed it.[43]

Another activist reported that in response to censures by any UN committee relating to indigenous rights, the New Zealand government tries to:

> brush them off and tries to discredit those (UN) organizations or those committees and so they must be biased, they must have spoken to the wrong people, and they don't take the criticism on the chin really.[44]

---

[42] Interview with Māori activist #5, Wellington, New Zealand, 27 February 2008.
[43] Interview with Māori activist #1, Wellington, New Zealand, 13 February 2008.
[44] *Ibid.*

Another activist spoke to the racism and colonial mentality that remains in New Zealand, which is in direct conflict with, and even masked by, its positive human rights reputation and self-image. He said:

> I guess that the issue I have with the New Zealand government in terms of the way that it engages on indigenous issues is that it tends not to deal with these issues with integrity. And I think that's different than the people across the way in Australia because for years and years the indigenous people in Australia knew what the attitude of the Australian government was. They'd come right out and say certain things and do certain things which are, quite frankly, racist. The cultural difference here is that they'll say and do whatever they can just to avoid the issue. ...Mainstream culture here in New Zealand is not one that comes right out in front and say certain things and I think that mainstream New Zealand is quite afraid of being called racist which is fair enough but what it doesn't do is allow you to actually deal with the issues and that's the problem. ...On the one hand they are trying to hold up New Zealand as this really racially harmonious society while at the same time being quite underhanded and quite nasty to indigenous peoples here as well.[45]

Māori Party member of Parliament Hone Harawira was a bit more optimistic on the results of the shaming strategy in indigenous rights. In his view,

> New Zealand's reputation in that area suffered hugely when they took away the foreshore and seabed because I think that for the first time, Māori appealed to the United Nations, to the CERD.[46] And we had a Rapporteur come over and basically caned the government for what they'd done, for the breach of the Treaty, for their denial of legal rights to us, etc., etc., which tended to lift everybody's vision to another level here. ...New Zealand, I think, has started to suffer from Māori determining to take their case to the international stage. You know, they talk about this thing, the clean, green image and, oh, we treat out Māori so well...yeah, yeah...there's starting to be these cracks. Yeah, it's starting to crack.[47]

---

[45] Interview with Māori activist #9, Wellington, New Zealand, 10 March 2008.

[46] The CERD refers to the monitoring body of the Convention on the Elimination of Racial Discrimination. New Zealand is a signatory to this Convention and, as a result, is subject to its review.

[47] Interview with Māori Party Member of Parliament Hone Harawira, Wellington, New Zealand, 20 February 2008.

Even though the government's response to UN criticism is often tepid and sometimes highly defensive, Harawira sees that there is actual embarrassment in the government and the society when indigenous issues are exposed on the international level. He said,

> Oh, the government was embarrassed, and it continues to be so, because we use it often in our speeches in the House, the Māori Party, and because the Reporter's report covered such a broad range of areas, we're able to use aspects of that report on numerous occasions, I'd say probably twenty times in twenty different speeches in the House last year we referred to the CERD report and different aspects of it. And the importance of New Zealand realizing that if they want to go down that track, we are here to remind them of this and that. And the world is now open and, of course, our speeches are on the Internet.[48]

New Zealand's Shifting Identity: Multiculturalism and Absorption of Maori Identity

In the decades since the 1970s rebirth of Māori activism and international indigenous activity, three discourses have developed which have produced a shift in New Zealand's identity, focused in two areas: multiculturalism and an absorption of Maori identity. These discourses, coupled with the "global human rights steward" discourse have intersected, converged and together produced a desire to reconcile New Zealand's colonial past.

Multiculturalism

The society of New Zealand has undergone tremendous changes which have also impacted the country's indigenous rights behavior and its interpretation of the Treaty relationship. With an influx of immigration in recent decades, particularly from Asia and the Pacific, New Zealand has become increasingly multiethnic. During the same period of time, the United Kingdom joined the European Union and began looking more

---

[48] *Ibid.*

towards Europe and, as a result, many Commonwealth nations like New Zealand have moved steadily away from their British origins. In this post-colonial globalized world, the question of what is New Zealand and what are its unique identifying features has become a near-obsession in this small, remote island nation in the South Pacific. Newspaper editorial pages are filled with columns and letters reflecting the national search for identity and place in the world. Politicians from all political parties also wrestle with the question of what defines the nationhood of New Zealand. In a famous 2004 speech entitled "Nationhood," National Party Leader Don Brash advocated that New Zealand's emerging national identity should reflect the nation's multiculturalism and principles of equality.[49] Prime Minister Helen Clark, from the opposing Labor Party, has also echoed this sentiment. In a speech to Parliament in early 2005, Clark stated that building national identity and pride was one of the primary objectives of her government and that a primary source of this identity and pride lies in "building a nation which offers fairness and opportunity, is tolerant and respectful of all."[50] In her opening remarks for a symposium marking the centennial anniversary of New Zealand's Dominion status, Clark elaborates these priorities:

> Whether we're talking about the past, the present, or the future, the question of what constitutes this place we call home is important for how we see ourselves and how the world sees us. Ideas about what contributes to our country's identity have changed a great deal over the course of the past century, partly as we've positioned ourselves in the world in our own style, and partly as we've become more comfortable with ourselves. Of most significance, perhaps is our growing willingness to acknowledge ...our growing diversity as a key component of what defines 21st century New Zealand. ...So many different peoples now contribute to New Zealand's identity, and we recognize, and should recognize, and

---

[49] Speech by Don Brash, Leader of the National Party, to the Orewa Rotary Club, 27 January 2004.
[50] Prime Minister Helen Clark. Statement to Parliament. 1 February 2005.

celebrate each one of them. ...And I would hope that the defining feature of 21st century New Zealand's identity will be that of inclusion and value of all who live here and make a contribution.[51]

These public remarks from the leaders of the two largest political parties--Labour and National--not only discuss the ongoing search for New Zealand's identity, but both speeches also highlight one of the three distinct, yet tightly inter-related, identity discourses currently at play in the social and political life of New Zealand. Clark and Brash both focused their remarks around the concept of multiculturalism and inclusion as defining features of New Zealand society.

Absorption of Maori Identity

Māori lawyer and activist Moana Jackson described the shifting identity of New Zealand and its defensive reactions as "schizophrenic,"

> because it always wants to be seen as honourable and good, but as colonizers, there is a fundamental contradiction because you can't be honourable in a fundamentally dishonourable process of dispossession. You can't show good faith while usurping the authority of others, an essentially bad faith act. And so I think there's a certain schizophrenia, not just in their human rights identity but in Pākehā identity which is why they struggle so much to identify who they are.[52]

Jackson also sees this identity struggle as the source of the third major identity discourse at play in New Zealand: the adoption of Māori identity as a defining feature of the national New Zealand identity. Jackson notes that the schizophrenia of colonialism leads to the obsessive identity quest which, then in turn leads into the taking on of Māori

---

[51] Prime Minister Helen Clark, Opening Remarks at "Concepts of Nationhood: Marking 100 Years Since the Proclamation of Dominion Status for New Zealand," Parliament, Wellington, New Zealand, 26 September 2007.
[52] Interview with Moana Jackson, Wellington, New Zealand, 11 March 2008.

identity by Pākehā New Zealand, as representing some formative part of Pākehā identity. Jackson says, "they steal from us to validate who they are, without recognizing that they are stealing from us."[53]

This adoption or absorption of Māori cultural identity into the national identity--the indigenization of New Zealand society--is evident throughout New Zealand and particularly salient whenever New Zealanders represent themselves overseas. A vocabulary of about 500 Māori words is used commonly and routinely by all in New Zealand, and without translation. It is simply assumed that everyone understands the meaning and the nuance of the relevant Māori vocabulary. New Zealand sports teams typically do a haka[54] before beginning international competition. Newspapers regularly publish photos of groups of Pākehā high school boys, or New Zealand troops in East Timor, or a graduating police class in Auckland all doing the haka. Tourists flock to buy a piece of greenstone as a souvenir. New Zealanders traveling overseas will also typically wear a piece of greenstone in a Māori moko design prominently around their neck to demonstrate to the world that they are from New Zealand. A report by the Ministry for Māori Development, Te Puni Kokiri, showed that Māori culture has a good reputation and is quickly growing internationally. The report advocated that New Zealand businesses should use Māori images to brand New Zealand products and to differentiate them overseas.[55] When New Zealand government officials travel overseas, they bring along a troupe of Māori not only to perform the haka, but also to engage other

---

[53] *Ibid.*

[54] The *haka* is a traditional Māori ritual of challenge to those who are entering a *marae*. It is characterized by foot stomping, chest beating and extended tongues. The idea is to look fierce in order to repel those who may do harm, although it could also be seen as preparation for battle if necessary.

[55] New Zealand Government. Te Puni Kokiri. *Te wa o te ao hurihuri ki te Ohanga Whanaketanga Māori/A Time for Change in Māori Economic Development.* Wellington, New Zealand, October 2007.

government officials in Māori rituals of encounter. Any official visitor, whether it be a minister, a head of state, or a diplomat, that comes to New Zealand will also go through a porihi[56] when they come to present their credentials, as well as celebrities, musicians, etc. The hongi[57] is always used when New Zealanders greet foreigners in any official capacity. As one Māori activist noted, "It's just part of how things are done here. People do these things without even thinking."[58]

> Pākehā are increasingly taking on a Māori identity because, as one activist noted,
>
> Māori culture is fashionable. Indigenous culture is fashionable. But, it's more vogue to be Māori overseas than it is to be Māori here. People overseas without all the baggage, they just see what they see and they like it. They like the beauty of the art. They like the sound of the language. They like the meaning of the culture.[59]

Another activist mentioned that,

> An interesting thing about New Zealanders is that the white settler population here even identifies itself with a Māori word, Pākehā. ...I guess what it is, is that a lot of them are trying to find a way to connect with this place, Aotearoa/New Zealand. ...It's often not until they leave this place that they realize that there are some really unique things about it and so they grasp on to Māori things. And I think that it's a really interesting thing because it's not about Māori identity, it's about white settler identity and they are trying to find a way to describe their connection.[60]

The Pākehā search for their identity and their connection to the land of New Zealand through the absorption of Māori identity reached a critical point in 1999 when Michael King published a book in which he argued that Pākehā are now every bit as

---

[56] A Māori ritual of encounter.

[57] Another Māori ritual of encounter and friendly greeting. It involves touching the bridge of one's nose to the bridge of the other person's nose, then taking a long, slow breath together.

[58] Interview by author with Māori activist #2, Wellington, New Zealand, 17 February 2008.

[59] Interview by author with Māori activist #1, Wellington, New Zealand, 13 February 2008.

[60] Interview by author with Māori activist #9.

indigenous to New Zealand as are Māori, writing that "the people who live in New Zealand by choice as distinct from an accident of birth, and who are committed to this land and its people and steeped in their knowledge of both, are no less 'indigenous' than Māori."[61] Race Relations Minister Trevor Mallard made a speech in 2004 which echoed King's sentiments. His speech emphasized the need to put the difficulties of the past behind us so that New Zealand can forge a collective sense of nationhood because Māori and Pākehā are both indigenous people now. He even stated unabashedly that "I regard myself as an indigenous New Zealander."[62]

Many Māori not only took offense at these claims of the indigeneity of Pākehā, but they also recognized the discursive maneuvering being done at the intersection of the three dominant discourses in New Zealand. One Māori activist pondered the possibility that declarations of Pākehā indigeneity may actually be an attempt to pretend that colonization didn't happen. Moana Jackson was more explicit about the colonial undertones and overtones in the absorption of Māori identity by Pākehā:

> I always say, if you want an identity, then acknowledge the beginnings of your place in this country. And then build your identity on an honest acknowledgement of what that is. But it's actually easier to indigenize yourself because what colonization does is it allows indigenous peoples to keep the safe and the exotic but it denies the things that exercise real power. So we can sing our songs and we can dance our dances. We can even speak our language, but we can't exercise the power that those songs and dances and language once expressed. And so I think that they feel very generous in allowing us to do that and in return for their generosity, they should be allowed to take those safe things as well and use them in whatever way they wish.[63]

---

[61] Michael King. 1999. *Being Pākehā: Reflections and Recollections of a White Native.* Auckland, New Zealand: Penguin Books.
[62] Race Relations Commissioner Trevor Mallard. "We Are All New Zealanders Now." Speech at Victoria University, Wellington, New Zealand, 28 July 2004.
[63] Jackson, 11 March 2008

These three discourses--the search for a national identity, a positive human rights self-image and a shifting national identity--have converged and intersected for the better part of three decades in New Zealand society and politics. Together, they have produced a desire to reconcile New Zealand's colonial past but, as Moana Jackson's remarks indicate, these discourses have produced a particular model of reconciliation: the Doctrine of Discovery understanding of both reconciliation and the Treaty of Waitangi. This model of reconciliation looks to settle past grievances but maintain unified Crown sovereignty in New Zealand. It is the contrasting view of reconciliation and of the Treaty of Waitangi, the Tino Rangatiratanga understanding, focused on land and self-determination rights, an understanding which requires a reordering and renegotiation of sovereignty in New Zealand, which remains highly controversial. One of the major sources of political conflict in New Zealand is the gap and tension between these two understandings.

Two Competing Understandings of Reconciliation and the Treaty of Waitangi

As discussed in the above section, discourses of reconciliation began developing in New Zealand in the 1970s, and particularly since the passage of the Treaty of Waitangi Act in 1975, the act of Parliament which established the Waitangi Tribunal and has led to the now three-decades old treaty settlements process. As I will demonstrate, the Waitangi Tribunal and the treaty settlements process in New Zealand, and especially the Foreshore and Seabed issue, each represent the Doctrine of Discovery understanding of reconciliation and the Treaty relationship between Māori and Pākehā, an understanding which has developed and become entrenched as New Zealand's identity has shifted

216

toward multiculturalism, human rights, and an absorption of Maori identity. New Zealand is willing to make legal and policy moves in indigenous rights within the framework of the Doctrine of Discovery understanding of reconciliation, but it always remains solidly within this framework. This framework encourages New Zealand to emphasize individual rights and soft collective rights (language, culture, education, etc.), while simultaneously resisting the hard rights of land and self-determination which are called for under the Tino Rangatiratanga understanding.

The Doctrine of Discovery understanding of reconciliation is based on the settlement and disposition of past grievances so that the nation can move forward as "one law, one people." One of the unquestioned assumptions in this understanding of reconciliation and the Treaty relationship is that the Crown legitimately holds and will retain full sovereignty in New Zealand. Major political parties--liberal or conservative--hold this assumption. Don Brash, the National Party leader in 2004, stated that New Zealand is "one country with many peoples," "a modern democratic society, embodying the essential notion of one rule for all in a single nation state."[64] He claimed that, "There are some Māori who claim that sovereignty never properly passed from Māori into the hands of the Crown. They are living in a fantasy world."[65] Brash concedes that "where there has been a clear breach of the Treaty - where land has been stolen, for example - then it is right that attempts to make amends should be made," but he is clear that the Treaty "did not create a partnership: fundamentally, it was the launching pad for the creation of one sovereign nation." In this same speech, Brash also highlighted the many efforts that New Zealand has made to "close the gaps" economically, socially and

---

[64] Brash, "Nationhood" Speech, 27 January 2004.
[65] Ibid.

217

educationally between Māori and Pākehā. He even addressed the importance of Māori culture and language in New Zealand and how much New Zealand society values it and take great strides to protect it: "The indigenous culture of New Zealand will always have a special place in our emerging culture, and will be cherished for that reason."[66]

The Labour Party's position, as a more liberal party on the New Zealand political spectrum, places a high priority on social policy and workers' rights, but the underlying assumptions about power and the discourses surrounding Māori, reconciliation and the Treaty are remarkably similar to the National Party. In her 2005 address to Parliament, Prime Minister Helen Clark, talked about how the nation "has to keep moving ahead, to become an even more compelling place to live in, work in, bring children up in, invest in, and above all take pride in."[67] Like Brash's focus on "closing the gaps", the Labour Party is also focused on correcting Māori disparities in society. Clark stated Labour's goal that "the decade and this century will see Māori emerge even more strongly as very significant stakeholders, asset holders and contributors to economic development"[68] and in fact, it is in this terrain that New Zealand's pro-Māori reputation is earned. Regarding reconciliation and the Treaty however, Labour's position is that in order to achieve Māori potential[69] it "is important to get historical claims settled" because "both Māori and Pākehā want us to complete treaty settlements to we can move forward together."[70] Like Brash, however, she does not allow any space for ongoing partnership in governance or anything but complete Crown sovereignty. She states, "There's no

---

[66] *Ibid.*
[67] Prime Minister Helen Clark, Address to Parliament, 1 February 2005.
[68] *Ibid.*
[69] Interestingly, this is the name the Labour Party has given to the Ministry for Māori Development, Te Puni Kokiri, which translates to "Realising Māori Potential".
[70] Prime Minister Helen Clark, Address to Parliament, 1 February 2005.

place for the kind of government that sets New Zealanders against each other." Rather, reconciliation with Māori is a process that has a discrete end point and will be successful when all Treaty settlements are finalized.[71] Clark told BBC reporters, "on historical claims, the time has come to seek finality."[72] Labour's focus is on improving Māori's position as individual citizens of New Zealand. As the Minister of Customs Nanaia Mahuta, speaking on behalf of the Minister of Foreign Affairs, stated during Parliament's discussion of the UN Indigenous Rights Declaration, this "Government is committed to ensuring that Māori participate equally and successfully in New Zealand's economy and society" and that the Government has made it a priority to improve "outcomes for Māori."[73] Once Māori grievances are settled, they are expected to take their places next to other New Zealand citizens as "one people" under "one law"--the Crown's law.[74]

This understanding of reconciliation, which is shared by both major political parties, thus attempts to effectively retain the colonial order in New Zealand and presumes the superiority of Pākehā culture and government. By contrast, the Tino Rangatiratanga understanding of reconciliation and the Treaty, which is centered on notions of respect, equality and cooperation between Treaty partners, presents a direct frontal challenge to the colonial order and assumptions. Another crucial difference is that the Tino Rangatiratanga understanding of reconciliation and the Treaty does not have an end date after which reconciliation will be complete. Rather, it sees reconciliation as an ongoing process which requires a renegotiation and a reordering of sovereignty in New

---

[71] The Labour Party's stated goal was to have all Treaty claims settled by 2020.
[72] BBC news. 4 August 2005.
[73] Transcript, Question Time in New Zealand Parliament, 12 September 2007. Document on file with the author.
[74] Interviewees #1, #2 #5, #7, #8 an #9 (all Māori activists) all expressed this sentiment, each in their own words. Interviews with government officials echoed the same sentiment, although the way they express it does differ, the meaning remains the same.

219

Zealand. This process will replace unified Crown sovereignty with a Treaty partnership

model of governance, as stated in the Māori language version of the Treaty of Waitangi.

One activist described the Tino Rangatiratanga vision as "Māori control over

Māori things."[75] Māori Party Member of Parliament (MP), Te Ururoa Flavell, expressed

that Tino Rangatiratanga means that Māori iwi are able "to run our own affairs based on

the Treaty of Waitangi, and we think we can do it better than the state."[76] Others testified

that "a significant transfer of land back to Māori" is required for a genuine reconciliation

so that iwi can be self-sustaining and self-governing.[77] Virtually all Māori activists

interviewed advocated for some form of constitutional change in New Zealand which will

entrench the Treaty, a move which will necessarily involve some sort of power sharing.

Some, like Māori Party MP Hone Harawira, have called for a two-house parliament--a

Māori house and a non-Māori house--with disputes resolved in an upper house.[78] Bill

Hamilton of the non-partisan Human Rights Commission, described a complex power

sharing proposal called "Paepae Rangatira" which is based on the principles of mutual

recognition, respect, and negotiation between the two Treaty partners: the Crown and

Māori. Under Paepae Rangatira, a partnership would be created that integrates a better

Treaty relationship. Each Treaty partner, the Crown and the Rangatira[79] would maintain

a set of human rights coupled with responsibilities on various levels of engagement.[80]

As Moana Jackson said in an interview, the only just path to reconciliation in New

---

[75] Interviewee #9, 10 March 2008.
[76] Interview with Māori Party MP Te Ururoa Flavell, Wellington, New Zealand, 6 March 2008.
[77] Interviewee #1, 13 February 2008.
[78] Interview with Māori Party MP Hone Harawira, Wellington, New Zealand, 20 February 2008.
[79] Māori word for chief, or the leadership of an iwi.
[80] Interview with Bill Hamilton, Human Rights Commission, Wellington, New Zealand, 26 February 2008.

Zealand is a rejection of colonization, coupled with an honest process of renegotiation of

power and governance in the country:

> One of the great myths in this country is that colonization has ended, but
> no one has yet been able to tell me when it ended. And if colonization is
> the systematic dispossession and the denial of rights and equality of
> indigenous peoples, then it has definitely not ended. Politicians come up
> with various constitutional milestones in the Westminster tradition, like
> when the settlers presumed to take self-government from the governor,
> passage of the statute of Westminster Act and so on. Poets take it from the
> discovery of a Pākehā identity. Sports people take it from the first
> international tour by a rugby team to England. But, for me, it has not
> ended and will not end until the culture of colonization has been
> dismantled. And that means not just a government process of treaty
> settlements, but a whole constitutional reorganization which acknowledges
> that Māori are the first people of this land, not just as some quaint
> metaphorical description, but are the first people in terms of authority, of
> law, of jurisdiction. ...And so part of ending the culture of colonization
> here is to have a proper and effective recognition of Māori jurisdiction and
> Māori law which then leads to a Māori-defined notion of Māori rights.[81]

I will now shift discussion to some recent political issues that demonstrate the gap

and tension between these two understandings of reconciliation and the Treaty of

Waitangi. The Waitangi Tribunal and the Treaty Settlements process illustrate how the

Doctrine of Discovery understanding manifests itself in indigenous policy, while another

recent and highly controversial issue, the 2004 Foreshore and Seabed Act, shows how the

state apparatus of New Zealand resists the emerging Tino Rangatiratanga interpretation

of reconciliation and the Treaty in an attempt to preserve the Doctrine of Discovery

understanding.

---

[81] Jackson, 11 March 2008.

The Waitangi Tribunal and the Treaty Settlements Process

The Waitangi Tribunal is a permanent commission of inquiry charged with making recommendations on claims brought forward by Māori relating to actions or omissions by the Crown that breach the Treaty of Waitangi. It does not have the authority to adjudicate claims. Only the Crown can make Treaty settlements, and it is free to take the Tribunal's recommendations into account or to completely ignore them.

The Treaty settlements process works as follows.[82] First, a claim is submitted by a claimant group to the Waitangi Tribunal. If the claim meets the requirements of the Treaty of Waitangi Act, it is registered and assigned a "WAI" number and all interested parties are notified. The claims are then carefully researched and Tribunal hearings are held. Evidence and submissions are presented first by claimants and then by the Crown and then by anyone else with an interest in the claim. The hearings and researching phase can take an extremely long period of time; the average time is 25 years. Yet, several Māori reported that this can be a healing time for an iwi. One Māori leader said,

> In order to present to the Tribunal, you have to open up the knowledge to that entire iwi because you have to piece together all the little bits of history that maybe five individuals know a lot, but they need all the little bits that tie it all together. So when you are going through an actual hearing process, you'll get Auntie so and so whose whole job in life has been to work at the *marae* in the kitchen, but she has a story or she has a photograph or she has a book and it has this really valuable piece of information, just a little piece, but it's really important. And so she gets to speak and everyone gets to hear her and it just changes the way that people feel about each other. It's a very inclusive process and everyone can participate.[83]

---

[82] Procedural information and settlement statistics were obtained directly from the Waitangi Tribunal Office, and also contained in a document called "The Waitangi Tribunal and the Settlement of Historical Treaty Claims," dated December 2005.

[83] Interview with Māori leader #8, Wellington, New Zealand, 8 March 2008.

When the research and hearings are complete, the Waitangi Tribunal issues its report on the claims, including its recommendations. If both the claimants and the Crown agree to negotiate, they can begin formal negotiations. If course, the Crown may or may not decide to accept the Tribunal's recommendations. If the claimants and the Crown agree on the terms of settlement, then a deed of settlement is signed. The settlement can be implemented and legislation passed if necessary to give effect to the settlement. At any stage in this process, the claimants can elect to skip to the end of the process and simply negotiate directly with the Crown, which is the scenario most preferred by the New Zealand government.

Final Deeds of Treaty Settlement have three components. First, there is a Crown apology, which includes a full account of historical events and acknowledgement of the treaty violations. These apologies are long (up to twelve pages) and they are read publically at a *marae* by an official of the Crown. Second, there must be cultural redress. This can include such things as changing geographical place names back to Māori or safeguarding rights of access to certain important areas for cultural or spiritual purposes. Finally, there is financial redress which can be cash settlements and/or return of Crown land to Māori. No privately held land can be returned--only Crown lands.

As of mid-2008, there were twenty-one completed settlements and another twenty-one in process at various stages. The total financial redress awarded in all of the completed settlements stood at NZ$600 million as of mid-2008. The first settlements between 1992 and 1998 were some of the largest, with three major settlements each accounting for NZ$170 of the NZ$600 million total. Even at this level, however, the settlement represented only 3% of the value of what had been lost, based upon the current

223

market value of the land that was illegally taken. Since that time, the dollar amount of treaty settlements has been limited by law. In recent years, a large settlement has been NZ$30-40 million, with most being in the range of $13-14 million. Settlements are now typically 1% or less than the value of the land that was lost. Once a settlement is signed, it is agreed by all parties that it is full and final. No treaty claims may ever be made again by that claimant group against the Crown.

The Waitangi Tribunal and the Treaty Settlements process is highly reflective of the Doctrine of Discovery understanding of reconciliation and the Treaty relationship. It attempts to settle past grievances, and often fairly generously, so that Māori can prosper and the nation can move forward together, under Crown sovereignty. The superiority of the Crown and its government are presumed, and its power remains firmly intact. Hone Harawira, Māori Party MP, summed up the settlements process from a Tino Rangatiratanga perspective:

> I'm not a fan of the settlements process because the thief has written the rules, the thief set up the Tribunal, the thief determines who's on the Tribunal, the thief determines what the Tribunal can review, the thief determines what the Tribunal can decide, and at the end of it, the thief says, "Well, if we don't like what you've done, we can ignore it." We Māori are so engaged in achieving settlements, that we seem to have missed the fact that no settlement to date has been settled for more than 3% of the value of the claim. And most of them are substantially lower. Not only are they substantially lower, but we are being conned into signing the clause that they are full and final, which means that we are effectively saying to our grandchildren that, "You don't have any Treaty claim after we are gone because we agreed to that." So when my grandson stands up and says, "You idiot! You settled for 2.5% and you want to roll over on that, no way." And he'll be right. He will be right. And so I try to say to people, look, if you must settle, then settle on the basis of compensation for that particular time, for that particular claim. And don't ever let it affect our Treaty rights, which are ongoing. Our ancestors didn't sign a Treaty so that it could be ended in 2008. Our ancestors signed the Treaty so that it would be a pluralistic management

and governance of this nation forever. It's not reconciliation at all, it's just set up to make us indigenous people feel like we're getting something back.[84]

Foreshore and Seabed Issue

One of the most politically explosive issues in indigenous rights in New Zealand's history came about in 2004, when the New Zealand Parliament passed the Foreshore and Seabed Act. This Act effectively unilaterally extinguished Māori aboriginal title to the foreshore[85] and seabed coastal areas of New Zealand. When Parliament passed this act, Māoridom exploded into protest. Protest marches, or *hikoi*, were held throughout New Zealand, including a very large and famous march of 30,000 - 50,000 people on the New Zealand Parliament. The Māori Party was birthed at this time, a direct result of Māori feeling betrayed and abandoned by the Labour Party which had pushed this Act through Parliament.

The issue of the foreshore and seabed began on 19 June 2003 with a Court of Appeal decision in the case of *Ngati Apa v. Attorney General*. In this case, the Court of Appeal departed from the previous understanding of the law regarding the foreshore and seabed, which was a presumption of Crown ownership. In this case, the Court of Appeal ruled that Māori native land title had survived the Crown's assumption of full sovereignty since 1840, and that Māori native title had never been extinguished. This ruling opened up the legal possibility that Māori could seek freehold title on the foreshore and seabed through the Māori Land Court.[86] The fear expressed in the wider public discourse was

---

[84] Harawira, 20 February 2008.
[85] The foreshore is the area of land that emerges between high and low tide.
[86] See Claire Charters, "An Imbalance of Powers: Māori Land Claims and an Unchecked Parliament." In *Cultural Survival Quarterly*, Spring 2006, p. 32-35.

the Māori could now pursue title to the entire coastline of New Zealand. In response to public concerns about access to the beaches, the Labour government announced that it would enact legislation to ensure public ownership and access to the coastline.

As soon as the Labour government's policy was announced, the case was immediately referred, as an urgent inquiry, to the Waitangi Tribunal. The Tribunal agreed to consider the case, noting that its resolution was important to New Zealand and its identity as a fair, human rights-supporting society:

> We proceed in the expectation that governments in New Zealand want to be good governments, whose actions, although carried by power are mitigated by fairness. Fairness is the value that underlies the norms of conduct with which good governments conform -- legal norms, international human rights norms, and in the New Zealand context, Treaty norms. ...We think that New Zealanders generally have an instinct for fairness, and that a policy that is intrinsically fair will, when properly explained, ultimately find favor.[87]

The Tribunal hearing took place over six days in January 2004 and a report was issued in February. The Tribunal report was highly critical of the government's policy, stating that "the policy clearly breaches the Treaty of Waitangi" but, more than that, the policy also "fails in terms of wider norms of domestic and international law that underpin good government in a modern, democratic state" and referred especially to principles of fairness and non-discrimination.[88] The Tribunal recommended to the Government that it "go back to the drawing board, and engage with Māori in proper negotiations about the way forward."[89] The Tribunal Report was clear that there was a need to search for an

---

[87] New Zealand. Waitangi Tribunal. 2004. Report on the Crown's Foreshore and Seabed Policy (Wai 1071). Wellington: Legislation Direct, p. xiii.

[88] Ibid., p. xiv.

[89] Ibid., p. xv.

outcome that "is faithful to the vision of the Treaty: two peoples living together in one nation, sharing authority and resources, with fundamental respect for each other."[90]

This vision of the Treaty expressed by the Tribunal was antithetical to the Government's understanding of its absolute and unfettered sovereignty. In response, Parliament passed the Foreshore and Seabed Act on 18 November 2004. This Act granted the Crown "absolute ownership of all foreshore and seabed land that is not held in fee simple, thereby extinguishing existing Māori common law aboriginal title."[91]

A group of Māori organizations lobbied the United Nations Committee on the Elimination of Racial Discrimination (UN CERD) to consider the legislation, and it sent Special Rapporteur Rudolfo Stavenhagen to investigate and report on the situation in New Zealand. The Special Rapporteur's report, which was highly critical of the New Zealand government, was issued in March 2005.[92]

The UN Report made several recommendations to the New Zealand government, including a recommendation to repeal or significantly amend the Foreshore and Seabed Act. The Report recognized some of the positive and significant achievements New Zealand can boast where the status of indigenous people is concerned. But, the Report stated that these achievements were not adequate to shield New Zealand from criticism, as the Foreshore and Seabed controversy could attest. The Special Rapporteur also made several additional recommendations, in light of emerging international human rights principles regarding indigenous peoples, which directly challenged the government's

---

[90] *Ibid.*, p. 144.

[91] Charters, 2006, p. 35.

[92] United Nations. Economic and Social Council. Commission on Human Rights. Report of the Special Rapporteur on the situation of human rights and fundamental freedoms of Indigenous people, Rudolfo Stavenhagen, 13 March 2006, E/CN.4/2006/78/Add.3.

presumption of full sovereignty. First, it called for a constitutional convention to "design a constitutional reform in order to clearly regulate the relationship between the Government and the Māori on the basis of the Treaty of Waitangi and the internationally recognized right of all peoples to self-determination."[93] The Report stated that the Treaty should be constitutionally entrenched so that Māori can exist "as a distinct people, possessing an alternative system of knowledge, philosophy and law."[94] Furthermore, the Special Rapporteur recommended that *iwi* and *hapu* should form the units for Māori self-governance.

As mentioned earlier, the Government outrightly rejected the UN Special Rapporteur's Report, fiercely defended any alteration in the structure of governance in New Zealand, with an attack on both the CERD and the Special Rapporteur, claiming that they were "on the outer edges of the UN system."[95]

Conclusion

I have offered an explanation for New Zealand's indigenous rights over-compliance which attempts to explain the paradox of New Zealand's excellence in certain indigenous rights areas while simultaneously resisting the international standard of indigenous rights. Thus, the constructivist cost of commitment explanation succeeds where other explanations fail.

According to the constructivist cost of commitment explanation, there are three discourses which have developed in New Zealand during the past three decades which

---

[93] *Ibid.*, p, 20.
[94] *Ibid.*
[95] Statement can be viewed at www.Beehive.govt.nz.

228

have intersected and produced an indigenous reconciliation effort in New Zealand: 1) a highly vocal indigenous movement connected to the global indigenous rights movement, 2) the nation's concern for its human rights reputation, and 3) a shift in the national identity, which is defining itself in terms of a super-tolerant liberal multiculturalism that is also increasingly integrating Māori identity as a central feature of the New Zealand national identity. When these three discourses combine and intersect, New Zealand is propelled toward reconciliation while simultaneously remaining constrained within a particular framework of reconciliation.

The first two discourses--a globally connected domestic indigenous rights movement and a "global human rights steward" identity--work together to push New Zealand toward indigenous reconciliation. The indigenous rights movement, through campaigns of shame and embarrassment, exposes how New Zealand has not and does not live up to its "global human rights steward" identity when it comes to Maori. In order for New Zealand's "global human rights steward" identity to be cleansed of the stains that the indigenous movement continually exposes, New Zealand engages in, and often excels in, the realm of indigenous "soft rights", that is, rights such as culture, language, religion, and education. Rationalist, liberal and other explanations such as high indigenous population and domestic politics, can certainly account for this side of the compliance picture. A domestic movement presses for a policy change and the New Zealand state makes accommodations, which also happen to be in its own best interest. While these rights have often been difficult to attain in New Zealand as many of these rights involve the acceptance of a body of collective rights by a country which has typically followed

229

the British tradition of the centrality of individual rights, this struggle has not been insurmountable, and in terms of explanation, not particularly difficult or controversial.

Rationalist, liberal and other explanations do fail, however, to account for the New Zealand's excellence in some areas of indigenous rights *and* its simultaneous resistance to other indigenous rights and particularly to the codification of those rights in an international declaration. A constructivist cost of commitment explanation does address this paradox by providing insight into the simultaneous positive and negative indigenous rights behavior of New Zealand. The third discursive change--a shift in New Zealand's identity toward multiculturalism and absorption of Maori identity--when combined with the first two discourses, produces the paradoxical pattern.

When all three discourses conjoin, the reconciliation impulse becomes constrained by the shift in New Zealand's identity and then a particular tension develops between the two understandings of reconciliation. First, the two identity shifts, multiculturalism and the "Maori-ization" of the nation, are both strong equalizing forces and both ultimately result in the negation of indigeneity (defined in terms of being indigenous to the land), in favor of placing Maori side-by-side, on an equal basis, with all other ethnic groups in New Zealand. In short, the identity shifts create a discursive environment which constrains the state from accepting any indigenous "hard rights," land or self-determination, because a multicultural "Maori-ized" nation would view these rights as "special rights" inappropriately recognized (or "granted") to a particular group of otherwise equal citizens. Second, the globally connected domestic indigenous rights movement advocates for both hard rights and soft rights under the Tino Rangatiratanga understanding of reconciliation, yet a tension remains as New Zealand pursues

230

reconciliation strictly under the Doctrine of Discovery understanding which emphasizes soft rights. The cost of commitment for New Zealand to pursue Tino Rangatiratanga reconciliation is high, as not only are soft rights demanded but also land and self-determination, requiring an alteration in the arrangement of governance and sovereignty in New Zealand. Tino Rangatiratanga reconciliation necessarily calls for a complete renouncement of the Doctrine of Discovery, a legal doctrine which is implicitly foundational to New Zealand's legitimate existence. Therefore, indigenous global politics in New Zealand is pushing for a complete renegotiation of the country's sovereignty, a move which New Zealand absolutely and consistently resists.

Chapter 6

Indigenous Rights in Canada

(Canadians) must humble themselves and be prepared to move beyond

their mythology and the politics of multiculturalism in order to deal with

indigenous peoples in an honorable way.

--Indigenous Activist from Canada, 2008

Canada is often viewed internationally as a beacon of engaging with indigeneity,

touting its "Canadian way" of various cultures living side by side harmoniously within

Canadian society. At the same time, Canada is highly criticized for failing to match its

ideals with reality when it comes to respecting the rights of indigenous people. While

Canada maintains an international reputation for engaging indigeneity, it is also widely

renounced for mistreating indigenous peoples. Indigenous peoples in Canada have

constitutional protection for their treaties, Canada engages multiple land claims

settlement processes, and Canada has more recently issued an apology for its century-

long policy of placing Native children into residential schools. Yet, at the same time,

Canadian police are regularly accused of abusing Aboriginal people[1] and Aboriginal

people remain consistently at the bottom of all socio-economic indicators in Canada,[2] and

First Nations peoples face continual pressures on their traditional lands by the

government and corporations seeking resource extraction and development[3] and, as

---

[1] "Aboriginal Rally Against Police Mistreatment," December 6, 2006 at http://nativenewsonline.org.
[2] See *The Canada Yearbook* published every year by Statistics Canada. Recent years available at www.statcan.gc.ca.
[3] For examples, see Keith Leslie. "First Nations Vow to Occupy Eastern Ontario Site to Block Uranium Mining." January 11, 2008. *The Canadian Press.* and Press Release, First Nations Leadership Council.

mentioned in earlier chapters, Canada campaigned against the Declaration on the Rights of Indigenous Peoples and was one of only four countries to vote against it. In short, the indigenous rights situation in Canada can best be described as a paradox, and far from settled for a country that is known around the world as a leader in human rights.

Like New Zealand, Canada takes its international reputation in human rights very seriously. The Government of Canada's "Action Plan Against Racism" touts the extent of Canada's commitment to international human rights, noting that Canada "is recognized internationally as a leader in human rights."[4] As the report points out, Canada is the birthplace of John Peters Humphrey, one of the authors of the Universal Declaration on Human Rights. In addition to serving as one of the driving forces behind the 1948 Universal Declaration on Human Rights, Canada's human rights record includes ratification of all the major international human rights treaties: the International Covenant on Civil and Political Rights and the first optional protocol (accession by Canada in 1970), the International Covenant on Economic, Social and Cultural Rights (ratified in 1976), the International Covenant on the Elimination of Racial Discrimination (accession in 1970), the Convention on the Rights of the Child and the optional protocols (ratified 1991, 2000 and 2005), the Convention on the Elimination of All Forms of Discrimination Against Women and the optional protocol (ratified 1981) and the Convention against Torture and Other Cruel, Inhuman or Degrading Treatment or Punishment (ratified 1987).[5] Canada has also signed and ratified numerous other international human rights

---

"First Nations Mining Summit Set for October in Prince George." July 8, 2008. Available at: http://www.fns.bc.ca/pdf/NR_BC_FN_MiningSummit0708.pdf.

[4] Government of Canada. Department of Canadian Heritage. Multiculturalism National Office. *Canada's Action Plan Against Racism: A Canada for All.* Gatineau, Quebec. 2005, p. 2.

[5] Government of Canada. Department of Canadian Heritage website. www.patromoinecanadien.gc.ca.

instruments, making it one of the world leaders in human rights treaty ratification.[6]

Canada has served as a member of the United Nations Human Rights Council since its inception in 2006. The Human Rights Council is charged primarily with "promoting universal respect for the protection of all human rights and fundamental freedoms for all" and with making "recommendations with regard to the promotion and protection of human rights."[7]

Even though Aboriginal peoples may disagree, the international community often references Canada's domestic record in Aboriginal rights and often deems it impressive and progressive. During the British colonial period when straightforward Doctrine of Discovery logic was typically applied by colonizing European powers, the Royal Proclamation of 1763 was a significant and notable departure from the global norm. Rather than asserting *terra nullius* and full Crown ownership in Canada, the Royal Proclamation of 1763 "acknowledges the Indians as continuing to own the lands which they have used and occupied."[8] The Royal Proclamation thus acknowledged some level of Indian title[9] very early in Canada's history, and even though the Royal Proclamation has remained a highly controversial subject, the fact that some level of Aboriginal title was acknowledged by the Crown in 1763 cannot be disputed, and this fact has influenced Canada's relationship with Aboriginal peoples throughout its history. As a result of the Royal Proclamation's recognition of Indian title, the British did not generally take land

---

[6] University of Minnesota Human Rights Library. *Ratification of International Human Rights Treaties.* Edited and Updated by Ilhan Isik (2004) and Taobo Zheng (2008). www1.umn.edu/humanrts/research/ratification-index.html.

[7] United Nations. General Assembly. Resolution adopted by the General Assembly. Human Rights Council. UN Doc A/Res/60/251.

[8] Paul Tennant. 1990. *Aboriginal Peoples and Politics: The Indian Land Question in British Columbia, 1849-1989.* Vancouver: University of British Columbia Press, p. 10.

[9] The term "Indian title" has since given way to "Aboriginal title."

arbitrarily, but rather they negotiated and signed treaties. "The treaties were the primary means by which diplomatic relations were conducted between Britain and the aboriginal peoples."[10] The treaty-making norm continued after Canada's Confederation in 1867. Canada negotiated and signed eleven numbered treaties[11] with Aboriginal peoples between 1871 and 1923.[12] While Canada did pass a very paternalistic Indian Act in 1876[13] which remains law in Canada today, the Indian Act has been subject to significant modifications over the years, largely in response to pressure from First Nations or as a result of litigation brought forward by First Nations or individual Aboriginal people. The Supreme Court's landmark *Calder* decision of 1973[14] "recognized that Aboriginal title over unceded lands could possibly have survived the assertion of sovereignty by the crown and the creation of the overlapping federal and provincial jurisdictions in British Columbia."[15] The uncertainty of Aboriginal title and its implications present in this Supreme Court decision prompted the Canadian federal government to act. The federal government launched a series of land claims settlement negotiations, which have culminated in such notable achievements as the modern-day British Columbia treaties and land claims settlements as well as the 1999 establishment of Nunavut, an Inuit territory in the Far North.

---

[10] John J. Borrows and Leonard I. Rotman. 1998. *Aboriginal Legal Issues: Cases, Materials & Commentary.* Toronto: Butterworths, p. 105.

[11] These are literally called Treaty No. 1, Treaty No. 2, etc.

[12] It is noteworthy that no treaty was negotiated and signed in British Columbia during this period.

[13] Indian Act, S.C. 1876, c.18. This act defines who is an Indian, recognizes reserves and how they are to be managed, specifies the benefits payable to Indians as well as articulating exemptions from taxation. The Indian Act identifies those Indians with "status" as distinct from those without "status." According to the Indian Act, only status Indians are eligible for benefits or exemption from taxation. Once status is lost, it cannot be regained. Status can only be retained by living on reserve. This Act is widely criticized by First Nations and Inuit, but especially by Métis and urban Aboriginal peoples.

[14] *Calder v. Attorney-General of B.C.,* [1973] S.C.R. 313.

[15] Michael Cassidy, "Treaties and Aboriginal-Government Relations, 1945-2000" in *Hidden in Plain Sight: Contributions of Aboriginal Peoples to Canadian Identity and Culture.* Edited by David R. Newhouse, Cora J. Voyageur, Dan Beavon. 2005. Toronto: University of Toronto Press, p. 45.

In 1982, Canada ratified its new constitution which included Section 35 (1). Section 35 provides constitutional protection for "any existing Aboriginal right." However, from an indigenous perspective, the constitutional protection, while valuable, does not go far enough since it only protects the rights secured up until that point in history. It does not include protections for indigenous collective land ownership and self-determination; these Aboriginal rights need to be negotiated or litigated on a case-by-case basis. There is currently a backlog of 800 to over 1000 land claims,[16] a fact which creates frustration among Aboriginal communities across Canada. Therefore, many Aboriginal peoples[17] in Canada have worked in the international sphere since the 1970s, attempting to use international pressure to encourage the Canadian government to recognize further indigenous rights to land and self-determination. The Canadian and international press report numerous road blocks and other forms of protest as Aboriginal groups attempt to cast light on Canada's shortcomings in indigenous rights.[18]

On the international level, Canada has ratified ILO No. 107, but not ILO No. 169. In addition, Canada campaigned and voted against the Draft Declaration in the Human Rights Council in late 2006 and was one of the four states to vote against the Declaration on the floor of the UN General Assembly in September 2007. Even as Canada cast its

---

[16] See Assembly of First Nations, http://www.afn.ca/article.asp?id=3214, for current figures on the backlog of land claims.

[17] "Aboriginal peoples" in Canada refers collectively to the three main indigenous groups in Canada: Indians (or First Nations), Inuit and Métis. The Métis are the descendants of mixed marriages between indians and Europeans. According to Statistics Canada (http://www12.statcan.ca/english/census01/Products/Analytic/companion/abor/canada.cfm), in the 2001 census, there were 1.3 million people who identified as Aboriginal, representing about 4.4% of Canada's total population. About 30% of the Aboriginal population identified as Métis, 62% identified as Indian, and 5% considered themselves Inuit. The remaining 3% identified as being from more than one of these groups.

[18] See, for example, Am Johal, "Native Tribes Fight to Block New Pipeline." September 22, 2006, *IPS News*. and "Armed Native Protesters Block Ontario Highway." *Toronto Sun,* June 29, 2007.

vote against the Declaration, the statement made by Ambassador John McNee to the General Assembly touted Canada's "commitment to actively advancing indigenous rights at home and internationally," in a poignant illustration of Canada's paradoxical behavior in indigenous rights. In his statement, the Ambassador claimed that the text of the Declaration "did not meet expectations" and the process was also unsatisfactory. He noted that "Canada's position has remained consistent and principled" and "Canada is proud of the fact that Aboriginal and treaty rights are given strong recognition and protection in its Constitution." Canada, he said, "take(s) effective action, at home and abroad, to promote and protect the rights of indigenous peoples."[19] While leaving the distinct impression that Canada's vote against the Declaration was rooted in its already superior domestic law, the Ambassador's statement concludes by curtly asserting that the Declaration is not legally binding, has no effect in Canada and does not represent customary law. In the months following the UN General Assembly vote on the Declaration, the Canadian House of Commons passed a resolution to endorse the Declaration,[20] and a group of more than 100 legal scholars issued an open letter asserting that no legal or constitutional barrier exists which should prevent Canada from endorsing the Declaration.[21] Rather, they wrote, the Declaration "is consistent with the Canadian Constitution and Charter and is profoundly important for fulfilling their promise."

---

[19] Statement by Ambassador John McNee, Permanent Representative of Canada to the United Nations. 13 September 2007.

[20] A motion presented to the House of Commons on 7 April 2008 - "That the government endorse the United Nations Declaration on the Rights of indigenous Peoples as adopted by the United Nations General Assembly on 13 September 2007 and that Parliament and Government of Canada fully implement the standards contained therein" (Third report of the Standing Committee on Status of Women). The resolution was carried by a majority vote on 8 April 2008. Documents available at www.parl.gc.ca.

[21] Open Letter, 1 May 2008. "UN Declaration on the Rights of indigenous Peoples: Canada needs to Implement This New Human Rights Instrument." Text available at www.amnesty.ca/index_resources/open_letters/un_ip_declaration_experts_letter.pdf.

Nevertheless, the Harper government remains resolutely opposed to endorsing the Declaration.[22]

Since Canada never ratified ILO No. 169 and it voted against the Declaration, it is not technically obligated to uphold collective rights or self-determination rights for indigenous peoples under its international commitments. Yet, Canada's record on indigenous rights indicates that it has enacted certain domestic policies which have brought it into at least partial compliance with some of the provisions of ILO No. 169 and the Declaration. In addition to a Constitutional recognition of treaty rights, a number of land and self-government agreements have been negotiated across Canada, including the establishment of the Inuit territory of Nunavut. Further, in 1995 the Canadian government adopted a policy that recognized the inherent right of First Nations to self-government.[23] Yet, at the time, the Harper government in Canada remains steadfast in its opposition to any international recognition of indigenous peoples' land and self-determination rights.

I argue that Canada's paradoxical policy behavior in indigenous rights has resulted from a convergence of several factors which have led to the Canadian model of indigenous reconciliation. As in the case of New Zealand, there is a vocal indigenous movement in Canada which has been actively involved in the global indigenous rights movement and has invoked the international human rights discourse in its domestic struggles. Also like New Zealand, Canada demonstrates a high level of concern for its

---

[22] Since the Parliament passed only a resolution in support of the Declaration, the Prime Minister is allowed by parliamentary procedure to simply ignore it. For more history on this procedure, see Christopher McCreery. *The Order of Canada*. Toronto: University of Toronto Press, 2005.

[23] Government of Canada. 1995. *Aboriginal Self-Government: The Government of Canada's Approach to Implementation of the Inherent Right and the Negotiation of Self-Government*. Ottawa: Minister of Public Work and Government Services.

world reputation in human rights advancement and even relies on this reputation for the construction of its self-image. As a smaller country in a globalized world, Canada is on an almost constant quest to find its identity, again in a very similar way that New Zealand struggles with national identity. There are also several structural, legal and societal elements, however, that distinguish Canada from New Zealand in terms of indigenous rights and yet the models of reconciliation are remarkably similar in both countries. I will show that while Canada has the structural and legal opportunity to create space for indigenous rights as articulated by the emerging global indigenous rights consensus, Canada remains constrained by a particular model of reconciliation which emphasizes absolution for past actions as well as certainty of both land tenure and Crown sovereignty in the future. In other words, Canada is resisting the challenges to liberalism and Westphalian sovereignty which are being presented by the emerging global indigenous rights consensus. As a result, Canada's behavior in indigenous rights, while often well-intentioned and advanced in certain respects, often ends with confusing, inconsistent and paradoxical policies.

In this chapter, I will explore Canada's indigenous reconciliation discourse and demonstrate how it is ultimately constrained by the very liberal framework through which it operates. I argue that Canada's model of reconciliation results from the emerging *argue* Canadian national identity narrative which forecloses the possibility of an alternative model of reconciliation which is advanced by indigenous leaders in Canada. This alternative, an indigenous model of reconciliation, would renounce the Doctrine of Discovery and adopt the principle of indigenous self-determination, both central features of the emerging global indigenous rights regime. In the end, the Canadian model of reconciliation, while demonstrating over-compliance in certain indigenous rights areas, is also an effort to resist indigenous rights in other areas.

I will look specifically at three cases which illustrate the Canadian model of reconciliation and over-compliance at work. Each case demonstrates how a Canadian Aboriginal policy initially appears to advance indigenous rights but, in actuality, each policy represents instances of Canadian *resistance* to indigenous land and self-determination rights. First, I will examine the creation of the territory of Nunavut. Second, I will explore the recent Apology for Residential Schools and the Truth and Reconciliation Commission which followed. Third, I will consider the British Columbia Treaty Process, with particular emphasis on the 1998 Nisga'a Treaty.

Indigenous Reconciliation in Canada

As in New Zealand, an atmosphere of indigenous reconciliation has arisen in Canada over the past several decades. Canada was compelled towards reconciliation by a convergence of factors that is remarkably similar to New Zealand in some ways, yet differs in other critical aspects. The end result is that the Canadian version of indigenous reconciliation differs notably from New Zealand's experience.

Like the Maori from New Zealand, indigenous groups from Canada have been extremely active in international indigenous politics for as long as there has been such a movement. One of the very first transnational indigenous organizations was the World Council on Indigenous Peoples, founded in 1972 by George Manuel, a Shusawp, and the National Indian Brotherhood of Canada. The World Council on Indigenous Peoples, which focused exclusively on an international struggle for indigenous rights, was one of the first two indigenous organizations to attain consultative status at the UN as an NGO. It was also one of the foundational indigenous organizations of the global indigenous rights movement that was birthed in Geneva in 1977. First Nations, Métis and Inuit groups from Canada have always been present and played a highly visible role in indigenous peoples' meetings at the United Nations. They have also brought the human rights framework of indigenous rights back to Canada.

Also like New Zealand, Canada has, in recent decades, become somewhat obsessed with its search for national identity as a small country in a globalized world which has also experienced a rapid shift in the diversity of its population, a fact which continues to distance Canada from its British past. As in New Zealand, Canada has increasingly become a nation of diverse immigrants. As recently as the 1960s, most immigration to Canada came from northern and western Europe, while in recent decades Canada has accepted large numbers of immigrants from many parts of the world, typically accepting upwards of 200,000 immigrants per year.[24] According to data from the Canadian government,[25] 47% of Canada's citizens have ethnic origins other than British, French or native-born Canadian. In 2006, almost 20% of Canada's population were immigrants and international migration accounted for almost two-thirds of Canada's population growth. Between 2001 and 2006, 60% of Canada's immigration was from Asia. In the cities of Vancouver and Toronto, more than a third of the population is a visible minority and one out of every five school children in each of these cities was a

---

[24] Government of Canada. Department of Canadian Heritage. *Canadian Diversity: Respecting Our Differences.* 2008. Ottawa. Available at www.pch.gc.ca/progs/multi/respect_e.cfm?nav=2.

[25] Demographic data has been collected and compiled from two separate reports: 1) Statistics Canada. 2003. *Canada's Ethnocultural Portrait : The Changing Mosaic.* 2001 Census Analysis series. Statistics Canada Catalogue number 96F0030XIE2001008. Ottawa. and 2) Statistics Canada. 2008. *Canadian Demographics at a Glance.* Statistics Canada Catalogue number 91-003-XIE. Ottawa.

new immigrant to Canada. For more than half of these children, the language spoken in the home was neither English nor French. These massive population changes over the past several decades have necessitated a renewed search for the definitive Canadian identity.

The Canadian challenge has always been to find unity in its diversity.[26] As Kernerman observes,

> The defining narrative of Canada is of an unwieldy political project, always in search of unity and forever attempting to constitute itself as a political community. …The results are a continued preoccupation with determining their common identity *as Canadians* (emphasis original) and a fixation on the sources of cohesion that will, at minimum, hold them together as members of a single political community.[27]

Governor General Michaëlle Jean also referred to the Canadian need to find unity in diversity during her 2005 installation speech: "We must eliminate the spectre of all the solitudes and promote solidarity among all citizens who make up the Canada of today."[28]

The popular press in Canada often reports the elusive nature of Canadian identity,[29] and defining Canadian identity has even become a stated goal of the current Harper government. Prime Minister Harper created a new sub-ministerial cabinet position dedicated to the search for Canadian identity, naming Jason Kenney as Secretary

---

[26] Kernerman, *Multicultural Nationalism: Civilizing Difference, Constituting Community*, 15-16.

[27] Gerald Kernerman, *Multicultural Nationalism: Civilizing Difference, Constituting Community* (Vancouver: University of British Columbia Press, 2005), 13.

[28] Installation Speech - The Right Honourable Michaëlle Jean Governor General of Canada on the occasion of her Installation. Ottawa. 27 September 2005.

[29] Examples of media coverage includes: CBC News. "Larry Zolf: Peacekeeping and the Canadian Identity" 7 February 2002; CBC News. "Queen 'treasures' her role in Canadian identity" 8 October 2002; CBC Radio. "A Changing Identity" 18 May 2004; and CBC Radio One. "The Current with Anna Maria Tremonti" 27 March 2008. The CBC has also complied a series of instructional materials for Canadian educators focused specifically on the search for Canadian identity. A non-governmental website has also emerged which is dedicated to defining the Canadian identity (www.canadianidentity.com) while a prominent blog is also titled, "I am Canadian, What am I?" (http://www.blogaholics.ca/archives/2005/02/i_am_canadian_w.html).

of State for Multiculturalism and Canadian Identity.[30] In July 2008, Citizenship and

Immigration Canada, along with the Dominion Institute, issued the results of a survey of

3000 Canadians conducted the previous year. The survey asked Canadians to identify the

people, places, events, accomplishments and symbols that best define Canada. While

symbols like the maple leaf, hockey and the Canadian flag were at the top of the list of

"101 Things that Most Define Canada," the societal characteristics which were identified

in the survey were peacekeeping, multiculturalism, human rights, freedom, democracy,

and being a "good country."[31] In January 2008, CBC Radio asked listeners to vote for

the 49 songs that the newly inaugurated U.S. President Barack Obama must hear which

will best represent Canada. According to CBC's Radio Director, "One of the best ways

to know Canada is through the depth and breadth of our artistic expression. We're

excited about the new president and we want him to be excited about us, so we're asking

our audience to help compile the list of our most definitive Canadian songs!"[32] As

columnist Dan Gardner of the Vancouver Sun noted, CBC radio was attempting to find a

song that "best captures the complex and subtle character of the Canadian identity that so

fascinates us."[33]

Canadians aim to stake out their unique place in the world not just by separating

themselves from Great Britain and their British heritage, but they also spend a great deal

of energy trying to separate their identity from the United States.[34] A 1999

---

[30] CBC News. "The 39th Parliament: Stephen Harper's first shuffle." 4 January 2007.

[31] Ipsos Reid. 2008. *Defining Canada: A Nation CHOOSES The 101 Things That Best Define Their Country.* Results of survey commissioned by Citizenship and Immigration Canada and the Dominion Institute. Results available at www.101things.ca/Listof101Things.pdf.

[32] Garnder, Dan. "Get over Yourself, Canada." *Vancouver Sun.* 19 January 2009.

[33] *Ibid.*

[34] Philip Resnick, *The European Roots of Canadian Identity.* Peterborough, Ontario: Broadview Press, 2005.

Macclean's/CBC survey reported that half of Canadian respondents believed that Canada was becoming more like America, and nearly a third felt that a full political union with the United States was likely at some point in the future. By the end of 2002 however, this sentiment had changed, with Canadians expressing a desire to distinguish themselves from their southern neighbor and those who stated that Canadians were "essentially different" from Americans grew to 57%.[35] As one commentator on Canadian national identity observed, "The real story is Canadians' need to be perceived, and to perceive themselves, as more tolerant than Americans."[36]

Tolerance and diversity, most often represented in the language of "multiculturalism," has come to represent a key theme of the emerging Canadian national identity. As Chief Justice Beverley McLachlin states on the Supreme Court of Canada website:

> Canadians are privileged to live in a peaceful country. Much of our collective sense of freedom and safety comes from our community's commitment to a few key values: democratic governance, respect for fundamental rights and the rule of law, and accommodation of difference.[37]

Prime Minister Jean Chretien echoed these sentiments about the centrality of multiculturalism to the national identity in a June 2000 speech:

> We have established a distinct Canadian way, a distinct Canadian model: Accommodation of cultures. Recognition of diversity. A partnership between

---

[35] "Becoming More American" The Canadian Encyclopedia. www.thecanadianencyclopedia.com. Accessed 10 January 2008.
[36] *Russell Lawrence Barsch, "Aboriginal Peoples and Canada's Conscience" in Newhouse (2005), p. 280.*
[37] http://www.scc-csc.gc.ca/Welcome/index_e.asp.

citizens and state. A balance that promotes individual freedom and economic prosperity while at the same time sharing risks and benefits.[38]

A federal government statement on diversity and multiculturalism states unequivocally that "Canada's experience with diversity distinguishes it from most other countries"[39] and that multiculturalism "is viewed as one of Canada's most important attributes, socially and economically."[40]

In 1971, Canada was the first country in the world to adopt multiculturalism as an official government policy, which meant that it would provide programs and services for different cultural associations.[41] The Trudeau government viewed multiculturalism as a way to diffuse the bilingual 'duopoly' problem between English- and French-speaking Canada, arguing that cultural rights were an element of individual freedom.[42] Since 1972, the cabinet in Canada has included a Minister for Multiculturalism. In the 1982 Canadian Constitution, multiculturalism gained constitutional recognition in Section 27 of the Charter of Rights and Freedoms, which specified that Canadian courts were to make rulings "in a manner consistent with the presentation and enhancement of the multicultural heritage of Canada."[43] In June 1988, the Canadian Multiculturalism Act was passed which legislatively established the official government policy of

---

[38] Government of Canada. 2000. "The Canadian Way in the 21st Century." Speech of Prime Minister Jean Chrétien to Conference on "Progressive Governance for the 21st Century", 2-3 June 2000.
[39] Government of Canada. 2008. "Canadian Diversity: Respecting Our Differences." Department of Canadian Heritage. Ottawa.
[40] *Ibid.*
[41] *Ibid.*
[42] Eva Mackey. 1999. *The House of Difference: Cultural Politics and National Identity in Canada.* London and New York: Routledge.
[43] Canadian Charter of Rights and Freedoms.

multiculturalism.[44] These initiatives by government reflect a growing sentiment that multiculturalism has become a defining feature of Canadian national identity. In fact, by 2006 a poll of Canadians reported that approximately 40% viewed multiculturalism as the core of Canadian identity.[45]

Of course, Canada has always been a nation of diversity, with its history of bilingualism and biculturalism between the English- and French-speaking settler populations alongside, and often blending with, extremely diverse Aboriginal populations. As the above discussion has illustrated, the search for the Canadian identity in recent decades has shifted the national narrative away from its historical bilingual/bicultural emphasis toward an emerging Canadian identity that focused around two important features: Canada's image as a global steward of human rights and multiculturalism. This emerging national identity has pushed Canada in the direction of indigenous reconciliation, and each of these features has had particular implications for the character of that reconciliation.

"Global Steward of Human Rights"

As a "good global steward of human rights" it is important for Canada to be perceived as a global leader in human rights and also in indigenous rights, for in order to maintain its global reputation as a peacemaker and honest broker in international politics, it must also be a world leader in indigenous rights and demonstrate that it has reconciled with Aboriginal peoples and moved beyond its colonial past. Interviews with indigenous leaders from Canada during 2007 and 2008 document how Canada's reputation and

---

[44] Parliament of Canada. 1988. Bill C-93: Canadian Multiculturalism Act.
[45] John Geddes, "Canadian Nationalism in Decline, Says Poll," Maclean's, 23 January 2006.

positive self-image in human rights is consciously utilized by indigenous activists as a tool to expose Canada's shortcomings in indigenous rights in order to compel Canada to act in ways that advance indigenous reconciliation.

One First Nations leader reported that "Canada has a constitutional guarantee of the rights of indigenous peoples. However, even with this guarantee, the protection of our rights is not easy."[46] Another leader added that "It is essential to show the world that Canada is not a paradise in relation to human rights because Canada does not take seriously the situation of First Nations."[47]

Canadian indigenous interviewees spoke often about how they have attempted to embarrass Canada about its vote against the Declaration of Indigenous Rights at the UN General Assembly, using Canada's "good human rights steward" identity against it on an international level. One First Nations leader said,

> We must denounce the Canadian government which chose to vote against the Declaration. We welcome the passage of the Declaration, but Canada has let us down. The Declaration is not the end of a process but is the beginning. There is a need for urgent action. We must bring shame upon Canada. Canada changed its reputation with respect to international human rights when it voted against the Declaration. Canada cannot be considered a great nation until it supports the Declaration.[48]

Another indigenous activist from Quebec stated that:

> Canada offers a rich society. It offers new immigrants the chance of a job, health care and reasonable housing. It makes reasonable attempts to integrate new cultures into the Canadian fabric. How then can we explain the desperate situation of us indigenous peoples in Canada?[49]

---

[46] Interview with Canadian indigenous leader. Canadian interviewee #5. May 2008.
[47] Interview with Canadian indigenous leader. Canadian interviewee #2. May 2008.
[48] *Ibid.*
[49] Interview with indigenous leader from Quebec. Canadian interviewee #4. April 2008.

Indigenous groups liberally used the shaming strategy in the Canadian press in order to place Canada's human rights self-image into question after Canada cast its vote against the Declaration. In a press release from the First Nations Leadership Council, Grand Chief Stewart Philip, President of the Union of British Columbia Indian Chiefs, was quoted as saying,

> Canada no longer enjoys a 'blue beret' reputation at the United Nations. Canada's disgraceful and disgusting conduct against Indigenous People at both the national and international level is being noted. It is simply shameful that, as a member of the Human Rights Council, Canada pretends to espouse the highest standards and protection of Human Rights.[50]

A year later, on the first anniversary of the Declaration's passage, the First Nations Leadership Council issued another press release, urging "all political parties (in the upcoming Canadian election) to publicly demonstrate their commitment to the Declaration and to the human rights of indigenous peoples across Canada."[51]

The shaming strategy of indigenous peoples toward Canada's human rights identity is also evident in UN meetings. Speaking at the 7th Session of the U.N. Permanent Forum on Indigenous Issues, Chief Ghislain Picard of the Assembly of First Nations of Quebec and Labrador, called out Canada's human rights reputation:

> I would like to shed new light on Canada which boasts being a model country on the international scene and encourages others to adopt its high standards on human rights, yet it refuses to endorse the Declaration on

---

[50] First Nations Leadership Council. Press Release: First Nations Leadership Council Troubled By Today's Vote at the United Nations; Inaction on Declaration on the Rights of Indigenous Peoples Inexcusable. 13 September 2007.

[51] First Nations Leadership Council. Press Release: First Nations Pressure Canada to Endorse the United Nations Declaration on the Rights of Indigenous Peoples on the Eve of the Anniversary of its Adoption. 12 September 2008.

Indigenous Rights, which shows its minimal norms for indigenous peoples.[52]

On another day of the 7th Session of the Permanent Forum on Indigenous Issues, both Wilton Littlechild, speaking on behalf of the Assembly of First Nations, and Beverly Jacobs of the Native Women's Organization of Canada, addressed the failure of Canada to endorse the Declaration as a minimum standard of indigenous rights. Both speakers called upon Canada to immediately implement the Declaration in order to salvage its global human rights reputation. The representative from the Canadian Ministry of Foreign Affairs was quick to respond and publicly defend Canada's human rights and indigenous rights record. She stated,

> Canada has long demonstrated its commitment to advancing indigenous peoples' rights both domestically and internationally. Canada did not support the Declaration because it could not support this particular set of political commitments. Canada continues to have concerns about the Declaration, but it is not our intention to stand in the way. ...Canadian policies will continue to remain based on existing human rights obligations and commitments.[53]

As a state party to the Convention on the Elimination of Racial Discrimination (CERD), Canada is obligated to submit periodic reports of its efforts against racial discrimination and is subject to biannual review. The CERD Committee then evaluates and makes recommendations to a state party. While CERD recommendations are not legally binding, they do, as CERD Committee member Francisco Cali said, "carry considerable weight and are meant to guide state parties as to their obligations under the

---

[52] Statement by Chief Ghislain Picard, Assembly of First Nations of Quebec and Labrador. 7th Session of the UN Permanant Forum on Indigenous Issues. New York, 30 April 2008.
[53] Statement by Canadian Ministry of Foreign Affairs. 7th Session of the UN Permanent Forum on Indigenous Issues. New York, 28 April 2008.

Convention. No country wants to be condemned by this committee."[54] As part of its review procedure, the CERD accepts "shadow reports" from groups representing affected minority populations. First Nations groups have made effective use of this option. When Canada was up for review by the CERD in 2007, a number of groups representing First Nations submitted shadow reports, all of which attempted to demonstrate to the world that Canada was not the "good human rights steward" that it purports to be.

The shadow report submitted by the International Indian Treaty Council and the Confederation of Treaty 6 First Nations, firmly accused Canada of "racism and racial discrimination towards the Indigenous Peoples whose traditional homelands are considered to be located within that country."[55] The IITC submission argued that Canada's failings included

> ongoing institutional racism and discrimination within the criminal justice and court systems, Treaty violations, a range of inequities in social services and living conditions, ...and the imposition of development projects impacting Indigenous Peoples' lands, waters, and traditional means of subsistence undertaken without their free, prior and informed consent.[56]

The Lubicon Lake Indian Nation was another First Nation to submit a shadow report to the CERD regarding Canada's periodic review. This submission also charged Canada with international dishonesty regarding the rights of indigenous Peoples:

---

[54] Presentation by Francisco Calí (Maya), Member of the CERD Committee. Human Rights Training Session held by the International Indian Treaty Council. Mille Lacs Indian Museum, Minnesota. 27 September 2007.
[55] Submission by the International Indian Treaty Council to the United Nations Committee on the Elimination of Racial Discrmination (CERD), dated 14 February 2007. Regarding the Report of the Government of Canada to the Committee on the Elimination of Racial Discrimination, concerning Canada's 17th and 18th Periodic Reports to the CERD (CERD/C/CAN/18) to be considered at its 70th session, 19 February - 9 March 2007.
[56] *Ibid.*

Canada has been the subject of several UN decisions regarding the abuse of the human rights and aboriginal rights of the Lubicon Lake Indian Nation under ...international human rights covenants to which Canada is a signatory. Canada has not only ignored these decisions but has misrepresented them to both Canadians and to members of the international community.[57]

These efforts by indigenous groups did achieve the desired effect of placing into question Canada's "good human rights steward" self-image and international reputation. On 8 March 2007, the UN CERD Committee called on Canada to reverse its position on the Declaration on the Rights of Indigenous Peoples. It also "voiced concerns" about the actions of trans-national mining companies registered in Canada and urged Canada to "take measures" to ensure their accountability with regard to the human rights of indigenous peoples.[58] This was the first time that the CERD had held multinational corporations accountable when it ruled that the state is responsible for the actions of corporations both within and operating outside the boundaries of the state.[59] As Ron Lameman, representative of the Confederation of Treaty Six First Nations stated,

> We learned the process and we helped set new standards. ...When we present shadow reports, then we have the ability to stand up to these lawyers. They have all this machinery; we don't have that. ...But, our efforts at the United Nations help hold Canada accountable to the international community. We have forced the government of Canada to change its actions.[60]

---

[57] Lubicon Lake Indian Nation. Submission to the 70th Session of the UN Committee on the Elimination of Racial Discrmination with Regard to the Lack of Canadian Compliance with UN Human Rights Decisions and General Recommendation No. 23 of the Committee on the Elimination of Racial Discrmination, 19 February - 9 March, 2007.

[58] Confederacy of Treaty Six First Nations and the International Indian Treaty Council. Press Release, 8 March 2007. "The UN Committee on the Elimination of Racial Discrmination calls upon Canada to immediately endorse the United Nations Declaration on the Rights of Indigenous Peoples."

[59] Statement by Andrea Carmen, Executive Director of the International Indian Treaty Council. Human Rights Training Session held by the International Indian Treaty Council. Mille Lacs Indian Museum, Minnesota. 27 September 2007.

[60] Statement by Ron Lameman (Beaver Creek First Nation), Confederacy of Treaty Six First Nations. Human Rights Training Session held by the International Indian Treaty Council. Mille Lacs Indian Museum, Minnesota. 27 September 2007.

Multiculturalism

Multiculturalism, both as a policy and as a discourse, has also helped shape the
Canadian model of indigenous reconciliation in two important ways. First, it exerts an
equalizing force, essentially moving to erase indigeneity in Canada. Second, it
encourages indigenous policies that focus primarily on correcting socio-economic
disparities between Aboriginal and non-Aboriginal Canadians.

Multiculturalism as an equalizing force which erases indigeneity is manifested
most commonly in statements such as one that appears in a Mount Allison University
publication on Multiculturalism in Canada:

> Canada is often described as a multicultural nation. But what does that
> mean? Simply stated, it means that Canadians are not of any one cultural
> background, race or heritage. Instead, Canadians today reflect a vast
> diversity of cultural heritages and racial groups. This multicultural
> diversity is a result of centuries of immigration. *All Canadians, including
> the Native People, can trace their origins to an immigrant past* (emphasis
> added).[61]

Another poignant example of this discursive move is an opinion piece published by Bob
Verdun in an online newspaper called *The Nation:*

> Canada is a nation of immigrants: the world's most international society.
> Canada is making huge strides in eliminating racism, and promoting true
> equality.
> Sadly, one group refuses to accept the reality of Canada. These are the
> Indians, or Natives, or Aboriginals, or whatever the politically-correct
> term happens to be. ...They refuse to accept the fact that *they are
> immigrants too, and that there were no truly original inhabitants of
> America.* They came from Asia! (emphasis added.)[62]

---

[61] Mount Allison University, Faculty of Arts, Canadian Studies. 2007. "About Canada: Multiculturalism in Canada." Sackville, New Brunswick.

[62] Bob Verdun "The Human Race: Reparation Repercussions." The Nation Newspaper. 15 April 2007. Available at www.nationnews.com.

While Verdun's comments come from the political far right and certainly do not represent the whole of Canadian society, the essential component of his statement, as in the official government document above, is the assertion that all Canadians, Aboriginal or not, are immigrants. This discursive move implies that Aboriginal people are not really "indigenous" to Canada, and Aboriginal Canadians are simply another instance of multiple cultures. When emphasis is placed on multiculturalism, all "cultures" become equivalent and then the erasure of indigeneity comes from the logic of multiculturalism itself. Under this logic, Aboriginal Canadians are in no way entitled to any Treaty rights, land claims, or self-determination rights.

Multiculturalism also encourages policies which focus on the socio-economic disparities between Aboriginal and non-Aboriginal populations. "Canada's Action Plan Against Racism: A Canada for All"[63] demonstrates this impulse. This report presents a Six Point Action Plan to "close the gaps in social and economic outcomes"[64] for all: women, visible minorities and Aboriginal people. The action plan has the following components: 1) combat discrimination, 2) promote diversity, 3) strengthen civil society, 4) strengthen regional and international cooperation, 5) diversity education, and 6) counter hate and bias. While Aboriginal people are mentioned throughout the report, the context is always one related to their socio-economic deficiencies and the need to reduce disparities. Land rights and self-determination for indigenous peoples and communities is notably absent from this fifty-six page report. The report concludes that, by implementing this plan, Canadians will "achieve a shared vision of an inclusive society--

---

[63] Government of Canada. Department of Canadian Heritage. 2005.
[64] *Ibid.*, p. 7.

a Canada for all--where everyone is treated with respect and dignity, and ...no one is left behind."[65] In other words, multiculturalism will be successful when the socio-economic gaps between all groups--Aboriginal and otherwise--are closed.

As the above discussion has demonstrated, the two defining features of emerging Canadian identity are shaping indigenous rights and the reconciliation discourse in particular ways, which together have created the Canadian model of reconciliation. The "good human rights steward" image encourages Canada to make positive actions in indigenous rights, in order to reconcile its colonial past and maintain its positive image. Multiculturalism, then, pushes that action into a particular framework that emphasizes equality and correcting socio-economic disparities as an end goal. These dual impulses-- good human rights image and multiculturalism--create the Canadian model of indigenous reconciliation. The Canadian model of indigenous reconciliation centers on two primary goals: 1) provide absolution to Canada for its past actions related to indigenous peoples, and 2) create certainty for the future by securing land tenure and state sovereignty, keeping all groups equal within the existing power structure.

The Canadian model of indigenous reconciliation looks vastly different from the indigenous model of reconciliation that has been advanced by the international indigenous rights movement and often advocated by Aboriginal people in Canada. The central feature of the indigenous model is a call for states to renounce the Doctrine of Discovery in their laws, policies and thought patterns, and, in its place, renegotiate, in good faith, land and self-determination agreements and partnerships. As Chief Oren Lyons (Haudenassaunee), stated at the 7th Session of the UN's Permanent Forum on

---

[65] *Ibid.*, p. 56.

Indigenous Peoples, "Canadian law always works against us. There is a barrier there that, for years, we couldn't see. The answer is that the Doctrine of Discovery is foundational to law. Canadian law and jurisprudence help legitimize colonial doctrines."[66] Regarding a renegotiated relationship between Aboriginal peoples and Canada, one indigenous activist commented,

> Canadian society is built on a foundation of theft. In order for a real reconciliation to occur, Canadians must first apologize for their collective actions in the past. Then, they must humble themselves and be prepared to move beyond their mythology and the politics of multiculturalism in order to deal with indigenous peoples in an honorable way.[67]

Chief Wabananick, speaking at the UN Permanent Forum on Indigenous Issues, also spoke to the indigenous model of reconciliation:

> We have the right to co-management. First Nations have been fighting about access to resources but First Nations never gave up the right to access territories. Under Canadian law, ancestral occupation gives us underlying title to the land. This means that provinces never had exclusive rights on public land. Their property right depends on Aboriginal title which can only be given up through negotiation...First Nations can only give up their inherent sovereignty under treaties. ...Treaties provide the opportunity to reconcile indigenous sovereignty and the sovereignty of the Crown.[68]

Although there are many similarities between Canada and New Zealand's visions of reconciliation, there are several structural and societal elements that distinguish the Canadian model of indigenous reconciliation from New Zealand's Doctrine of Discovery understanding of the Treaty of Waitangi, as discussed in the previous chapter. First of

---

[66] Statement by Chief Oren Lyons, Haudenassaunee. 7th Session of the UN Permanent Forum on Indigenous Issues. New York, 29 April 2008.
[67] Interview with indigenous activist from Canada, May 2008.
[68] Statement of Chief Wabananick, Assembly of First Nations of Quebec and Labrador. 7th Session of the UN Permanent Forum on Indigenous Issues. New York, 1 May 2008.

all, Canada is a federal system while New Zealand has a unified national government. As a result, Canada is better prepared structurally to accommodate various layers of sovereignty, as demanded by indigenous advocates for self-determination. Second, although Canada and New Zealand are both engaged in a constant search for the national identity, Canada has not absorbed Aboriginal identity into the national identity in the same way that Maori identity has come to represent New Zealand. Even with these significant differences, however, the end product, i.e. the model of reconciliation employed, looks remarkably similar in both Canada and New Zealand, suggesting that there is another element, common to both countries, which encourages them both to resist the indigenous model of reconciliation.

In the next section, three recent cases of reconciliation in Canada will be briefly examined: the creation of the territory of Nunavut, the Harper government's apology for residential schools and the resulting Truth and Reconciliation Commission, and the British Columbia treaty process. Each of these cases will illustrate how Canada excels within the framework of the Canadian model of reconciliation, even moving to accept indigenous cultural rights as recognized collective rights in Canada. However, this framework ultimately forecloses the possibility of the indigenous model of reconciliation.

The Creation of the Territory of Nunavut

> A bold attempt to right past wrongs and bring hope to an entire region was launched as this day began and the map of Canada was redrawn to make room for the new territory of Nunavut.

> At midnight, with the wind chill here hovering around 45 below zero, and a rare blue moon encircled by a halo of light, Ottawa divided the old

256

Northwest Territories in two and Nunavut, which means, "our land" was created from the eastern 60% of the region.

... "What we affirm today, with the stroke of a pen, is the end of a very long road," said Prime Minister Chretien.
--New York Times, April 2, 1999[69]

In April 1999, the creation of the territory of Nunavut, the first time the map of Canada has been redrawn in 50 years, was widely heralded in the Canadian and international press as a significant Canadian achievement in indigenous rights. Like the above article implies, Canada "gave" the Inuit, or Eskimos, "a land of their own."

A division of the Northwest Territories was first discussed in 1976 during land claims negotiations between the Inuit Tapiriit Kanatami and the Canadian government. A referendum on the possible division of the Northwest Territories was held in 1982, which passed with a majority of Northwest Territories residents voting in favor of the division.[70] The final land claims agreement was reached in September of 1982 and ratified by nearly 85% of the voters in Nunavut.[71] On 9 July 1993, the Canadian Parliament passed both the Nunavut Land Claims Agreement Act[72] and the Nunavut Act.[73] The territory of Nunavut was officially created on 1 April 1999. Paul Okalik, the first premier of the newly launched territory, proudly proclaimed, "We have regained control of our destiny and will now determine our own path."[74]

Certain features of Nunavut demonstrate Canada's tolerance for an advanced level of indigenous rights, particularly in the soft rights areas of language, cultural arts and

---

[69] Anthony DePalma, "Canada's Eskimos Get a Land of Their Own." *New York Times*, 2 April 1999.
[70] www.gov.nu.ca
[71] *Ibid.*
[72] S.C. 1993, c.29, 10 June 1993.
[73] S.C. 1993, c.28, 10 June 1993.
[74] "For Canada's Inuits, this land is 'our land' (Nunavut)", *Christian Science Monitor*, 5 April 1999.

even involving internal governance. For example, the territory of Nunavut has two official languages, in addition to English and French: Inuktitut and Inuinnaqtun.[75] Inuit in Nunavut have "their inherent right to use the Inuit language in full equality with other Official Languages. ...This exceeds any other legal protection in place for any other Aboriginal group in Canada."[76] Also, Canada now, as a whole, widely utilizes the *Inukshook*[77] as a cultural symbol, even dedicating it as the symbol for the 2010 Winter Olympics in Vancouver. Nunavut's internal governance structure even reflects Canada's accommodation of Inuit culture. There are no parties in the Legislative Assembly and the legislature operates on a consensus-basis, in accordance with Inuit culture.[78] There is also an advisory council of elders whose task is to help incorporate Inuit culture into the Nunavut government.

While, on the surface, it appears that Nunavut demonstrates an advanced level of Canadian indigenous rights compliance in language, culture and even self-government, a more in-depth examination shows that the Nunavut land claims settlement and the creation of the public government of Nunavut are more reflective of the Canadian model of reconciliation than of the indigenous model of reconciliation. Rather that an accommodating the hard rights of indigenous land and self-determination, Nunavut actually demonstrates a pattern of Canadian *resistance* to these rights. First of all, the land claims settlement, like other Aboriginal land claims settlements in Canada, moves

---

[75] www.gov.nu.ca

[76] Government of Nunavut. Department of Culture, Language, Elders & Youth. Statement to the 7th Session of the U.N. Permanent Forum on Indigenous Issues, New York, 29 April 2008.

[77] An Inukshook is a piece of Inuit art comprised of a series of stacked stones which resembles a human figure. The name itself means "likeness of a person." Inukshooks are widely available wherever tourist souvenirs are sold in Canada, even in places very far away from Inuit territory. It has come to be a cultural symbol of Canada.

[78] CBC News. "On the Nunavut Campaign Trail." March 5, 2008.

land from Aboriginal title to fee simple title.[79] In other words, Inuit lands, which were

formerly held in collective Aboriginal title, are placed into individual ownership with the

completion of a land claims settlement. Far from recognizing the indigenous form of

collective land rights, Canada demands that land claims be settled in a way that results in

land ownership by individuals or Aboriginal corporate entities. Since Canada serves both

as defendant and arbiter in the land claims settlement process, it is in the position to make

such demands, regardless of what type of land title is desired by indigenous peoples.

Aboriginal title is tied conceptually to indigeneity, implying attachment to and

responsibility for certain lands. Fee simple title lands can be bought and sold to anyone.

Therefore, the Nunavut land claim settlement erased, rather than recognized, indigeneity.

Second, through the Nunavut land claims process, Canada also sought certainty of

land tenure for the future. With all Aboriginal title eradicated, and all lands in Nunavut

converted to fee simple title, Canada could move forward with development and resource

extraction plans, unimpeded by possible obstructions by the Supreme Court.

Third, the public government in Nunavut remains strictly under Canadian federal

control, particularly since the territory is almost completely dependent upon Ottawa to

fund its governmental operations. In the end, Canada is tightly maintaining Crown

sovereignty over Nunavut. "By negotiating both the real estate deals simultaneously but

separately, Ottawa was able to avoid creating an ethnic state," said former Northwest

Territories premier Dennis Patterson. "And by setting up Nunavut as a territory,

constitutionally on par with the other two territories (the Yukon and remaining Northwest

---

[79] Agreement Between the Inuit of the Nunavut Settlement Area and Her Majesty the Queen In Right of Canada. Text available at:
http://www.nucj.ca/library/bar_ads_mat/Nunavut_Land_Claims_Agreement.pdf.

Territories), the creation of a fourth level of government was avoided."[80] Even though

the Nunavut territory is expensive for Ottawa, Inuit leader John Amagoalik said "that it

has been money well spent because the building up of Nunavut and its communities has

been an effective way for Canadians to assert Arctic sovereignty, a pressing issue for the

Harper government."[81]

Apology Followed by Truth and Reconciliation Commission

On 11 June 2008, Prime Minister Stephen Harper stood up in the Canadian House

of Commons and delivered an apology to the former students of Indian residential

schools in Canada. The residential school policy, which had operated in Canada from the

1880s until the 1970s, had been a key part of the government's cultural assimilation

policy for Aboriginal peoples during that period of time. More than 160,000 Native

children passed through the residential school system during its years of operation,[82]

many of them the victims of physical and sexual abuse. All of them were victims of a

harsh educational program which removed Native children from their homes and

communities and forbade them from speaking their languages or practicing their cultures

so that they would assimilate as quickly as possible into Canadian society.

Harper's apology relied heavily on both Canada's "good human rights steward"

and multiculturalism identity discourses. "These objectives were based on the

assumption that aboriginal cultures and spiritual beliefs were inferior or unequal. ...Today

---

[80] *Christian Science Monitor*, 5 April 1999.
[81] Katherine O'Neill. "Nunavut's birthday sparks debate about its future." *Globe and Mail*. 31 March 2009.
[82] Am Johal. "Canada Must be Back by Action, Native Leaders Say." Inter Press Service News Agency. 17 June 2008. Available at http://www.ipsnews.net.

we recognize that this policy of assimilation was wrong, has caused great harm and has no place in our country."[83] Noting that "the absence of an apology has been an impediment to healing and reconciliation," Harper offered the apology on behalf of the government and society, "to Aboriginal peoples for Canada's role in the Indian residential schools system."[84] Again, near of the end of the text, Harper declared, "There is no place in this country for the attitudes that inspired the Indian residential school system."[85]

Directly invoking the Canadian reconciliation impulse, Harper next stated that in order to move in the direction of "healing, reconciliation and resolution of the sad legacy of Indian residential schools,"[86] Harper pointed out the importance of the Indian Residential Schools Settlement Agreement from 2007, which offered some compensation to the victims of abuse, along with the establishment of a Truth and Reconciliation Commission, whose five year work plan revolves around a series of public hearings.[87] This agreement, he said, is "a positive step in forging a new relationship between aboriginal peoples and other Canadians."[88] He then characterized this new relationship in multicultural terms, as one in which Aboriginal and non-Aboriginal Canadians will "move forward together with a renewed understanding that ...vibrant cultures and traditions will contribute to a stronger Canada for all of us."[89]

---

[83] Canwest News Service. "Text of the Apology." 11 June 2008.
[84] *Ibid.*
[85] *Ibid.*
[86] *Ibid.*
[87] The total settlement agreement was Can$1.9 billion. The Truth and Reconciliation Commission is the first ever established in a Western industrialized democracy. It will began work on 1 June 2008. CBC News, 29 May 2008.
[88] *Ibid.*
[89] *Ibid.*

A number of alternative voices in Canada offered critical reactions to the apology, noting in particular how it did not live up to the renegotiated power relationship envisioned in the indigenous model of reconciliation. In this vision, the apology was flawed because it was limited to the residential schools issue and did not make any mention of land loss, continued institutionalized racism, or most importantly, a renegotiated land and power arrangement. As Kahentinetha Horn, Mohawk Nation News, wrote:

> There has finally been an official apology. ...This is a start. Now we have to deal with other big issues, sovereignty and resources. ...Don't be fooled! The evil program is still in full swing. Canada has no intention to stop. They continue to drive us off our land, to criminalize us, incarcerate us and refuse to return control of our land and resources to us. ...Saying sorry doesn't cut it. ...Real reconciliation means restoring the traditional homelands and resources of the various indigenous people who have been dispossessed. Anything less is a farce.[90]

The text of this apology reflects the Canadian model of reconciliation, combining the discourses of multiculturalism and the "good steward of human rights." Driven by the desire to maintain a "good steward of human rights" image, Canada was compelled to act in some way to remove the stain from its conscience, as residential school survivors had begun airing the issue publicly during the 1990s. Beginning in the 1990s and continuing until 2005, a series of class action lawsuits were filed against the federal government and the Catholic and Anglican churches which had operated the schools. By 2005, the Assembly of First Nations filed a massive class action lawsuit against the federal government, citing the scope of abuse that had been perpetrated against Aboriginal children. Seeking to stop the lawsuits and, of course, salvage Canada's

---

[90] Kahentinetha Horn, "Canada Confesses to Part of its Crimes Against Humanity." *Mohawk Nation News*, 14 June 2008.

human rights image, the Canadian government approved a settlement package for residential school survivors. Survivors had until August 2007 to accept a government settlement or to pursue an individual case. The government offered a common experience settlement to all survivors with a supplemental settlement if there had been abuse. The common settlement was $10,000 for the first year of residence and $3,000 for each additional year of residence after the first year.[91] Again, like the Nunavut settlement, this was a Canadian effort to individualize a collective Aboriginal issue.

The text of the residential school apology is also an effort to seek reconciliation, framed in terms of Canada's multicultural identity, mentioning that "the vibrant cultures" of Canadian society would now be able to "move forward together." The implication here is that now that this apology has been offered, Aboriginal peoples can now rightfully take their place alongside other cultures in Canada. This is another effort by Canada to erase the uniqueness of the indigenous experience in Canada.

So these two elements--good human rights steward and multiculturalism--combine in the residential school apology in the Canadian model of reconciliation, rather than the indigenous model. While there is a recognition of the collective indigenous experience, Canada moves quickly to individuate the collective indigenous experience. Harper's apology does not aim to pursue a future of nation-to-nation relationships between indigenous peoples and the Canadian government but rather, looks for absolution for Canada's past sins while simultaneously seeking to maintain the certainty of present power structures.

---

[91] Information on the class action lawsuits and the government settlement were provided by Cohen Highley Lawyers, London, Ontario and the Assembly of First Nations.

263

The British Columbia Treaty Process

As discussed in an earlier section, the Royal Proclamation of 1763 had established the principle of Aboriginal title,[92] which differed from fee simple title. Even though the Royal Proclamation claimed to extend British sovereignty over the West, it also maintained that British sovereignty was not incompatible with Indian land ownership under Aboriginal title. Aboriginal title remained intact unless it was specifically transferred to the Crown. These principles were largely followed in eastern Canada, but were mostly ignored in British Columbia.[93]

Governor James Douglas made a total of fourteen land agreements with tribal nations on Vancouver Island during his tenure.[94] These agreements, later referred to as the Douglas Treaties, were similar to treaties in other parts of Canada which left Aboriginal title intact. Gov. Douglas mysteriously stopped making treaties in 1854 in favor of a Doctrine of Discovery approach which denied Aboriginal title and assumed Crown sovereignty and ownership of land.[95] This approach generated the "Aboriginal Land Problem" in British Columbia that would last for the next century and a half.

While First Nations had engaged in low-level protests and resistance since the 1850s, the official land claims process in British Columbia emerged during the early-1970s era of heightened global indigenous activism when the Supreme Court of Canada handed down its *Calder* ruling in 1973. In this ruling, the Nisga'a lost the actual case, but they did receive an acknowledgement of Aboriginal title in the written Court opinion.

---

[92] This concept has been previously referred to as Indian title.

[93] Paul Tennant. 1990. *Aboriginal Peoples and Politics: The Indian Land Question in British Columbia, 1849-1989.* Vancouver: University of British Columbia Press.

[94] Morales, Robert. "New Treaty, Same Old Problems," *Cultural Survival*, Spring 2006.

[95] Tennant, 1990.

Since this Supreme Court opinion threw into question most of the land tenure in British Columbia, the Trudeau government asked the Nisga'a and other First Nations groups to negotiate directly with the federal government rather than litigate. The federal government began direct negotiations with the Nisga'a in 1976 and the provincial government later joined the negotiations in 1990.[96]

The independent British Columbia Treaty Commission (BCTC) was appointed in 1993 in order to manage and monitor the British Columbia treaty negotiation process.[97] Although it is completely funded by the government, its full range of functions include: beginning negotiations, allocating funding to Aboriginal groups, reporting on the progress of negotiations and assisting to resolve differences.[98] The BCTC treaty process is comprised of six stages, beginning with the "Statement of Intent to Negotiate" and proceeding through "Negotiation Of An Agreement in Principle," Treaty Finalization and Treaty Implementation.[99]

The establishment of the BCTC marked the beginning of the modern-day treaty making in British Columbia, reflected in the province's official "New Relationship" policy. According to a joint statement issued by the Province of British Columbia and the First Nations Leadership Council, the "New Relationship" policy reflects a commitment "to a new government-to-government relationship based on respect, recognition and accommodation of aboriginal title and rights and to reconciliation of

---

[96] Government of Canada. Department of Indian and Northern Affairs. "Fact Sheet: The Nisga'a Treaty."
[97] Morales, 2006.
[98] Government of Canada. Department of Indian and Northern Affairs. *Nisga'a Final Agreement Act Issue Papers.* 1998.
[99] British Columbia Treaty Commission. "Six Stages: Policies and Procedures." Vancouver. 2007.

Aboriginal and Crown titles and jurisdictions."[100] According to Mike deJong, Aboriginal

Relations Minister for British Columbia, "Treaties which include self-governing

provisions that include a treaty settlement land base are a further expression of the new

relationship."[101] As of the end of 2008, the BCTC reported that sixty First Nations were

participating in 49 sets of negotiations through the commission.[102] There were forty-

three First Nations in the process of negotiating agreements,[103] and five had completed

final agreements.[104]

Since the absence of treaties in British Columbia created a great deal of

uncertainty regarding the use and management of lands, a central feature of the BC treaty

process has been the quest for "certainty."[105] The "certainty" characteristic places the BC

Treaty process firmly within the Canadian model of reconciliation, a model that seeks

absolution for past actions and assurance for the future of state sovereignty and power

relations.

The first modern BC Treaty was the 1998 Nisga'a Final Agreement, which

provided CAN$196 million in government transfers over a five year period, recognized

Nisga'a ownership of certain mineral resources, recognized an entitlement to a share of

salmon and other fish and seafood, recognized Nisga'a legal jurisdiction over Nisga'a

[100] Joint Statement on the New Relationship.
http://ubcic.bc.ca/files/PDF/JointStatementOnTheNewRelationship_Sept2007.pdf.
[101] United Native News "Historic B.C. Treaty opens the often caustic B.C. legislature with a party." 15 October 2007. nnns.wordpress.com/2007.
[102] BC Treaty Commission. Negotiation Update. www.bc.treaty.net/files/updates.php. Accessed 10 January 2009.
[103] *Ibid.*
[104] British Columbia. Ministry of Aboriginal Relations and Reconciliation. Update on Aboriginal Treaties. www.gov.bc.ca/arr/treaty. Accessed 10 January 2009.
[105] Carole Blackburn, "Searching for Guarantees in the Midst of Uncertainty: Negotiating Aboriginal Rights and Title in British Columbia." *American Anthropologist*, Vol. 107, Issue 4, p. 586-596.

children, repatriated artifacts and protected certain Nisga'a sites.[106] Canadian Indian

Affairs Minister Jane Stewart, who signed the agreement on behalf of Canada, referred to

it as a "treaty of recognition and reconciliation."[107] It was also hailed by Nisga'a

President Joseph Gosnell, Sr. as a document which makes "history as we correct the

mistakes of the past (and) ...talk about reconciliation and a new understanding between

cultures."[108] The Nisga'a President's equation of reconciliation with correcting (some)

past mistakes reflects the first part of the Canadian model, absolution for past actions.

This also shows how the two models of reconciliation, which I call Canadian and

indigenous, do not necessarily imply that one must be indigenous or Canadian to ascribe

to the different visions of reconciliation. Here, the leader of an indigenous nation clearly

supports the Canadian vision of reconciliation. Gosnell continued, in the same statement,

to assert the importance of the certainty of land tenure and state sovereignty as well. He

stated that, "Today we join Canada and BC as free citizens, full and equal participants in

the social, economic and political life of this country."[109]

As many indigenous voices have observed, the certainty aspect in BC Treaty

negotiations is heavily slanted in the direction of the government. Robert Morales, Chair

of the Chief Negotiators of the First Nations Summit, pointed out that the BC Treaty

process through the BCTC represents not a "New Relationship" between the government

and First Nations, but it is merely an "extinguishment policy" towards First Nations

peoples. By erasing the indigeneity of Aboriginal peoples, the Canadian vision of

reconciliation thus also has the practical effect of closing down the possibility of a nation-

---

[106] Nisga'a Final Agreement. 1998.

[107] Debra Lockyer, "Nisga'a celebrate final agreement," *Windspeaker,* 4 August 1998.

[108] *Ibid.*

[109] *Ibid.*

to-nation relationship which the indigenous model of reconciliation would compel. In short, it reinscribes the Doctrine of Discovery in existing state sovereignty, by implying that the colonial Canadian state has the right to hold full and complete sovereignty while indigenous nations' place is to "join Canadian society." The BC Treaty process does this in several ways. First of all, return of any Aboriginal title lands to First Nations is not open for negotiation. There is also no possibility of co-management of the land or resources, or any sharing of revenue generated from those lands. Since the treaty process is meant to be "forward looking," there is not to be any compensation for the earlier illegal taking of Aboriginal lands. In addition, if a First Nation finds itself frustrated by the negotiations and wishes to resort to litigation, the treaty negotiation process will immediately and permanently cease. Finally, since the objective of the process is to achieve "certainty," all settlement agreements are to be full and final related to Aboriginal title and rights claims.[110]

Several other limitations of the BC Treaty process, specifically the privatization of land ownership and the model of governance which are compelled by the treaty process, not only reflect the Canadian model of reconciliation but move further, to actually pre-empt any possible future renegotiation of sovereignty and power relations as envisioned by the indigenous model of reconciliation. Under the Nisga'a Final Agreement, for example, all Nisga'a lands convert to individualized and privatized fee simple title. All Nisga'a and their lands also lose their tax-exempt status.[111] So, in order to be removed from the Indian Act, the Nisga'a needed to accept full privatization and individualization of their lands.

---

[110] Morales 2006.
[111] Nisga'a Final Agreement. 1998.

268

Second, the model of governance for the Nisga'a also changed character under the 1998 Final Agreement. The Nisga'a Tribal Council was replaced by the Nisga'a Lisims Government.[112] The Nisga'a Government has the power to make certain laws related to internal Nisga'a self-governance (e.g. Nisga'a citizenship, language, culture, marriages and social services) but is subject to both provincial and federal authority. Notably, in a move that completely subsumes indigenous nations under Canadian state sovereignty, the Nisga'a Final Agreement stated that "the Nisga'a Government will be quite recognizable as a local government compatible with other local governments in Canada."[113] As one indigenous commentator observed, "This is a form of self-government that imitates municipal government. It's being portrayed as Nisga's government but it's not. If it was, it would have involved the hereditary chiefs. It didn't."[114] Elected Nisga'a President Joseph Gosnell acknowledged the assimilative character of the land and governance provisions of the Nisga'a Final Agreement when he argued, "We are negotiating our way into Canada, not out of it."[115]

Conclusion

Canada is a country that wishes to create and maintain an image of itself as a harmonious multicultural society and "good human rights steward." As the above discussion has illustrated, the "good human rights steward" image propels Canada toward reconciliation, although that reconciliation remains constrained by a particular

---

[112] Canada. Department of Indian and Northern Affairs. "Nisga'a Final Agreement 2001 Annual Report." Ottawa. 2001.
[113] Nisga'a Final Agreement. 1998.
[114] Paul Barnsley, "Final agreement debated across the country." *Windspeaker.* 10 August 1998.
[115] Nisga'a Final Agreement. 1998.

framework, the Canadian model of reconciliation. Under this model, Canada seeks to be fully absolved of its "past" egregious behavior against indigenous peoples, and it also seeks certainty for the future, especially in land tenure and sovereignty.

Canada's emerging multicultural identity also helps shape the character of reconciliation as many efforts in Canada are focused on "closing the gaps" between Aboriginal and non-Aboriginal Canadians, framed strictly in socio-economic terms. Multiculturalism has created space for Aboriginal rights as collective rights and thus has allowed Canada to become a world leader in such "soft rights" areas as language and culture. However, reconciliation efforts in Canada, from the creation of the Territory of Nunavut, to the Apology for Residential Schools, to the British Columbia Treaty Process, all substantial achievements when considered from an international perspective, nevertheless all operate within the framework of the Canadian model of reconciliation. This model of reconciliation not only excludes features of the indigenous model of reconciliation, such as co-management of resources, but in certain cases like the BC Treaty process, actually acts preemptively to avoid a renegotiation of power relations between First Nations and Canada. In short, Canadian over-compliance is actually a form of state *resistance* to the emerging global consensus in indigenous rights. Canada is willing to move forward in certain "soft rights" areas in order to resist developments in "hard rights" areas that would threaten the liberal framework and the sovereignty status quo.

Chapter 7

Conclusions, Implications and Suggestions for Future Research

I began with a broad goal: to discern what indigenous global politics is and how it is challenging the international order both in theory and in practice. More specifically, I asked what the Declaration on the Rights of Indigenous Peoples is, why it took so long and how states have responded to it. Through a historical analysis of the Declaration process, a qualitative analysis of the patterns of indigenous rights compliance by states, and comparative case studies of indigenous rights in two "over-compliant" states, I have generated several major findings in this study.

Research Findings

First, the transnational indigenous rights movement, by constituting itself in terms of land and self-determination rights, created a type of global politics which was distinctive from other rights movements. Indigenous global politics battles both indigenous discrimination and assimilation. Because states have viewed land and self-determination in zero-sum terms, indigenous global politics set up a conflict with states and with the international system itself, challenging some central tenets of international politics, namely sovereignty, territoriality and the universal, individual-rights based, human rights system. Indigenous global politics seeks a re-articulation of sovereignty, territoriality and human rights toward more pluralistic conceptions, which can better accommodate indigenous peoples' rights to land and self-determination, thereby

271

combating not only discrimination and marginalization of indigenous peoples but also assimilative efforts to integrate indigenous peoples into states, societies and the international system. Indigenous global politics has also challenged existing modes of practice in international politics, forcing shifts in rules and procedures in order to accommodate indigenous ways of thinking and acting.

Second, state responses to the emerging indigenous rights regime falls into four categories: compliance (further subdivided into compliance-high and compliance-low), partial compliance, under-compliance, and a new category which I have identified as "over-compliance." Over-compliance means that a state's policies and/or behavior exceed its international legal and/or normative commitments. States, as a whole, are most likely to partially comply or under-comply with the emerging indigenous rights regime. Common law parliamentary countries, however, are the only type of country that over-complies in indigenous rights, compelling a more in-depth examination of such countries' indigenous rights situations.

Third, "over-compliance" in indigenous rights occurs when several conditions develop and intersect to propel a state towards a colonizer-centric model of reconciliation: a) the presence of a domestic indigenous movement which invokes the international discourse on indigenous rights, b) the state has a high human rights self-image and international reputation; and c) the state is experiencing a shifting identity, increasingly situated in multiculturalism which, to varying degrees, also incorporates indigenous identity. Over-compliance occurs when a state focuses on, and excels in, "soft rights" (e.g. language, culture, religion, etc.) for indigenous peoples while

272

simultaneously resisting "hard rights" (i.e. land rights and self-determination.) Colonizer-centric models of indigenous reconciliation address indigenous individuals' discrimination and soft collective rights, while leaving in place an implicit or explicit reliance on the Doctrine of Discovery, while either avoiding or attempting to deflect conversations about hard rights. Often, colonizer-centric reconciliation models attempt to shift hard rights out of the conversation by insisting on an individualization of land and a model of indigenous "self"-governance which adheres to the liberal democratic standard.

Implications

Indigenous global politics is a politics of resistance and counter-resistance, both in theory and in practice. Its narrative encapsulates not only resistance by indigenous peoples against states and the legacy of colonialism in the international system, but it also includes a counter narrative of resistance by states to an emerging indigenous rights regime in order to maintain the international status quo. I have examined these multiple paths of resistance in the preceding chapters in order to address the question of how indigenous global politics is forging international change. I contend that indigenous global politics is creating much larger challenges to the international system than is typically recognized by practitioners or theorists of international politics. While indigenous peoples' struggles are hardly noticed in a world characterized by terrorism, nuclear proliferation, economic distress and climate change, and the Declaration on the Rights of Indigenous Peoples was barely a blip on the international media radar in September 2007 when it passed the UN General Assembly, the changes being forged by

273

indigenous global politics are not likewise small and inconsequential. Indigenous global politics actually represents significant international challenges in a variety of areas.

First, indigenous global politics reveals how the Doctrine of Discovery remains embedded in both international law and the domestic law of at least several common law states.[1] The Doctrine of Discovery presumes the superiority of Europeans, their cultures and forms of governance. It then subsequently presumes the right of European-based peoples to dictate non-Europeans' forms of governance, thus reducing the humanity of non-Europeans, and creating and maintaining a hierarchy in the international system. Such a colonial doctrine, which clearly discriminates against some groups of people in favor of other groups, has no legitimate place in a decolonized international system or in purported "post-colonial" liberal democratic states. Indigenous global politics fights against this doctrine on multiple levels.

Second, indigenous global politics focuses attention on a global dilemma: how to apply universals that allow for difference? Indigenous global politics reveals how injustice can result from the application of universals. For example, the individual rights focus of the international human rights system during its first six decades aimed for universal application of individual human rights in an effort to protect persons from violence and abuse by their governments. However, by exclusively individualizing human rights, the human rights system performed a particular injustice to indigenous peoples who often articulated the necessity of protecting some of their collective rights (e.g. land, religion, language, culture) from the violence and abuse caused by assimilation

---

[1] The Doctrine of Discovery may be embedded in the domestic law of states other than common law states, but this will be explored in future studies. This study focused specifically on those common law states that were over-complying in indigenous rights.

on the part of governments and surrounding societies. Indigenous global politics helps problematize certain taken-for-granted universals like individual human rights that, in their effort to protect all persons equally, can actually *cause* discrimination in some cases. Indigenous global politics also challenges the universal of state sovereignty within the nation-state system since the existing nation-state framework has also performed an injustice against indigenous peoples' rights to land, resources, and self-determination by only recognizing sovereign nation-states in the international system. Indigenous global politics challenges such tenets that encourage assimilation into a global mass. Indigenous global politics, rather, centers on a right to maintain difference.

Third, indigenous global politics imagines and practices international relations differently, incorporating indigenous culture, spirituality, world views and a consensus decision making processes into international politics. It also demonstrates how unity and solidarity can be maintained over an extended period of time and through extremely difficult circumstances. Much of the success of the transnational indigenous rights movement can be attributed to protest and pure tenacity, but some of the credit belongs to the manner in which the indigenous movement conducted global politics. The consensus style, rooted in a respect for the diversity of indigenous cultures and unified by a common indigenous identity, strengthened the solidarity of the indigenous rights movement.

Fourth, the passage of the Declaration on the Rights of Indigenous Peoples enhanced the international protection of indigenous peoples' rights as individuals, but it also forged a particular set of international changes in the nature of human rights and self-determination, which necessarily begins to alter the existing meaning of sovereignty and territoriality. The passage of the Declaration added collective rights to the international human rights consensus, opening a door to collective rights recognition which had always been closed. It also pushed the meaning of self-determination beyond a purely statist and territorial conception by recognizing indigenous peoples' right to self-determination while offering additional protections for state sovereignty. These challenges are significant, and bordering on revolutionary, but they have been largely ignored by the field of international relations. I have also argued that the primary reason for the strong resistance to the emerging indigenous rights regime from a set of normally rights-advocating liberal democratic states emanates from these states' strong investment in the status quo of the international order, particularly centered around explicit and/or implicit reliance on the Doctrine of Discovery.

Fifth, indigenous global politics reveals that the indigenous rights situation, even in advanced liberal democracies typically known for their high standards on human rights, is insufficient. Reconciliation efforts in these countries remain colonizer-centric and represent continued efforts on the part of these states to individualize and assimilate indigenous peoples into their multicultural states and societies, rather than working through a genuine conversation between colonizer and indigenous perspectives on reconciliation. Worst of all, the models of reconciliation being invoked in these countries are leaving the Doctrine of Discovery intact, in both legal and discursive senses. Indigenous global politics aims to expose the shortcomings of these countries in order to help frame future indigenous and indigenous-state discussions.

276

Finally, the move toward a non-statist conception of self-determination[2] and land is the most foundational change being forged by indigenous global politics, and it is the change most actively resisted by states. Since the 1970s, the transnational indigenous rights movement has pushed to shift the international conversation away from one focused solely on discrimination against individuals toward one which also focuses on the right of indigenous nations to self-determination. This push aims to move international politics beyond both a state-centered and individual rights focus to recognize the nationhood status, even if not the statehood status, of indigenous nations. In other words, this international conversation necessarily and inevitably leads to discussions about collective rights and plural sovereignty arrangements if indigenous nationhood is to be recognized without disrupting existing statehood. Indigenous global politics thus forces a rethinking of relationships between indigenous peoples and the state toward a new and just relationship. Such a new relationship requires, first, a global renouncement of the Doctrine of Discovery, a doctrine which in still exists in explicit and implicit formulations in international law and common law countries, and results in a dehumanization of indigenous peoples. Second, achieving new and just relationships then requires a new negotiation of territory and sovereignty based on mutual respect between negotiating partners and accepting indigenous peoples as fully human.

In her 1993 book on indigenous politics at the global level, Franke Wilmer asked if transnational indigenous politics represents a significant development in international politics.[3] In the preceding chapters, I have argued that indigenous global politics does

---

[2] Anaya, *Indigenous Rights in International Law*, 51
[3] Wilmer, *The Indigenous Voice in World Politics, 25.*

indeed present significant challenges to international politics. Indigenous global politics not only theorizes international relations differently, it also practices international relations differently. In addition, it is a normative project which seeks a particular set of changes which challenge some of the fundamental tenets of the international system of sovereign nation-states and the liberal world order. Lest we get too carried away in our exposition of the global change being pushed for by indigenous global politics, however, it is also important to recognize that indigenous global politics also recognizes its limitations. The early workings of a theory of indigenous global politics that I have sketched out here contain more elements of IR realism, and even liberalism, than Wilmer and other scholars of transnational indigenous politics either expect or recognize. While indigenous global politics seeks international change, it remains constrained by many of the recalcitrant features of the existing world order and attempts to work within them in order to make critical changes to them.[4] To hearken back to Moana Jackson's assessment of indigenous global politics, "Our people have never been naively optimistic about the international human rights process. ...We see it not as a panacea but as another tool that can be used"[5] in the broad and larger fight for indigenous rights.

Suggestions for Future Research

This study represents an initial effort to analyze indigenous global politics through the lens of international relations, but much work remains to be done in this area.

---

[4] See James Tully, "The Struggles of Indigenous People for and of Freedom" in *Political Theory and the Rights of Indigenous Peoples,* D. Ivison, P. Patton, and W. Sanders, ed. (Cambridge, Cambridge University Press, 2000).
[5] Interview with Moana Jackson, Wellington, New Zealand, 11 March 2008.

278

I would like to conclude with some suggestions for future projects which can be launched based upon my findings here.

Because there were only two country cases examined in this study, further comparative case work may reveal more conditions and discourses which are significant in states' indigenous rights behavior. The other two recalcitrant states on the Declaration (Australia and the United States) should be further investigated in order to refine the initial findings that I have presented here. While the United States is not an over-compliant country in indigenous rights, it should still be included as a case in future research based upon its vote against the Declaration, since it would serve as a good country for cross-comparison. In addition, a deviant case analysis could be performed by including some countries that voted for the Declaration in order to locate the differences in conditions which led those countries to support, rather than oppose, the Declaration. Further comparative analysis should also be conducted on parliamentary versus presidential systems and their patterns of indigenous rights commitment and compliance.

A similar study could also be conducted which would focus on indigenous rights outcomes in the countries that have already put legal and/or constitutional protections for indigenous peoples into place. Such countries would include Canada, Bolivia, Colombia, and Ecuador. A study of this type would provide an even deeper understanding of the complexities of indigenous rights compliance behavior by individual states. Furthermore, a study of compliant-high countries versus compliant-low countries would also reveal insights about indigenous rights outcomes.

Further investigation of the concept of over-compliance is also called for. A multivariate analysis should be conducted on the compliance data presented in Chapter 4. For purposes of this study, I conducted only a qualitative comparison, examining the data for patterns and trends, but these patterns and trends should be tested through more rigorous quantitative methods. In addition, other human rights areas like children's rights or women's rights should also be examined to see if the indigenous rights compliance pattern of compliance, under-compliance, partial compliance and over-compliance travels to other issue areas or if it is a pattern of state response which is unique to indigenous peoples' rights.

Finally, more qualitative and comparative work should be conducted on the various indigenous visions of reconciliation and new relationships with states. There is already a body of work which examines indigenous reconciliation efforts from the state- and colonizer-centric perspective but very little which puts forward varied indigenous perspectives, indigenous visions of justice, and indigenous peoples' proposed models for renegotiated, plural sovereignty arrangements between indigenous nations and states. If indigenous peoples do not effectively articulate and communicate their perspectives on what these re-negotiated relationships should look like, states and their majority populations will continue to view indigenous hard rights issues in threatening zero-sum terms. A cross-national study which presents alternative models to Doctrine of Discovery-based nation-state sovereignty could be immediately useful in a practical sense, helping to reduce and diffuse the threat that states' see in indigenous rights. Such a study could play a significant role in the larger indigenous rights project, and help move indigenous global politics from its current position of *challenging* existing conceptions of sovereignty, territoriality and liberalism, to a position of affecting real *change* in the understandings of these concepts and toward a more just and post-colonial international order.

Selected Bibliography

"Open Letter: UN Declaration on the Rights of Indigenous Peoples: Canada Needs to Implement the Human Rights Instrument." 1 May 2008.

"The 39th Parliament: Stephen Harper's First Shuffle." *CBC News*, 4 January 2007.

"Nunavut's Challenges." *Christian Science Monitor*, 5 April 1999.

"On the Nunavut Campaign Trail." *CBC News*, 5 March 2008.

"Aboriginal Rally against Police Mistreatment." *nativenewsonline.org*, 6 December 2006.

"Queen 'Treasures' Her Role in Canadian Identity." *CBC Radio*, 8 October 2002.

"Becoming More American." In *The Canadian Encyclopedia*, 10 January 2008.

"Open Letter to the President of the UN Commission on Human Rights, from 130 Indigenous Nations and Organizations." 15 March 2005.

"Historic BC Treaty Opens on Often Caustic BC Legislature with a Party." *United Native News*, 15 October 2007.

"The Current with Anna Maria Tremonti." *CBC Radio One*, 27 March 2008.

"African Group Package, United Nations Declaration on the Rights of Indigenous Peoples." 30 August 2007.

"Indigenous Peoples: Pressing for Greater Rights." *UN Chronicle*, 1993, 95.

"Draft Declaration on Indigenous Peoples Approved." *UN Chronicle*, 1994, 73.

"People or Peoples: Equality, Autonomy, and Self-Determination: The Issues at Stake in the International Decade of the World's Indigenous Peoples." edited by ICHRDD. Montreal: ICHRDD, 1996.

Abbott, K.W. "Elements of a Joint Discipline, International Law and International Relations Theory: Building Bridges." *American Society of International Legal Practice* 86, (1992): 167-68.

Achen, C. and D. Snidal. "Rational Deterrence Theory and Comparative Case Studies." *World Politics* 4, no. 2 (1989): 143-69.

Alfred, Taiaiake. *Peace, Power and Righteousness: An Indigenous Manifesto*. Don Mills, Ontario: Oxford University Press, 1999.

————. "Sovereignty." In *A Companion to American Indian History*, edited by Philip J. and Neal Salisbury Deloria. Malden, MA: Blackwell, 2004.

Algozzine, Dawson R. Hancock and Bob. *Doing Case Study Research: A Practical Guide for Beginning Researchers*. New York: Columbia University Teachers College, 2006.

Alix, Lola Garcia. *"The Permanent Forum for Indigenous Issues"- the Struggle for a New Partnership*. Copenhagen: International Work Group for Indigenous Affairs, 1999.

Alston, Philip. *The United Nations and Human Rights: A Critical Appraisal*. Oxford: Clarendon Press, 1992.

Alves, D. *The Maori and the Crown: An Indigenous People's Struggle for Self-Determination*. New York: Oxford University Press, 1999.

Anaya, S. J., ed. *International Law and Indigenous Peoples*, The Library of Essays in International Law Series. New York: Oxford, 2003.

————. *Indigenous Peoples in International Law*. New York: Oxford University Press,

2004.

Archer, Clive. *International Organizations*. London: Routledge, 1992.

Archie, Carol. *Maori Sovereignty: The Pakeha Perspective*. Auckland, New Zealand: Hodder Moa Beckett, 1995.

Asch, Michael, ed. *Aboriginal and Treaty Rights in Canada: Essays on Law, Equality, and Respect for Difference*. Vancouver, BC: UBC Press, 1998.

Ashely, Richard K. "The Poverty of Neorealism." In *Neorealism and Its Critics*, edited by Robert Keohane. New York: Columbia University, 1986.

Ashley, Richard and R.B.J. Walker. "Introduction: Speaking the Language of Exile: Dissident Thought in International Studies." *International Studies Quarterly* 34, (1990): 259-68.

Banner, Stuart. *Possessing the Pacific: Land, Settlers, and Indigenous Peoples from Australia to Alaska*. Cambridge, MA: Harvard University Press, 2007.

Bargh, Maria, ed. *Resistance*. Wellington, New Zealand: Huia, 2007.

Barkawi, Tarak and Mark Laffey, ed. *Democracy, Liberalism, and War: Rethinking the Democratic Peace Debate*. Boulder, CO: Lynne Rienner, 2001.

―――. "Retrieving the Imperial: Empire and International Relations." *Millennium* 31, no. 1 (2002): 109-27.

Barker, Joanne, ed. *Sovereignty Matters: Locations of Contestation and Possibility in Indigenous Struggles for Self-Determination*. Lincoln, NE: University of Nebraska Press, 2005.

Barnett, Michael and Martha Finnemore. *Rules for the World: International Organizations in Global Politics*. Ithaca, NY: Cornell University Press, 2004.

Barnsley, Paul. "Final Agreement Debated across the Country." *Windspeaker*, 10 August 1998.

Barsch, Russell L. "Indigenous Peoples: An Emerging Object of International Law." *The American Journal of International Law* 80, no. 2 (1986): 369-85.

―――. "Indigenous Peoples and the Un Commission on Human Rights: A Case of the Immovable Object and the Irresistible Force." *Human Rights Quarterly* 18, (1996): 782-813.

―――. "Aboriginal Peoples and Canada's Conscience." In *Hidden in Plain Sight: Contributions of Aboriginal Peoples to Canadian Identity and Culture*, edited by David R Newhouse: Toronto, 2005.

Battiste, Marie, ed. *Reclaiming Indigenous Voice and Vision*. Vancouver, BC: UBC Press, 2000.

Bearce, David and Stacy Bondanella. "Intergovernmental Organizations, Socialization, and Member-State Interest Convergence." *International Organization* 61, no. 4 (2007): 703-33.

Belgrave, Michael, Mareta Kawharu, and David Williams, ed. *Waitangi Revisited: Perspectives on the Treaty of Waitangi*. South Melbourne, Victoria, Australia: Oxford University Press, 2005.

Belgrave, Michael. *Historical Frictions: Maori Claims & Reinvented Histories*. Auckland, New Zealand: Auckland University Press, 2005.

Bennett, Andrew. "Case Study Methods: Design, Use, and Comparative Advantages." In

Methods, Numbers, and Cases: Methods for Studying International Relations, edited by Deltlef F. Sprinz and Yael Wolinsky-Nahmias, 19-45. Ann Arbor, MI: University of Michigan Press, 2004.

Bennington, Seddon. "'Finding Common Ground' Te Papa 2008 Treaty Debate Series, Te Papa National Museum of New Zealand." Wellington, New Zealand, 31 January 2008.

Berg, Bruce L. *Qualitative Research Methods for the Social Sciences, Seventh Edition*. Boston: Allyn & Bacon, 2009.

Bern, John and Susan Dodds. "On the Plurality of Interests: Aboriginal Self-Government and Land Rights." In *Political Theory and the Rights of Indigenous Peoples*, edited by D. Ivison, P. Patton, and D. Sanders. Cambridge: Cambridge University Press, 2000.

Bhaha, Homi. *The Location of Culture*. London: Routledge, 1994.

Bishop, Russell. "Freeing Ourselves from Neocolonial Domination in Research: A Kaupapa Māori Approach to Creating Knowledge." In *The Sage Handbook of Qualitative Research, Third Edition*, edited by Norman K. Denzin, and Yvonna S. Lincoln, 109-38. Thousand Oaks, CA: Sage, 2005.

Black, Ezra. "New Zealand's Police Accused of Representing Indigenous Maori." *McGill Daily*, 25 October 2007.

Blackburn, Carole. "Searching for Guarantees in the Midst of Uncertainty: Negotiating Aboriginal Rights and Title in British Columbia." *American Anthropologist* (2005): 586-96.

Boast, Richard. *Foreshore and Seabed*. Wellington, New Zealand: LexisNexis New Zealand, 2005.

Bodley, John H. *Victims of Progress*. Mountain View, CA: Mayfield Publishing, 1999.

Boldt, Menno, and J. Anthony Long, ed. *The Quest for Justice: Aboriginal Peoples and Aboriginal Rights*. Toronto: University of Toronto Press, 1985.

Boldt, Menno. *Surviving as Indians: The Challenge of Self-Government*. Toronto: University of Toronto Press, 1998.

Boli, John and George Thomas, ed. *Constructing World Culture: International Nongovernmental Organizations since 1875*. Stanford: Stanford University Press, 1999.

Borrows, John. *Recovering Canada: The Resurgence of Indigenous Law*. Toronto: University of Toronto Press, 2007.

Borrows, John J. and Leonard I. Rotman. *Aboriginal Legal Issues: Cases, Materials & Commentary*. Toronto: Butterworths, 1998.

Bositis, David. *Research Designs for Political Science: Contrivance and Demonstration in Theory and Practice*. Carbondale, IL: Southern Illinois University Press, 1990.

Brash, Don. "Speech to the Orewa Rotary Club." 27 January 2004.

Brierly, J.L. *The Law of Nations: An Introduction to the International Law of Peace*. Oxford: Clarendon, 1978.

Briggs, Kara. "U.N. Declaration Rights Is Gaining Momentum." *Indian Country Today*, 14 May 2008.

Brookfield, F.M. *Waitangi & Indigenous Rights: Revolution, Law & Legitimation*.

Auckland: Auckland University Press, 2006.

Brown, Russell. *Great New Zealand Argument: Ideas About Ourselves*. Auckland, New Zealand: Activity Press Ltd, 2005.

Brysk, Allison. *The Politics of Human Rights in Argentina: Protest, Change and Democratization*. Stanford: Stanford University Press, 1994.

———. *From Tribal Village to Global Village: Indian Rights and International Relations in Latin America*. Stanford: Stanford University Press., 2000.

Buergenthal, Thomas. *International Human Rights in a Nutshell*. 2nd ed. St. Paul, MN: West Publishing, 1995.

Bull, Hedley. "The Grotian Conception of International Society." In *Diplomatic Investigations: Essays in the Theory of International Politics*, edited by H. and M. Wight Butterfield. London: Allen & Unwin, 1966.

———. *The Anarchical Society: A Study of World Politics*. New York: Columbia University Press, 1977.

———. "The Importance of Grotius in the Study of International Relations." In *Hugo Grotius and International Relations*, edited by H. Bull, B. Kingsbury, and A. Roberts. Oxford: Clarendon Press, 1992.

Burger, J. *Report from the Frontier: The State of the World's Indigenous Peoples*. London: Zed Press, 1987.

———. "Indigenous Peoples and the United Nations." In *The Human Rights of Indigenous Peoples*, edited by Cynthia Price Cohen, 3-16. Ardsley, NY: Transnational Publishers, 1998.

Burgers, J. Herman. "The Road to San Francisco: The Revival of the Human Rights Ideas in the Twentieth Century " *Human Rights Quarterly* 14, no. 4 (1992): 447-77.

Burgos-Debray, Elisabeth, ed. *I, Rigoberta Menchú: An Indian Woman in Guatemala*. London: Verso, 1984.

Byers, Michael. *Intent for a Nation: What Is Canada For? A Relentlessly Optimistic Manifesto for Canada's Role in the World* Vancouver, BC: Douglas & MacIntyre, 2007.

Byrnes, Giselle. *The Waitangi Tribunal and New Zealand History*. South Melbourne, Victoria, Australia: Oxford University Press, 2004.

Calí, Francisco. "Presentation on the CERD, Human Rights Training Session." Mille Lacs Indian Museum, Minnesota, 27 September 2007.

Camp Keith, Linda. "The United Nations International Covenant on Civil and Political Rights: Does It Make a Difference in Human Rights Behavior." *Journal of Peace Research* 36, no. 1 (1999): 95-118.

Campbell, Donald T. "'Degrees of Freedom' and the Case Study." In *Methodology and Epistemology for Social Science*, edited by E. Samuel Overman, 377-88. Chicago: Chicago University Press, 1975 (1988).

Carden, Steven. *New Zealand Unleashed: The Country, Its Future and the People Who Will Get It There*. Auckland, New Zealand: Random House, 2007.

Cardinal, Harold. *The Unjust Society*. Vancouver, BC: Douglas and MacIntyre, 1999.

Carmen, Andrea. "Statement at Human Rights Training Session." Mille Lacs Indian Museum, Minnesota, 27 September 2007.

Carr, Edward Hallet. *The Twenty Year's Crisis, 1919-1939* New York: Perennial, 2000
   (1939).

Cassidy, Michael. "Treaties and Aboriginal-Government Relations, 1945-2000." In
   *Hidden in Plain Sight: Contributions of Aboriginal Peoples to Canadian Identity
   and Culture*, edited by David R Newhouse. Toronto: University of Toronto Press,
   2005.

Center for Human Rights. "The Rights of Indigenous Peoples: Human Rights Fact Sheet
   No. 2." Geneva: United Nations, 1990.

Central Intelligence Agency. "The 2008 World Factbook ", 2008.

Chakrabarty, Dipesh. *Provincializing Europe: Postcolonial Thought and Historical
   Difference*. Princeton, NJ: Princeton University Press, 2000.

Champagne, Duane, Karen Jo Torjesen and Susan Steiner. *Indigenous Peoples and the
   Modern State*. Walnut Creek, CA: Alta Mira Press, 2005.

Charters, Claire. "An Imbalance of Powers: Māori Land Claims and an Unchecked
   Parliament." *Cultural Survival Quarterly* (2006): 32-35.

Chartrand, A.H., ed. *Who Are Canada's Aboriginal Peoples? Recognition, Definition,
   and Jurisdiction*. Saskatoon, SK: Purich Publishing Ltd, 2002.

Chavez, Frank. "Bolivia: Morales Gets Boost from the Un Declaration on the Rights of
   Indigenous Peoples." *www.ipsnews.net*, 10 September 2007.

Chayes, A. and A. Chayes. "On Compliance." *International Organization* 47, no. 2
   (1993): 175-205.

Chivers, C.J. "Russia Plants Underwater Flag at North Pole." *New York Times*, 2 August
   2007.

Chowdhry, Geeta and Sheila Nair, ed. *Power, Postcolonialism and International
   Relations: Reading Race, Gender and Class*. New York: Routledge, 2002.

Chretien, Prime Minister Jean. "The Canadian Way in the 21st Century. Speech.", 203
   June 2000.

Christie, Gordon, ed. *Aboriginality and Governance: A Multidisciplinary Perspective*.
   Ottawa, ON: Theytus Books, 2006.

Clark, Ann Marie. *Diplomacy of Conscience: Amnesty International and Changing
   Human Rights Norms*. Princeton: Princeton University Press, 2001.

Clark, Prime Minister Helen. "Statement to Parliament." 1 February 2005.

———. "Address to Parliament." Wellington, New Zealand, 1 February 2005.

———. "Opening Remarks At "Concepts of Nationhood: Marking 100 Years since the
   Proclamation of Dominion Status for New Zealand." Parliament, Wellington,
   New Zealand, 26 September 2007.

Coates, Kenneth S. *A Global History of Indigenous Peoples: Struggle and Survival*.
   Hampshire: Palgrave Macmillan, 2004.

Coates, Ken S. and P.G. McHugh. *Living Relationships/Kōkiri Ngatahi: The Treaty of
   Waitangi in the New Millennium*. Wellington, New Zealand: Victoria University
   Press, 1998.

Cobo, José Martinez. *Study of the Problem of Discrimination against Indigenous
   Populations, Volume V: Conclusions*. New York: United Nations, 1987.

Cohen, Andrew. *The Unfinished Canadian: The People We Are*. Toronto: McClennand &

Stewart Ltd., 2007.

Cohen, Cynthia Price. *Human Rights of Indigenous Peoples*. Ardsley, NY: Transnational Publishers, 1998.

Cole, Wade M. "Sovereignty Relinquished? Explaining Commitment to the International Human Rights Covenants, 1966-1999." *American Sociological Review* 70, (2005): 472-95.

Collier, D. "Degrees of Freedom and the Case Study." *Comparative Political Studies* 8, no. 2 (1995): 178-94.

Commission, British Columbia Treaty. "Six Stages: Policies and Procedures." Vancouver, 2007.

Confederacy of Treaty Six First Nations and the International Indian Treaty Council (IITC). "Press Release: The Un Committee on the Elimination of Racial Discrimination Calls Upon Canada to Immediately Endorse the United Nations Declaration on the Rights of Indigenous Peoples." 8 March 2007.

Consedine, Robert and Joanna Consedine. *Healing Our History: The Challenge of the Treaty of Waitangi*. Auckland, New Zealand: Penguin, 2005.

Council, First Nations leadership. "Press Release: First Nations Mining Summit Set for October in Prince George." 8 July 2008.

Cox, Lindsay. *Kotahitanga: The Search for Māori Political Unity*. Oxford: Oxford University Press, 1993.

Cox, Robert W. "Gramsci, Hegemony and International Relations: An Essay in Method." *Millennium* 12, no. 2 (1983): 162-75.

Cram, F. "Rangahau Māori: Tona Tika, Tona Pono--the Validity and Integrity of Māori Research." In *Research Ethics and Aotearoa New Zealand*, edited by M Tolich, 2001.

Cullis-Suzuki, Severn, Kris Frederickson, Ahmed Kayssi, Cynthia MacKenzie, ed. *Notes from Canada's Young Activists: A Generation Stands up for Change*. Vancouver, BC: Douglas and MacIntyre, 2007.

Curry, Steven. *Indigenous Sovereignty and the Democratic Project*. Burlington, VT: Ashgate, 2004.

Daes, Erica-Irene A. "Equality of Indigenous Peoples under the Auspices of the United Nations: Draft Declaration on the Rights of Indigenous Peoples." *St. Thomas Law Review* 7, (1995): 493-519.

———. "Some Considerations on the Right of Indigenous Peoples to Self-Determination." In *International Law and Indigenous Peoples*, edited by S. James Anaya. Burlington, VT: Ashgate, 2003.

Danspeckgrubr, Wolfgang. *The Self-Determination of Peoples: Community, Nation, and State in an Interdependent World*. Boulder, CO: Lynne Rienner, 2002.

Darby, Philip. "Pursuing the Political: A Postcolonial Rethinking of Relations International." *Millennium* 33, no. 1 (2004): 1-32.

Davis, Megan. "Indigenous Struggles in Standard-Setting: The United Nations Declaration on the Rights of Indigenous Peoples." *Melbourne Journal of International Law* 9, (2008).

de Bres, Joris. "'Finding Common Ground' Te Papa 2008 Treaty Debate Series, Te Papa

National Museum of New Zealand." Wellington, New Zealand, 7 February 2008.

de Bres, JorisDurie, Mason. "'Finding Common Ground' Te Papa 2008 Treaty Debate Series, Te Papa National Museum of New Zealand." Wellington, New Zealand, 31 January 2008.

de la Cadena, Marisol and Orin Starn, ed. *Indigenous Experience Today*. Oxford: Berg, 2007.

Dean, Bartholomew and Jerome M. Levi, ed. *At the Risk of Being Heard: Identity, Indigenous Rights, and Postcolonial States*. An Arbor, MI: The University of Michigan Press, 2003.

Deloria, Jr., Vine. *Custer Died for Your Sins*. Norman, OK: University of Oklahoma Press, 1969 (1988).

———. *Behind the Trail of Broken Treaties*. Austin, TX: University of Texas Press, 1974.

Deloria, Jr., Vine and David E. Wilkins. *Tribes, Treaties and Constitutional Tribulations*. Austin, TX: University of Texas Press, 1999.

Deloria, Jr., Vine. *For This Land: Writings on Religion in America*. New York: Routledge, 1999.

Denoon, Donald, Philippa Mein-Smith. *A History of Australia, New Zealand and the Pacific*. Oxford: Blackwell Publishers, 2000.

DePalma, Anthony. "Canada's Eskimos Get Land of Their Own." *New York Times*, 2 April 1999.

Der Derian, James and Michael J. Shapiro, ed. *International/Intertextual Relations: Postmodern Readings of World Politics*. Lexington, MA: Lexington Books, 1989.

Dion, D. "Evidence and Inference in the Comparative Case Study." In *Necessary Conditions: Theory, Methodology, and Applications*, edited by G. and H. Starr Goertz. Boulder, CO: Rowman and Littlefield, 2003.

Donnelly, Jack. "International Human Rights: A Regime Analysis." *International Organization* 40, no. 3 (1986): 599-642.

———. *Universal Human Rights in Theory and Practice*. Ithaca, NY: Cornell University Press, 1989.

———. *International Human Rights*. Boulder, CO: Westview, 1998.

Doty, Roxanne. *Imperial Encounters*. Minneapolis, MN: University of Minnesota Press, 1996.

Downs, G.W., D. Rocke, et. al. "Is the Good News About Compliance Good News About Cooperation?" In *International Institutions: An International Organization Reader*, edited by L. Martin and Beth A. Simons, 279-306. Cambridge, MA: MIT Press, 2001.

Doyle, Michael W. "Liberalism and World Politics." *The American Political Science Review* 80, no. 4 (1986): 1151-69.

———. *Ways of War and Peace: Realism, Liberalism, and Socialism*. New York: W.W. Norton & Co., 1997.

Dunbar-Ortiz, Roxanne. "The First Decade of Indigenous Peoples at the United Nations." *Peace & Change* 31, no. 1 (2006): 58-74.

Durie, E.G. and G.S. Orr. "The Constitutional Status of the Treaty of Waitangi: An

Historical Perspective." *New Zealand Law Review* 14, (1990): 9-36.

Durie, Mason. *Te Mana, Te Kāwanatanga: The Politics of Māori Self-Determination.* Oxford: Oxford University Press, 1998.

Eisner, E. *The Enlightened Eye: Qualitative Inquiry and the Enhancement of Educational Practice.* Columbus, OH: Merrrill, 1997.

Epp, Charles. *The Rights Revolution.* Chicago: University of Chicago Press, 1998.

Erueti, Andrew and Claire Charters, ed. *Maori Property Rights and the Foreshore and Seabed: The Last Frontier.* Wellington, New Zealand: Victoria University Press, 2007.

Eudaily, Sean Patrick. *The Present Politics of the Past: Indigenous Legal Activism and Resistance to (Neo)Liberal Governmentality.* New York: Grove Press, 2004.

Evison, Harry C. *The Treaty of Waitangi and the Waitangi Tribunal: Fact or Fiction.* Christchurch, New Zealand: Ngai Tahu Māori Trust Board, 1990.

Ewen, Alexander and the Native American Council of New York City, ed. *Voice of Indigenous Peoples: Native People Address the United Nations.* Santa Fe: Clear Light Publishers, 1994.

Faculty of Arts, Canadian Studies, Mount Allison University. "About Canada: Multiculturalism in Canada." Sackville, New Brunswick, 2007.

Fanon, Franz. *The Wretched of the Earth.* New York: Grove Press, 1963.

Finnemore, Martha. "Norms, Culture and World Politics: Insights from Sociology's Institutionalism." *International Organization* 50, no. 2 (1996): 325-47.

Finnemore, Martha and Kathryn Sikkink. "International Norm Dynamics and Political Change." *International Organization* 52, no. 4 (1998): 887-917.

———. "Taking Stock: The Constructivist Research Program in International Relations and Comparative Politics." *Annual Review of Political Science* 4, (2001): 391-416.

First Nations Leadership Council. "Press Release: First Nations Pressure Canada to Endorse the United Nations Declaration on the Rights of Indigenous Peoples on the Eve of Its Adoption.", 12 September 2008.

———. "Press Release: First Nations Leadership Council Troubled by Today's Vote at the United Nations, Inaction on Declaration on the Rights of Indigenous Peoples Inexcusable.", 13 September 2007.

Fleras, Augie and Paul Spoonley. *Recalling Aotearoa: Indigenous Politics and Ethnic Relations in New Zealand.* Auckland, New Zealand: Oxford University Press, 1999.

Foot, Rosemary, Neil McFarlane and Michael Mastanduno. *Us Hegemony and International Organizations.* New York: Oxford University Press, 2002.

Franck, T.M. *Fairness in International Law and Institutions.* New York: Clarendon Press, 1995.

Gardiner, Wira. *Haka: A Living Tradition, Second Edition.* Auckland, New Zealand: Hodder Moa Books, 2007.

Gardner, Dan. "Get over Yourself, Canada." *Vancouver Sun*, 19 January 2009.

Geddes, B. "How the Cases You Choose Affect the Answers You Get: Selection Bias in Comparative Politics." *Political Analysis* 2, no. 31-50 (1990).

Geddes, John. "Canadian Nationalism in Decline, Says Poll." *Maclean's*, 23 January 2006.

George, Alexander L. and Andrew Bennett. *Case Studies and Theory Development in the Social Sciences*. Cambridge, MA: MIT Press, 2005.

Gerring, John. "What Is a Case Study and What Is It Good For?" *American Political Science Review* 98, (2004): 341-54.

———. *Case Study Research: Principles and Practices*. Cambridge: Cambridge University Press, 2007.

Gilpin, Robert *War and Change in World Politics*. Cambridge: Cambridge University Press, 1983.

Goodwin, Jeff and James M. Jasper. *Rethinking Social Movements: Structure, Meaning and Emotion*. Lanham, MD: Rowman & Littlefield, 2004.

Government of Canada. *Aboriginal Self-Government: The Government of Canada's Approach to Implementation of the Inherent Right and the Negotiation of Self-Government*. Ottawa: Minister of Public Work and Government Services, 1995.

Government of Canada. Canadian Ministry of Foreign Affairs. "Statement at the 7th Session of the Permanent Forum on Indigenous Issues." New York, 28 April 2008.

Government of Canada. Department of Canadian Heritage.: www.patromoinecanadien.gc.ca.

———. *Canadian Diversity: Respecting Our Differences*. Ottawa2008.

Government of Canada. Department of Canadian Heritage. Multiculturalism National Office. "Canada's Action Plan against Racism: A Canada for All." Gatineau, Quebec, 2005.

Government of Canada. Department of Indian and Northern Affairs. "Nisga'a Final Agreement Act Issue Papers." 1998.

Government of Canada. Department of Canadian Heritage. "Canadian Diversity: Respecting Our Differences ". Ottawa., 2008.

Government of Canada. Department of Indian and Northern Affairs. "Fact Sheet: Nisga'a Treaty." 2000.

———. "Nisga'a Final Agreement 2001 Annual Report." 2001.

Government of Nunavut. "Statement to the 7th Session of the Un Permanent Forum on Indigenous Issues." New York, 29 April 2008.

Graham, Bill. *Case Study Research Methods*. London: Continuum, 2000.

Gregory, Derek. *The Colonial Present: Afghanistan, Palestine, Iraq*. Malden, MA: Blackwell, 2004.

Gruber, Lloyd. *Ruling the World: Power Politics and the Rise of Supranational Institutions*. Chicago: University of Chicago Press, 2000.

Hardt, Michael and Antonio Negri. *Multitude: War and Democracy in the Age of Empire*. New York: Penguin, 2004.

Harring, Sidney L. "Indian Law, Sovereignty, and State Law." In *A Companion to American Indian History*, edited by Philip J. and Neal Salisbury Deloria. Malden, MA: Blackwell, 2004.

Harris, Aroha. *Hīkoi: Forty Years of Māori Protest* Wellington, New Zealand: Huia

Publishers, 2004.

Hathaway, A. O. "The Cost of Commitment." *Stanford Law Review* 55, no. 3 (2003): 1821-62.

Havemann, P., ed. *Indigenous Peoples' Rights in Australia, Canada and New Zealand.* Oxford: Oxford University Press, 2000.

———. "Introduction." In *Political Theory and the Rights of Indigenous Peoples*, edited by P. Patton D. Ivison, W. Sanders. Cambridge: Cambridge University Press, 2000.

Hawkins, Darren and Wade Jacoby. "Partial Compliance: A Comparison of the European and Inter-American Courts for Human Rights." Paper Presented at the 2008 Annual Meeting of the American Political Science Association, Boston, 2008.

Hayward, Janine and Nicola R. Wheen, ed. *The Waitangi Tribunal: Te Roopu Whakamana I Te Tiriti O Waitangi.* Wellington, New Zealand: Bridget Williams Books, 2004.

Hill, Ronald Paul. "Blackfellas and Whitefellas: Aboriginal Land Rights, the *Mabo* Decision, and the Meaning of Land." *Human Rights Quarterly* 17, no. 2 (1995): 303-22.

Hill, Richard S. *State Authority, Indigenous Autonomy: Crown-Maori Relations in New Zealand/Aotearoa 1900-1950.* Wellington, New Zealand: Victoria University Press, 2004.

Hocking, Barbara Ann, ed. *Unfinished Constitutional Business? Rethinking Indigenous Self-Determination.* Canberra: Aboriginal Studies Press, 2005.

Holder, Cindy L. and Jeff Corntassel. "Indigenous Peoples and Multicultural Citizenship: Bridging Collective and Individual Rights." *Human Rights Quarterly* 24, no. 1 (2002): 126-51.

Horn, Katherine. "Canada Confesses to Part of Its Crimes against Humanity." *Mohawk Nation News*, 14 June 2008.

Howard, Bradley Reed. *Indigenous Peoples and the State: The Struggle for Native Rights.* DeKalb, IL: Northern Illinois University Press 2003.

Human Rights Council. "Resolution 1995/32." 3 March 1995.

Ignatieff, Michael. "Human Rights: The Midlife Crisis." *New York Review of Books* (1999).

Ikenberry, G. John. *After Victory: Institutions, Strategic Restraint and the Rebuilding of Order after Major Wars.* Princeton, NJ: Princeton University Press, 2001.

Inayatullah, Naeem and David Blaney. *International Relations and the Problem of Difference.* New York: Routledge, 2003.

Indigenous Caucus. "Statement." Geneva, 25 October 1996.

———. "Press Release: Hunger Strike by Indigenous Peoples' Representatives at the United Nations." Geneva, 29 November 2004.

Indigenous Peoples' Caucus. "Press Release: Indigenous Peoples' Caucus Calls for Change to Un Rules." 28 October 1996.

Indigenous Peoples' Caucus Regional Steering Committee. "Press Release: United Nations General Assembly Adopts the United Nations Declaration on the Rights of Indigenous Peoples." 13 September 2007.

291

International Indian Treaty Council (IITC). "Submission to the Un Committee on the Elimination of Racial Discrimination (CERD)." 14 February 2007.

———. "Statement at the Open-Ended Inter-Sessional Working Group on the Draft Declaration." Geneva, 20 November 1995.

———. "Statement on Behalf of the Indigenous Caucus." Geneva, 25 October 1996.

———. "The Geneva Conference: International Ngo Conference on Discrimination against Indigenous Peoples in the Americas." New York: International Indian Treaty Council, 1977.

International Work Group for Indigenous Affairs (IWGIA). *The Indigenous World 2006*. Copenhagen: IWGIA, 2006.

———. *The Indigenous World 2007*. Copenhagen: IWGIA, 2007.

Ivison, D., P. Patton, and D. Sanders, ed. *Political Theory and the Rights of Indigenous Peoples*. Cambridge: Cambridge University Press, 2000.

Jean, The Right Honourable Michaëlle. Governor General of Canada. "Installation Speech." 27 September 2005.

Jervis, Robert. "Cooperation under the Security Umbrella." *World Politics* 30, (1978): 167-214.

Johal, Am. "Native Tribes Fight to Block Pipeline." *IPS News*, 22 September 2006.

Johnson, Harold. *Two Families: Treaties and Government*. Saskatoon, SK: Purich Publishing, 2007.

Kawharu, I.H., ed. *Waitangi: Maori & Pakeha Perspectives of the Treaty of Waitangi*. Auckland, New Zealand: Oxford University Press, 1996.

Keal, Paul. *Conquest and the Rights of Indigenous Peoples*. Cambridge: Cambridge University Press, 2003.

Kearns, Rick. "U.N. Declaration Becomes Law of the Land in Bolivia." *Indian Country Today*, 12 December 2007.

Keck, Margaret E. and Kathryn Sikkink. *Activists Beyond Borders: Advocacy Networks in International Politics*. Ithaca, NY: Cornell University Press, 1998.

Kennedy, David. "The International Human Rights Movement: Part of the Problem?" *Harvard Human Rights Journal* 15, (2002): 101-26.

Keohane, Robert and Lisa Martin. "The Promise of Institutionalist Theory." *International Security* 20, no. 1 (1995): 39-51.

———. "Institutional Theory as a Research Program." In *Progress in International Relations Theory: Appraising the Field*, edited by Colin and Miriam Elman Elman. Cambridge, MA: MIT Press, 2003.

Keohane, Robert O. "International Relations and International Law: Two Optics." *Harvard Journal of International Law* 38, no. 2 (1997): 487-501.

Kernerman, Gerland. *Multicultural Nationalism: Civilizing Difference, Constituting Community*. Vancouver, BC: UBC Press, 2005.

King, Gary, Robert O. Keohane, and Sidney Verba. *Designing Social Inquiry: Scientific Inference in Qualitative Research*. Princeton, NJ: Princeton University Press, 1994.

King, Michael. *Being Pakeha Now: Reflections and Recollections of a White Native*. Auckland: Penguin, 1999.

King, Michael. *The Penguin History of New Zealand*. Auckland, New Zealand: Penguin Books, 2003.

————. *Nga Iwi O Te Motu*. Auckland, New Zealand: Reed Publishing (NZ) Ltd Te Karuhi Tā Tāpui o Reed (Aotearoa), 2006.

Kingsbury, B. "The Concept of Compliance as a Function of Competing Conceptions of International Law." *Michigan Journal of International Law* 19, no. 2 (1998): 345-75.

————. "Indigenous Peoples' in International Law--a Constructivist Approach to the Asian Controversy." *The American Journal of International Law* 92, (1998): 414-57.

Kirgis, Jr., Frederic L. . "The Degrees of Self-Determination in the United Nations Era." *The American Journal of International Law* 88, (1994): 304-10.

Klotz, Audie and Deepa Prakash, ed. *Qualitative Methods in International Relations: A Pluralist Guide*. New York: Palgrave MacMillan, 2008.

Kly, Y.N. and D. Kly, ed. *In Pursuit of the Right to Self-Determination: Collected Papers & Proceedings of the First International Conference on the Right to Self-Determination & the United Nations, Geneva 2000*. Atlanta, GA: Clarity Press, 2001.

Koh, H. "Why Do Nations Obey International Law?" *Yale Law Review* 106, no. 8 (1997): 2598-659.

Korman, Sharon. *The Right of Conquest: The Acquisition of Territory by Force in International Law and Practice*. Oxford: Clarendon Press, 1996.

Kowert, Paul and Jeffrey Legro. "Norms, Identity, and Their Limits: A Theoretical Reprise." In *The Culture of National Security*, edited by Peter J. Katzenstein. New York: Columbia University Press, 1996.

Krasner, Stephen D. *International Regimes*. Ithaca, NY: Cornell University Press, 1983.

————. "Sovereignty, Regimes, and Human Rights." In *Regime Theory and International Relations*, edited by Volker Rittberger. Oxford: Clarendon Press, 1993.

————. *Sovereignty: Organized Hypocrisy*. Princeton: Princeton University Press, 1999.

Kvale, Steinar and Svend Brinkmann. *Interviews: Learning the Craft of Qualitative Interviewing*. Los Angeles: Sage, 2009.

Kymlicka, Will, ed. *The Rights of Minority Cultures*. Oxford: Oxford University Press, 1995.

————. "Theorizing Indigenous Rights." *University of Toronto Law Journal* 49, (1999): 281-93.

————. *Multicultural Odysseys: Navigating the New International Politics of Diversity*. Oxford: Oxford University Press, 2007.

Laffey, Mark and Tarak Barkawi. "Retrieving the Imperial: Empire and International Relations." *Millennium: Journal of International Studies* 31, no. 1 (2002): 109-27.

Lake, David A. "Anarchy, Hierarchy, and the Variety of International Relations." *International Organization* 50, no. 1 (1996): 1-33.

Lâm, Maivan Clech. *At the Edge of the State: Indigenous Peoples and Self-Determination*. Ardsley, NY: Transnational Publishers, 2000.

293

Lameman, Ron, Confederacy of Treaty Six First Nations. "Statement at Human Rights Training Session." Mille Lacs Indian Museum, Minnesota, 27 September 2007.

Langer, Erick D. and Elena Muñoz. *Contemporary Indigenous Movements in Latin America*. Wilmington, DE: SR Books, 2003.

Langton, Marcia, Maureen Tehan, Lisa Palmer and Kathryn Shain, ed. *Honour among Nations? Treaties and Agreements with Indigenous Peoples*. Melbourne, Victoria, Australia: Melbourne University Press, 2004.

Lauren, Paul Gordon. *The Evolution of International Human Rights* Philadelphia: University of Pennsylvania Press, 1996.

Lawrey, A. "Contemporary Efforts to Guarantee Indigenous Rights under International Law." *Vanderbilt Journal of Transnational Law* 23, no. 4 (1990): 703-77.

Leslie, Keith. "First Nations Vow to Occupy Eastern Ontario Site to Block Uranium Mining." *The Canadian Press* 11 January 2008.

Levy, Jack. "Case Studies: Type, Designs, and the Logics of Inference." *Conflict Management and Peace Science* 25, (2008): 1-18.

Levy, Marc A., Oran R. Young and Michael Zurn. "The Study of International Regimes." *European Journal of International Relations* 1, no. 3 (1995): 268-312.

Library, University of Minnesota Human Rights. "Ratification of International Human Rights Treaties." edited by Ilhan and Taobo Zheng Isik, 2008.

Lijphart, Arend. "Comparative Politics and Comparative Method." *American Political Science Review* 65, (1971): 682-93.

———, ed. *Parliamentary Versus Presidential Government*. Oxford: Oxford University Press, 1992.

Lijphart, A. *Patterns of Democracy: Government Forms and Performance in Thirty-Six Countries*. New Haven, CT: Yale University Press, 1999.

Lijphart, Arend. "The Comparable Cases Strategy in Comparative Research." In *Case Study Research, Volume Iii*, edited by Matthew David. London: Sage, 2006.

Lockyer, Debra. "Nisga'a Celebrate Final Agreement." *Windspeaker*, 4 August 1988.

Lubicon Lake Indian Nation. "Submission to the 70th Session of the Un Committee on the Elimination of Racial Discrmination with Regard to the Lack of Canadian Compliance with Un Human Rights Decisions and General Recommendation No. 23." March 2007.

Lutz, Ellen L. and Kathryn Sikkink. "International Human Rights Law and Practice in Latin America." *International Organization* 54, no. 3 (2000): 633-59.

Lynch, Brian, ed. *Celebrating New Zealand's Emergence*. Wellington, New Zealand: New Zealand Institute of International Affairs 2005.

———, ed. *New Zealand and the World: The Major Foreign Policy Issues, 2005-2010*. Wellington, New Zealand: New Zealand Institute of International Affairs, 2006.

Lyons, Chief Oren. "Statement at the 7th Session of the Un Permanent Forum on Indigenous Issues." New York, 29 April 2008.

Maaka, R. and A, Fleras. "Engaging with Indigeneity: Tino Rangatiratanga in Aotearoa." In *Indigenous Peoples' Rights in Australia, Canada and New Zealand*, edited by P. Patton D. Ivison, W. Sanders. Oxford: Oxford University Press, 2002.

Maaka, Roger and Augie Fleras. *The Politics of Indigeneity: Challenging the State in*

Canada and Aotearoa New Zealand. Dunedin, New Zealand: University of Otago Press, 2005.

Mackey, Eva. *The House of Difference: Cultural Politics and National Identity in Canada.* London: Routledge, 1999.

Magallanes, C. J. "International Human Rights and Their Impact on Domestic Law on Indigenous Peoples' Rights in Australia, Canada and New Zealand." In *Indigenous Peoples' Rights in Australia, Canada and New Zealand*, edited by P. Havemann, 235-76. Oxford: Oxford University Press, 1999.

Malezar, Les. "Urgent Message - Indigenous Peoples - Global Consultation - Important Notice." 1 September 2007.

Malezar, Les, and Mililani Trask, Pacific Regional Coordinators on the Draft Declaration on the Rights of Indigenous Peoples. "Urgent Request and Update Relating to Final Un Action on the Declaration on the Rights of Indigenous Peoples." 2 September 2007.

Mallard, Trevor, Race Relations Commissioner "We Are All New Zealanders Now." Wellington, New Zealand, 28 July 2004.

Martin, Lisa. "Interests, Power and Multilateralism." In *International Institutions: An International Organization Reader*, edited by Lisa and Beth Simmons Martin. Cambridge, MA: MIT Press, 2001.

Martin, Lisa and Beth Simmons. "International Organizations and Institutions." In *Handbook of International Relations*, edited by Walter Carlsneas, Thomas Risse and Beth Simmons. London: Sage, 2002.

Martinez, Enrique Javier Ochoa, First Secretary, Humanitarian and Social Issues, Permanent Mission of Mexico to the United Nations as a Progress Report on the Declaration on the Rights of Indigenous Peoples. "Statement." Church Center at the UN, New York, 12 April 2007.

Matthews, Robert O. and Cranford Pratt, ed. *Human Rights in Canadian Foreign Policy.* Montreal: McGill-Queen's University Press, 1988.

Maxwell, Joseph A. *Qualitative Research Design: An Interpretive Approach, Second Edition.* Thousand Oaks, CA: Sage, 2005.

Maybury-Lewis, David, ed. *The Politics of Ethnicity: Indigenous Peoples in Latin American States.* Cambridge, MA: Harvard University Press, 2002.

Mbembe, Achille. *On the Postcolony.* Berkeley: University of California Press, 2001.

McAdam, Doug, John D. McCarthy, and Mayer N. Zald. *Comparative Perspectives on Social Movements.* Cambridge: Cambridge University Press, 1996.

McKreery, Christopher. *The Order of Canada.* Toronto: University or Toronto, 2005.

McNee, John, Ambassador, Permanent Representative of Canada to the United Nations. "Statement." (13 September 2007).

Mearsheimer, John J. "The False Promise of International Institutions." *International Security* 19, (1994): 5-49.

———. *The Tragedy of Great Power Politics.* New York: W.W. Norton & Co., 2001.

Mehta, Uday Singh. *Liberalism and Empire.* Chicago: University of Chicago Press, 1999.

Melbourne, Hineani. *Maori Sovereignty: The Maori Sovereignty.* Auckland, New Zealand: Hodder Moa Beckett, 1995.

Memmi, Albert. *The Colonizer and the Colonized*. Boston: Beacon Press, 1965.

Meron, T. *Human Rights Norms and Humanitarian Norms as Customary Law*. Oxford: Clarendon Press, 1989.

Merriam, S. *Qualitative Research and Case Study Applications in Education*. San Francisco: Jossey-Bass, 1998.

Meuhlebach, Andrea. "'Making Place' at the United Nations: Indigenous Cultural Politics at the U.N. Working Group on Indigenous Populations." *Cultural Anthropology* 16, no. 3 (2001): 415-48.

Mignolo, Walter D. *Local Histories/Global Designs*. Princeton, NJ: Princeton University Press, 2000.

———. *The Darker Side of the Renaissance*. Ann Arbor, MI: University of Michigan Press, 2003.

Miller, Raymond, ed. *New Zealand Government and Politics*. South Melbourne, Victoria, Australia: Oxford University Press, 2003.

Miller, Robert J. *Native America, Discovered and Conquered: Thomas Jefferson, Lewis & Clark and Manifest Destiny*. Westport, CT: Praeger, 2006.

Mills, P. Dawn. *For Future Generations: Reconciling Gitxsan and Canadian Law*. Saskatoon, SK: Purich Publishing Ltd, 2008.

Milner, Helen. *Interests, Institutions, and Information: Domestic Politics and International Relations*. Princeton, NJ: Princeton University Press, 1997.

Mitchell, Ronald. "Regime Design Matters." In *International Institutions: An International Organization Reader*, edited by Lisa and Beth Simmons Martin. Cambridge, MA: MIT Press, 2001.

Mohawk, John. "Discovering Columbus: The Way Here." In *View from the Shore: American Indian Perspectives on the Quincentenary*, edited by Jose Barreriro. Ithaca, NY: Cornell University Press, 1990.

Molloy, Tom. *The World Is Our Witness: The Historic Journey of the Nisga'a into Canada*. Calgary, Alberta: Fifth House Ltd., 2000.

Monture-Angus, Patricia. *Journeying Forward: Dreaming First Nations Independence*. Halifax, NS: Fernwood Publishing, 2002.

Moon, Paul. *The Newest Country in the World: A History of New Zealand in the Decade of the Treaty*. North Shore, New Zealand: Penguin, 2007.

Morales, Robert. "New Treaty, Same Old Problems." *Cultural Survival* (2006).

Moravcsik, A. "Taking Preferences Seriously: A Liberal Theory of International Politics." *International Organization* 51, no. 4 (1997): 513-53.

———. "The Origins of Human Rights Regimes: Democratic Delegation in Postwar Europe." *International Organization* 54, no. 2 (2000): 217-52.

Morgenthau, Hans J. *Politics among Nations*. Edited by Kenneth W. Thompson. 6th ed. New York: McGraw-Hill, 1985 (1948).

Morsink, Johannes. *The Universal Declaration of Human Rights: Origins, Drafting, and Intent*. Philadelphia: University of Pennsylvania, 1999.

Mulgan, Richard. "Should Indigenous Peoples Have Special Rights?" *Orbis* 33, (1989): 375-88.

———. *Māori, Pākehā and Democracy*. Auckland, New Zealand: Oxford University

Press, 1989.

Mulholland, Malcolm, ed. *State of the Māori Nation: Twenty-First-Century Issues in Aotearoa.* Auckland, New Zealand: Reed Publishing (NZ) Ltd Te Karuhi Tā Tāpui o Reed (Aotearoa), 2006.

Muppidi, Himadeep. *Producing the Global.* Minneapolis, MN: University of Minnesota Press, 2004.

Muthu, Sankar. *Enlightenment against Empire.* Princeton, NJ: Princeton University Press, 2003.

Neizen, Ronald. *The Origins of Indigenism: Human Rights and the Politics of Identity.* Berkeley: University of California Press, 2003.

Nettheim, Garth, Gary D. Meyers, Donna Craig. *Indigenous Peoples and Governance Structures: A Comparative Analysis of Land and Resource Management Rights.* Canberra, Victoria, Australia: Aboriginal Studies Press, 2002.

New Zealand Government. Human Rights Commission/Tu Kahui Tika Tangata. *Human Rights in New Zealand Today: New Zealand Action Plan for Human Rights.* Auckland, New Zealand: Human Rights Commission, 2004.

New Zealand Government. Ministry of Foreign Affairs and Trade. "New Zealand Handbook on International Human Rights." Wellington, New Zealand: Ministry of Foreign Affairs and Trade, 2003.

New Zealand Government. Te Puni Kokiri. *Te Wa O Te Ao Hurihuri Ki Te Ohanga Whanaketanga Māori/a Time for a Change in Māori Economic Development.* Wellington, New Zealand, October 2007.

New Zealand Human Rights Commission/Te Kahui Tika Tangata. "The New Zealand Draft Curriculum for Consultation 2006: Human Rights Issues." Wellington, New Zealand: Human Rights Commission, October 2006.

New Zealand Mission to the United Nations/Te Mangai O Aotearoa. "United Nations General Assembly, Declaration on the Rights of Indigenous Peoples. Explanation of Vote by New Zealand Permanent Representative H.E. Rosemary Banks.", 13 September 2007.

New Zealand. Waitangi Tribunal. "Report on the Crown's Foreshore and Seabed Policy (Wai 1071)." p. xiii. Wellington, New Zealand, 2004.

Newcomb, Steven T. *Pagans in the Promised Land: Decoding the Doctrine of Christian Discovery.* Golden, CO: Fulcrum Publishing, 2008.

Njolstad, O. "Learning from History? Case Studies and the Limits to Theory-Building." In *Arms Races: Technological and Political Dynamics,* edited by O. Njolstad. Los Angeles: Sage, 1990.

Notes, Akwesasne, ed. *Basic Call to Consciousness.* Summertown, TN: Native Voices, 2005.

Nunes, Keith D. "We Can Do ...Better: Rights of Singular Peoples and the Draft Declaration on the Rights of Indigenous Peoples." *St. Thomas Law Review* 7, (1995): 521-55.

O'Brien, Sharon. "Federal Indian Policies and the International Protection of Human Rights." In *American Indian Policy in the Twentieth Century,* edited by Jr. Deloria, Vine. Norman, OK: University of Oklahoma Press, 1985.

O'Neill, Katherine. "Canada Must Be Backed by Action, Native Leaders Say." *Inter Press Service Agency*, 17 June 2008.

O'Sullivan, Dominic. *Beyond Biculturalism: The Politics of an Indigenous Minority.* Wellington, New Zealand: Huia 2007.

Orange, Claudia. *The Treaty of Waitangi*. Wellington, New Zealand: Allen & Unwin, 1987.

Orton, F. and H. Beach. "A New Era for the Saami People of Sweden." In *Human Rights of Indigenous Peoples*, edited by Cynthia P. Cohen. Ardsley, NY: Transnational Publishers, 1998.

Osiander, Andreas. "Sovereignty, International Relations, and the Westphalian Myth." *International Organization* 55, no. 2 (2003).

Owen, John M. "How Liberalism Produces Democratic Peace." *International Security* 19, no. 2 (1994): 87-125.

Palmer, Matthew. "'Finding Common Ground' Te Papa 2008 Treaty Debate Series, Te Papa National Museum of New Zealand." Wellington, NZ, 31 January 2008.

Palmer, Matthew S. R. *The Treaty of Waitangi in New Zealand's Law and Constitution.* Wellington, New Zealand: Victoria University Press, 2008.

Parliament, New Zealand. "Question Time." Wellington, New Zealand, 12 September 2007.

Parlow, Anita. *Cry Sacred Ground: Big Mountain, USA.* Washington, DC: Christie Institute, 1988.

Peang-Meth, Abdulgaffar. "The Rights of Indigenous Peoples and the Fight for Self-Determination (Political Development in the Pacific)." *World Affairs* 164, (2002): 2-23.

Penikett, Tony. *Reconciliation: First Nations Treaty Making in British Columbia.* Vancouver, BC: Douglas & McIntyre, 2006.

Permanent Mission of the United States to the United Nations. "Observations of the United States with Respect to the Declaration on the Rights of Indigenous Peoples." 13 September 2007.

Petersen, Kim. "Indigenous Rights and the Mayan Victory in Belize." *The Dominion*, 23 January 2008.

Pevar, Stephen L. *The Rights of Indians and Tribes, Third Edition.* Carbondale, IL: Southern Illinois University, 2002.

Picard, Chief Ghislain, Assembly of First Nations of Quebec and Labrador. "Statement." 30 April 2008.

Ponting, J. Rick. *The Nisga'a Treaty: Polling Dynamics and Political Communication in Comparative Context.* Peterborough, Ontario: Broadview Press, 2006.

Price, Richard. "Transnational Civil Society and Advocacy in World Politics." *World Politics* 55, (2003): 579-606.

Pritchard, Sarah. "United Nations and the Making of a Declaration on Indigenous Rights." *Aboriginal Law Review* 3, (1997): 4-9.

Queensbury, Stephen V. "Recent United Nations Initiatives Concerning the Rights of Indigenous Peoples." In *Contemporary Native American Political Issues*, edited by Troy R Johnson. Walnut Creek, CA: Alta Mira Press, 1999.

Quentin-Baxter, ed. *Recognising the Rights of Indigenous Peoples*. Wellington, New Zealand: Institute of Policy Studies, 1998.

Raustiala, Kal. "Compliance and Effectiveness in International Regulatory Cooperation." *Case Western Reserve Journal of International Law* 32, (2000): 387-440.

Raustiala, K. and A. Slaughter. "International Law, International Relations and Compliance." In *Handbook of International Relations*, edited by T. Risse and B.A. Simmons W. Carlsnaes, 538-58. London: Sage, 2002.

Reconciliation., British Columbia. Ministry of Aboriginal Relations and. "Update on Aboriginal Treaties." 10 January 2009.

Reid, Ipsos. "Defining Canada: A Nation Chooses the 101 Things That Best Define Their Country." 2008.

Resnick, Philip. *The European Roots of Canadian Identity*. Peterborough, ON: Broadview Press, 2005.

Reus-Smit. "The Strange Death of Liberal International Theory." *European Journal of International Law* 12, no. 3 (2001): 573-93.

Rigney, L. "Internationalization of an Indigenous Anticolonial Cultural Critique of Research Methodologies." *Wicazo Sa Journal of American Indian Studies Review* 14, no. 2 (1999): 109-21.

Risse, T., S. Ropp and K. Sikkink. *The Power of Human Rights: International Norms and Domestic Change*. Cambridge: Cambridge University Press, 1999.

Robertson, Lindsay G. *Conquest by Law: How the Discovery of America Dispossessed Indigenous Peoples of Their Lands*. Oxford: Oxford University Press, 2005.

Rodriguez-Piñero. *Indigenous Peoples, Postcolonialism, and International Law: The ILO Regime (1919-1989)*. Oxford: Oxford University Press, 2005.

Roy, Bernadette Kelly and Gudmunder Alfredsson. "Indigenous Rights: The Literature Explosion." *Transnational Perspectives* 13, (1987): 19-24.

Rubin, Herert J. and Irene S. Rubin. *Qualitative Interviewing: The Art of Hearing Data, Second Edition*. Thousand Oaks, CA: Sage, 2005.

Ruggie, John G. "International Regimes, Transactions and Change: Embedded Liberalism in the Postwar Economic Order." *International Organization* 36, no. 2 (1983): 379-416.

———. "Reconstituting the Global Public Domain - Issues, Actors, and Practices." *European Journal of International Relations* 10, no. 4 (2004): 499-531.

Russell, P.H. "High Courts and the Rights of Aboriginal Peoples: The Limits of Judicial Independence." *Saskatchewan Law Review* 61, (1998): 247-79.

Said, Edward W. *Orientalism*. New York: Vintage Books, 1979.

———. *Culture and Imperialism*. New York: Vintage Books, 1994.

Sanders, Douglas. "The Re-Emergence of Indigenous Questions in International Law." In *International Law and Indigenous Peoples*, edited by S. J. Anaya. Burlington, VT: Ashgate Publishing, 1983.

———. "Draft Declaration on the Rights of Indigenous Populations." *Human Rights Quarterly* 11, (1989): 406-33.

———. "The Un Working Group on Indigenous Populations." *Human Rights Quarterly* 11, (1989): 406-33.

———. "Draft Declaration on the Rights of Indigenous Peoples--Commentaries: A Text and a New Process." *Canadian Law Reporter* 1, (1994): 48-49.

Saul, John Ralston. *A Fair Country: Telling Truths About Canada*. Toronto: Penguin, 2008.

Schmitz, H.P. and K. Sikkink. "International Human Rights." In *Handbook of International Relations*, edited by T. Risse and B.A. Simmons W. Carlsnaes. London: Sage, 2002.

Schuler, D. and A. Namoika. *Participatory Design: Principles and Practices*. Hillsdale, NJ: Erlbaum, 1993.

Scott, James C. *Weapons of the Weak*. New Haven, CT: Yale University Press, 1985.

Sen, Amartya. "An Argument for the Primacy of Political Rights: Freedom and Needs." *The New Republic* 31, no. 10/17 January (1994).

Service, Canwest News. "Text of the Apology." 11 June 2008.

Setear, J.K. "An Iterative Perspective on Treaties: A Synthesis of International Relations Theory and International Law." *Harvard International Law Journal* 37, (1996): 139, 42-47.

Seufart-Barr, Nancy. "Seeking a New Partnership: International Year for the World's Indigenous People, 1993." *UN Chronicle* 30, (1992): 40-51.

Shively, W. Phillips. *The Craft of Political Research, 3rd Edition*. Englewood Cliffs, NJ: Prentice Hall, 1990.

———. *The Craft of Political Research*. Englewood Cliffs, NJ: Prentice-Hall, 2004.

Simmons, Beth. "International Law and State Behavior: Commitment and Compliance in International Monetary Affairs." *American Political Science Review* 94, no. 4 (2000): 819-35.

Slack, David. *Civil War {...& Other Optimistic Predictions} Where Is New Zealand Going?* Auckland, New Zealand: Penguin, 2005.

Slaughter, A. "International Law in a World of Liberal States." *European Journal of International Law* 6, no. 4 (1995): 503-38.

Smith, Graham Hingangaroa. "Protecting and Respecting Indigenous Knowledge." In *Reclaiming Indigenous Voice and Vision*, edited by Marie Battiste. Vancouver, BC: UBC Press, 2000.

Smith, Jackie, Charles Chatfield, and Ron Pagnucco, ed. *Transnational Social Movements and Global Politics: Solidarity Beyond the State*. Syracuse: Syracuse University Press, 1997.

Smith, Keri E. Iayll. *The State and Indigenous Movements*. New York: Routledge, 2006.

Smith, Linda Tuhiwai. *Decolonizing Methodologies: Research and Indigenous Peoples*. Dunedin, New Zealand: University of Otago Press, 1999.

———. "On Tricky Ground: Researching the Native in the Age of Uncertainty." In *The Sage Handbook of Qualitative Research, Third Edition*, edited by Norman K. Denzin and Yvonna S. Lincoln, 85-108. Thousand Oaks, CA: Sage, 2005.

Smith, Linda Tuhiwai Te Rina. "Kaupapa Māori Research." In *Reclaiming Indigenous Voice and Vision*, edited by Marie Battiste, 225-47. Vancouver, BC: UBC Press, 2000.

Smith, Philippa Mein. *A Concise History of New Zealand*. Cambridge: Cambridge

University Press, 2005.

Smith, Steve. "Positivism and Beyond." In *International Theory: Positivism and Beyond*, edited by Ken Booth Steve Smith, and Marysia Kalewski. New York: Cambridge University Press, 1996.

Snedden, Patrick. *Pakeha and Treaty: Why It's Our Treaty Too*. Auckland, New Zealand: Random House, 2005.

Snidal, D. "The Game Theory of International Politics." *World Politics* 38, (1985): 226.

Sommer, Rebecca. "Adoption of the Declaration on the Rights of Indigenous Peoples." USA: Sommer Films, 2007.

Special NGO Committee on Human Rights. "Final Report. International Ngo Conference on Indigenous Peoples and the Land, Organized by the Sub-Commission on Racism, Racial Discrimination, Apartheid and Decolonisation, 15-18 September." Geneva, 1981.

Spivak, Gayatri Chakravorty. *A Critique of Postcolonial Reason: Toward a History of the Vanishing Present*. Cambridge: Harvard University Press, 1999.

Stamatopoulou, Elsa. "Indigenous Peoples and the United Nations: Human Rights as a Developing Dynamic." *Human Rights Quarterly* 1, (1994): 58-81.

Stasiulis, Daiva and Nira Yuval-Davis, ed. *Unsettling Settler Societies: Articulations of Gender, Race, Ethnicity and Class*. London: Sage, 1995.

Statistics Canada. "The Canada Yearbook." Ottawa: Statistics Canada, 2009.

Stenson, Marcia. *The Treaty: Every New Zealander's Guide to the Treaty of Waitangi*. Auckland, New Zealand: Random House, 2004.

Stewart-Harawira, Makere. *The New Imperial Order: Indigenous Responses to Globalization*. Wellington, New Zealand: Huia Press, 2005.

Swepston, L. "The Indigenous and Tribal Peoples Convention (No. 169): Eight Year after Adoption." In *The Human Rights of Indigenous Peoples*, edited by Cynthia P. Cohen, 17-36. Ardsley, NY: Transnational Publishers, 1998.

Tennant, Chris. "Indigenous Peoples, International Institutions, and the International Legal Literature from 1945-1993." *Human Rights Quarterly* 16, (1994): 1-57.

Tennant, Paul. *Aboriginal Peoples and Politics: The Indian Land Question in British Columbia, 1849-1989*. Vancouver, BC: UBC Press, 1992.

Thornberry, Patrick. "Self-Determination, Minorities, Human Rights: A Review of International Instruments." *The International Law Quarterly* 38, (1989): 867-89.

———. *Indigenous Peoples and Human Rights*. Manchester, Juris Publishing2002.

Tickner, Ann. *Gendering World Politics*. New York: Columbia University Press, 2001.

Todorov, Tzvetan. *The Conquest of America: The Question of the Other*. Norman, OK: University of Oklahoma Press, 1999.

Topa, Wahinkpe (Four Arrows) aka Don Trent Jacobs, ed. *Unlearning the Language of Conquest: Scholars Expose Anti-Indianism in America*. Austin, TX: University of Texas Press, 2006.

Tully, J. *Strange Multiplicity: Constitutionalism in an Age of Diversity*. Cambridge: Cambridge University Press, 1995.

———. "The Struggles of Indigenous Peoples for and of Freedom." In *Political Theory and the Rights of Indigenous Peoples*, edited by P. Patton D. Ivison, W. Sanders.

Cambridge: Cambridge University Press, 2000.

Turner, Dale. *This Is Not Peace Pipe: Towards a Critical Indigenous Philosophy.* Toronto: University of Toronto Press, 2006.

Turnpel, M.E. "Draft Declaration on the Rights of Indigenous Peoples--Commentaries." *Canadian Native Law Reporter* 1, (1994): 50-52.

UN Commission on Human Rights, Sub-Commission on Prevention of Discrimination and Protection of Minorities Thirty-Fifth Session. "Study of the Problem of Discrimination against Indigenous Populations. Report of the Working Group on Indigenous Populations on Its First Session.": E/CN.4/Sub.2/1982/33, 25 August 1982.

UN Commission on Human Rights, Sub-Commission on Prevention of Discrimination and Protection of Minorities. "Report of the Working Group on Indigenous Populations on Its Second Session." E/CN.4/Sub.2/1983/22, 1983.

———. "Report of the Working Group on Indigenous Populations on Its Third Session." E/CN.4/Sub.2/1984/20, 1984.

———. "Report of the Working Group on Indigenous Populations on Its Fourth Session." E/CN.4/Sub.2/1985/22, 1985.

———. "Report of the Informal Drafting Groups Established to Consider the First Revised Text of the Draft Universal Declaration on Indigenous Rights." E/CN.4/Sub.2/AC.4/1990/7/Add.1, 1990.

UN Special Rapporteur. "Indigenous Peoples Rights: Experiences and Challenges." Copenhagen: International Centre for Human Rights and Democratic Development, International Work Group for Indigenous Affairs (IWGIA), Tebtebba Foundation, Canadian Friends Service Committee., 2007.

United Nations. Economic and Security Council. "Resolution 1982/34." 7 May 1982.

United Nations. Economic and Security Council. Commission on Human Rights. "Report of the Special Rapporteur on the Situation of Human Rights and Fundamentally Freedoms of Indigenous Peoples, Rudolfo Stavenhagen.", 13 March 2006.

United Nations. Sub-Commission on Prevention of Discrimination and Protection of Minorities. "Resolution 8 (Xxiv) ", 18 August 1971.

United Nations. General Assembly. Human Rights Council. "Resolution Adopted by the General Assembly." A/Res/60/251.

United Nations. UN Department of Public Information. "General Assembly Adopts Declaration on the Rights of Indigenous Peoples." GA/10612, 13 September 2007.

van Boven, Theodor C. "The Role of Non-Governmental Organizations in International Human Rights Standard-Setting: A Prerequisite of Democracy." *California Western International Law Journal* 20, no. 2 (1989): 207-25.

Van Evera, Stephen *Guide to Methods for Students of Political Science.* Ithaca, NY: Cornell University Press, 1997.

Vasil, Raj. *Biculturalism: Reconciling Aotearoa with New Zealand.* Wellington, New Zealand: Institute of Policy Studies, 1988.

———. *What Do the Maori Want? New Maori Political Perspectives.* Auckland, New

Zealand: Random Century, 1990.

Venne, Sharon Helen. *Evolving International Law Regarding Indigenous Rights.* Penticton, BC: Theytus Books Ltd, 1998.

Verdun, Bob. "The Human Race: Reparation Repercussion." *The Nation Newspaper*, 15 April 2007.

Wabananick, Chief, Assembly of First Nations of Quebec and Labrador. "Statement at 7th Session of the Un Permanent Forum on Indigenous Issues." New York, 1 May 2008.

Waitangi Tribunal. "Montunui Waitora Report Wai 6." Wellington, New Zealand: Waitangi Tribunal, March 1983.

Walker, Ranginui. *Ka Whawhai Tonu Matou: Struggle without End.* Auckland, New Zealand: Penguin Books, 2004.

Waltz, Kenneth. *Man, the State, and War.* New York: Columbia University Press, 1959.
———. *Theory of International Politics.* Reading, MA: Addison-Wesley, 1979.

Ward, Alan. *An Unsettled History: Treaty Claims in New Zealand Today.* Wellington, New Zealand: Bridget Williams Books, 1999.

Warren, Kay B. and Jean E. Jackson, ed. *Indigenous Movements, Self-Representation, and the State in Latin America.* Austin, TX: University of Texas Press, 2002.

Warry, Wayne. *Ending Denial: Understanding Aboriginal Issues.* Peterborough, ON: Broadview Press, 2007.

Washburn, Wilcomb E. *Red Man's Land, White Man's Law.* Norman, OK: University of Oklahoma Press, 1971 (1995).

Wendt, Alexander. "Anarchy Is What States Make of It the Social Construction of Power Politics." *International Organization* 26, no. 2 (1992): 391-425.
———. *Social Theory of International Politics.* New York: Cambridge University Press, 1999.

Wendt, Alexander and Daniel Friedheim. "Hierarchy under Anarchy: Informal Empire and the East German State." *International Organization* 49, no. 4 (1995): 689-721.

Wiessner, S. "Rights and Status of Indigenous Peoples: A Global Comparative and International Analysis." In *International Law and Indigenous Peoples*, edited by S. J. Anaya, 257-328. Burlington, VT: Ashgate Publishing, 2003.

Wight, Martin. "Western Values in International Relations." In *Diplomatic Investigations: Essays in the Theory of International Politics*, edited by H. and M. Wight Butterfield. London: Allen & Unwin, 1966.
———. In *International Theory: The Three Traditions*, edited by G. and B. Porter Wight. Leicester: Holmes and Meier Publishers, 1991.

Wilkins, David E. *American Indian Sovereignty and the U.S. Supreme Court: The Masking of Justice.* Austin, TX: University of Texas Press, 1997.

Wilkins, David E. . *American Indian Politics and the American Political System.* Lanham, MD: Rowman & Littlefield, 2002.

Wilkins, David E. and K. Tsianina Lomawaima. *Uneven Ground: American Indian Sovereignty and Federal Law.* Norman, OK: University of Oklahoma Press, 2001.

Willia, Jerry W. *Foundations of Qualitative Research: Interpretive and Critical Methods.*

Thousand Oaks, CA: Sage, 2007.

Williams, Jr., Robert A. *The American Indian in Western Legal Thought: The Discourses of Conquest.* New York: Oxford University Press, 1990.

———. "Encounters on the Frontiers of International Human Rights Law: Redefining the Terms of Indigenous Peoples' Survival in the World." In *International Law and Indigenous Peoples*, edited by S. J. Anaya. Burlington, VT: Ashgate Publishing, 1990.

———. *Like a Loaded Weapon: The Rehnquist Court, Indian Rights and the Legal History of Racism in American.* Minneapolis, MN: University of Minnesota Press, 2005.

Willis, Jerry W. *Foundations of Qualitative Research: Interpretive & Critical Approaches.* Thousand Oaks, CA: Sage, 2007.

Wilmer, Franke. *The Indigenous Voice in World Politics.* Thousand Oaks, CA: Sage, 1993.

Wilson, Margaret and Anna Yeatman, ed. *Justice & Identity: Antipodean Practices.* St. Leonards, NSW, Australia: Allen & Unwin, 1995.

Working Group on the Draft Declaration. "Organization of Work (Participation)." Geneva: E/CN.4/1996/WG.15/CRP.7, 1996.

———. "Revised Chairman's Summary and Proposal." E/CN.4/2005/WG.15/2, 2005.

Wotherspoon, Terry and Vic Satzewich. *First Nations: Race, Class, and Gender Relations.* Regina, SK: Canadian Plains Research Centre, 2000.

Yashar, Deborah. "Contesting Citizenship: Indigenous Movements and Democracy in Latin America." *Comparative Politics* 31, no. 1 (1998): 23-42.

———. *Contesting Citizenship in Latin America: The Rise of Indigenous Movements and the Postliberal Challenge.* Cambridge: Cambridge University Press, 2005.

Yellow Bird, Michael. "What We Want to Be Called: Indigenous Peoples' Perspectives on Racial and Ethnic Identity Labels." *American Indian Quarterly* 23, (1999): 1-21.

Yin, Robert K. *Case Study Research, Design & Methods, 2nd Edition.* Newbury Park: Sage, 1994.

Zolf, Larry. "Peacekeeping and the Canadian Identity." *CBC News*, 7 February 2002.

Appendix 1:

Declaration of Principles, 1977

Declaration of Principles
for the Defense
of the Indigenous Nations and Peoples
of the Western Hemisphere

PREAMBLE:

Having considered the problems relating to the activities of the United Nations for the promotion and encouragement of respect for human rights and fundamental freedoms,

Noting that the Universal Declaration of Human Rights and related international covenants have the individual as their primary concern, and

Recognizing that individuals are the foundation of cultures, societies, and nations, and

Whereas, it is a fundamental right of any individual to practice and perpetuate the cultures, societies and nations into which they are born, and

Recognizing that conditions are imposed upon peoples that suppress, deny or destroy the culture, societies or nations in which they believe or of which they are members,

Be it affirmed that,

1. RECOGNITION OF INDIGENOUS NATIONS

Indigenous peoples shall be accorded recognition as nations, and proper subjects of international law, provided the people concerned desire to be recognized as a nation and meet the fundamental requirements of nationhood, namely:

    a. Having a permanent population
    b. Having a defined territory
    c. Having a government
    d. Having the ability to enter into relations with other states

2. SUBJECTS OF INTERNATIONAL LAW

Indigenous groups not meeting the requirements of nationhood are hereby declared to be subjects of international law and are entitled to the protection of this Declaration, provided they are identifiable groups having bonds of language, heritage, tradition, or other common identity.

3. GUARANTEE OF RIGHTS

No indigenous nation or group shall be deemed to have fewer rights, or lesser status for the sole reason that the nation or group has not entered into recorded treaties or agreements with any state.

4. ACCORDANCE OF INDEPENDENCE

Indigenous nations or groups shall be accorded such degree of independence as they may desire in accordance with international law.

5. TREATIES AND AGREEMENTS

Treaties and other agreements entered into by indigenous nations or groups with other states, whether denominated as treaties or otherwise, shall be recognized and applied in the same manner and according to the same international laws and principles as the treaties and agreements entered into by other states.

6. ABROGATION OF TREATIES AND OTHER RIGHTS

Treaties and agreements made with indigenous nations or groups shall not be subject to unilateral abrogation. In no event may the municipal laws of any state serve as a defense to the failure to adhere to and perform the terms of treaties and agreements made with indigenous nations or groups. Nor shall any state refuse to recognize and adhere to treaties or other agreements due to changed circumstances where the change in circumstances has been substantially caused by the state asserting that such change has occured.

7. JURISDICTION

No state shall assert or claim to exercise any right of jurisdiction over any indigenous nation or group or the territory of such indigenous nation or group unless pursuant to a valid treaty or other agreement freely made with the lawful representatives of the indigenous nation or group concerned. All actions on the part of any state which derogate from the indigenous nations' or groups' right to exercise self-determination shall be the proper concern of existing international bodies.

8. CLAIMS TO TERRITORY

No state shall claim or retain, by right of discovery or otherwise, the territories of an indigenous nation or group, except such lands as may have been lawfully acquired by valid treaty or other cessation freely made.

9. SETTLEMENT OF DISPUTES

All states in the Western Hemisphere shall establish through negotiations or other appropriate means a procedure for the binding settlement of disputes, claims, or other matters relating to indigenous nations or

25

groups. Such procedures shall be mutually acceptable to the parties, fundamentally fair, and consistent with international law. All procedures presently in existence which do not have the endorsement of the indigenous nations or groups concerned, shall be ended, and new procedures shall be instituted consistent with this Declaration.

10. NATIONAL AND CULTURAL INTEGRITY

It shall be unlawful for any state to take or permit any action or course of conduct with respect to an indigenous nation or group which will directly or indirectly result in the destruction or disintegration of such indigenous nation or group or otherwise threaten the national or cultural integrity of such nation or group, including, but not limited to, the imposition and support of illegitimate governments and the introduction of non-indigenous religions to indigenous peoples by non-indigenous missionaries.

11. ENVIRONMENTAL PROTECTION

It shall be unlawful for any state to make or permit any action or course of conduct with respect to the territories of an indigenous nation or group which will directly or indirectly result in the destruction or deterioration of an indigenous nation or group through the effects of pollution of earth, air, water, or which in any way depletes, displaces or destroys any natural resource or other resources under the dominion of, or vital to the livelihood of an indigenous nation or group.

12. INDIGENOUS MEMBERSHIP

No state, through legislation, regulation, or other means, shall take actions that interfere with the sovereign power of an indigenous nation or group to determine its own membership.

13. CONCLUSION

All of the rights and obligations declared herein shall be in addition to all rights and obligations existing under international law.

Appendix 2:

Declaration of Principles, Working Group on Indigenous Populations, 1985

E/CN.4/Sub.2/1985/22
Annex IV
page 1

ANNEX IV

Draft declaration of principles proposed by the Indian Law
Resource Center, Four Directions Council, National Aboriginal
and Islander Legal Service, National Indian Youth Council,
Inuit Circumpolar Conference, and the International Indian
Treaty Council 1/

Declaration of principles

1. Indigenous nations and peoples have, in common with all humanity, the right
to life, and to freedom from oppression, discrimination, and aggression.

2. All indigenous nations and peoples have the right to self-determination, by
virtue of which they have the right to whatever degree of autonomy or self-
government they choose. This includes the right to freely determine their
political status, freely pursue their own economic, social, religious and
cultural development, and determine their own membership and/or citizenship,
without external interference.

3. No State shall assert any jurisdiction over an indigenous nation or people,
or its territory, except in accordance with the freely expressed wishes of the
nation or people concerned.

4. Indigenous nations and peoples are entitled to the permanent control and
enjoyment of their aboriginal ancestral-historical territories. This includes
surface and subsurface rights, inland and coastal waters, renewable and non-
renewable resources, and the economies based on these resources.

5. Rights to share and use land, subject to the underlying and inalienable
title of the indigenous nation or people, may be granted by their free and
informed consent, as evidenced in a valid treaty or agreement.

6. Discovery, conquest, settlement on a theory of terra nullius and
unilateral legislation are never legitimate bases for States to claim or retain
the territories of indigenous nations or peoples.

7. In cases where lands taken in violation of these principles have already
been settled, the indigenous nation or people concerned is entitled to immediate
restitution, including compensation for the loss of use, without extinction of
original title. Indigenous peoples' desire to regain possession and control of
sacred sites must always be respected.

8. No State shall participate financially or militarily in the involuntary
displacement of indigenous populations, or in the subsequent economic
exploitation or military use of their territory.

9. The laws and customs of indigenous nations and peoples must be recognized by
States' legislative, administrative and judicial institutions and, in case of
conflicts with State laws, shall take precedence.

1/ Appeared also in document E/CN.4/Sub.2/AC.4/1985/WP.4/Add.4.

10. No State shall deny an indigenous nation, community, or people residing within its borders the right to participate in the life of the State in whatever manner and to whatever degree they may choose. This includes the right to participate in other forms of collective action and expression.

11. Indigenous nations and peoples continue to own and control their material culture, including archeological, historical and sacred sites, artifacts, designs, knowledge, and works of art. They have the right to regain items of major cultural significance and, in all cases, to the return of the human remains of their ancestors for burial in accordance with their traditions.

12. Indigenous nations and peoples have the right to be educated and conduct business with States in their own languages, and to establish their own educational institutions.

13. No technical, scientific or social investigations, including archeological excavations, shall take place in relation to indigenous nations or peoples, or their lands, without their prior authorization, and their continuing ownership and control.

14. The religious practices of indigenous nations and peoples shall be fully respected and protected by the laws of States and by international law. Indigenous nations and peoples shall always enjoy unrestricted access to, and enjoyment of sacred sites in accordance with their own laws and customs, including the right of privacy.

15. Indigenous nations and peoples are subjects of international law.

16. Treaties and other agreements freely made with indigenous nations or peoples shall be recognized and applied in the same manner and according to the same international laws and principles as treaties and agreements entered into with other States.

17. Disputes regarding the jurisdiction, territories and institutions of an indigenous nation or people are a proper concern of international law, and must be resolved by mutual agreement or valid treaty.

18. Indigenous nations and peoples may engage in self-defence against State actions in conflict with their right to self-determination.

19. Indigenous nations and peoples have the right freely to travel, and to maintain economic, social, cultural and religious relations with each other across State borders.

20. In addition to these rights, indigenous nations and peoples are entitled to the enjoyment of all the human rights and fundamental freedoms enumerated in the International Bill of Human Rights and other United Nations instruments. In no circumstances shall they be subjected to adverse discrimination.

Appendix 3:

Draft Declaration on the Rights of Indigenous Peoples, Sub-Commission Text, 1994

1   Affirming that indigenous peoples are equal in dignity and rights to all other peoples, while recognizing the right of all peoples to be different, to consider themselves different, and to be respected as such,

2   Considering that all peoples contribute to the diversity and richness of civilizations and cultures, which constitute the common heritage of humankind,

3   Affirming that all doctrines, policies and practices based on or advocating superiority of peoples or individuals on the basis of national origin, racial, religious, ethnic or cultural differences are racist, scientifically false, legally invalid, morally condemnable and socially unjust,

4   Reaffirming also that indigenous peoples, in the exercise of their rights, should be free from discrimination of any kind,

5   Concerned that many indigenous peoples have been deprived of their human rights and fundamental freedoms, resulting, inter alia, in the dispossession of their lands, territories and resources, thus preventing them from exercising, in particular, their right to development in accordance with their own needs and interests,

6   Recognizing the urgent need to respect and promote the inherent rights and characteristics of indigenous peoples, especially their rights to their lands, territories and resources, which derive from their cultures, spiritual traditions, histories and philosophies, as well as from their political, economic and social structures,

7   Welcoming the fact that indigenous peoples are organizing themselves in order to bring an end to all forms of discrimination and oppression wherever they occur,

8   Convinced that increasing the control of indigenous peoples over ~~development~~ development affecting them and their lands, territories and resources will enable them to continue to strengthen their institutions, cultures and traditions, as well as to promote their development in accordance with their aspirations and needs,

9   Recognizing also that respect for indigenous knowledge and practices contributes to sustainable development and management of the environment,

Emphasizing the need for demilitarization of the lands and territories of indigenous peoples, which will contribute to peace, economic and social progress and development, understanding and friendly relations among nations and peoples of the world,

Recognizing in particular the interest of indigenous families and communities to retain shared responsibility for the upbringing, training and education of their children,

Believing that indigenous peoples have the right freely to determine their relationships with States in a spirit of coexistence, mutual benefit and full respect,

Considering that treaties, agreements and other constructive arrangements between States and indigenous peoples continue to be matters of international concern and responsibility,

Noting that the Charter of the United Nations, the International Covenant on Economic, Social and Cultural Rights and the International Covenant on Civil and Political Rights affirm the fundamental importance of the right of self-determination of all peoples, by virtue of which they freely determine their political status and freely pursue their economic, social and cultural development,

Bearing in mind that nothing in this Declaration may be used to deny any peoples their right of self-determination,

Encouraging States to comply with and effectively implement all international instruments, in particular those related to human rights, as they apply to indigenous peoples, in consultation and cooperation with the peoples concerned,

Believing that this Declaration is an important step forward for the recognition, promotion and protection of the rights and freedoms of indigenous peoples and in the development of relevant activities of the United Nations system in this field,

Solemnly proclaims the following Declaration on the Rights of Indigenous Peoples:

PART I

Article 1

Indigenous peoples have the right to the full and effective enjoyment of all human rights and fundamental freedoms recognized in the Charter of the United Nations and in international human rights law;

Article 2

Indigenous peoples are free and equal to all other human beings and peoples in dignity and rights, and have the right to be free from any kind of discrimination, in particular that based on their indigenous origin or identity;

Article 3

Indigenous peoples have the right of self-determination. By virtue of that right they freely determine their political status and freely pursue their economic, social and cultural development;

Article 4

Indigenous peoples have the right to participate fully, if they so wish, in the political, economic, social and cultural life of the State while maintaining their distinct political, economic, social and cultural characteristics as well as their legal systems;

PART II

Article 5

Indigenous peoples have the collective right to exist in peace and security as distinct peoples and to be protected against genocide.

In addition, they have the individual rights to life, physical and mental integrity, liberty and security of person;

Article 6

Indigenous peoples have the collective and individual right to be protected against ethnocide and cultural genocide, including the prevention of and redress for:

(a) Removal of indigenous children from their families and communities under any pretext;

(b) Any action which has the aim or effect of depriving them of their integrity as distinct societies, or of their cultural or ethnic characteristics or identities;

(c) Any form of assimilation or integration by other cultures or ways of life imposed on them by legislative, administrative or other measures or means;

(d) Dispossession of their lands, territories or resources;

(e) Any propaganda directed against them;

Article 7

Indigenous peoples have the collective and individual right to maintain and develop their distinct characteristics and identities, including the right to identify themselves as indigenous and to be recognized as such;

Article 8

The right of an indigenous person to belong to an indigenous nation or community, in accordance with indigenous traditions and customs, is a matter of his or her individual choice and no disadvantage of any kind may arise from the exercise of such a choice;

Article 9

Indigenous peoples shall not be forcibly removed from their lands or territories. No relocation shall take place without the free and informed consent of the indigenous peoples concerned and after agreement on just and fair compensation and, where possible, with the option of return;

Article 10

Indigenous peoples have the right to special protection and security in periods of armed conflict.

States shall observe international standards for the protection of civilian populations in circumstances of emergency and armed conflict, and shall not:

(a) Recruit indigenous persons against their will into the armed forces and, in particular, for use against other indigenous peoples;

(b) Recruit indigenous children into the armed forces under any circumstances;

(c) Force indigenous persons to abandon their lands and territories and means of subsistence and relocate them in special centres for military purposes;

PART III

Article 11

Indigenous peoples have the right to revitalize and practice their cultural traditions. This includes the right to maintain, protect and develop the past, present and future manifestations of their cultures, such as archaeological and historical sites, artifacts, designs, ceremonies, technologies and visual and performing arts and literature, as well as the right to the restitution of cultural, religious and spiritual property taken without their free and informed consent or in violation of their laws, traditions and customs;

Article 12

Indigenous peoples have the right to manifest, practise and teach their spiritual and religious traditions, customs and ceremonies; the right to maintain, protect, and have access in privacy to their religious and cultural sites; the right to the use and control of ceremonial objects; and the right to the repatriation of human remains.

States shall take effective measures to ensure that indigenous sacred places including cemeteries be preserved, respected and protected;

Article 13

Indigenous peoples have the right to revitalize, use, develop and transmit to future generations their languages, oral traditions, writing systems and literatures, and to designate and retain their own names for communities, places and persons.

States shall take effective measures to ensure that indigenous peoples can understand and be understood in political, legal and administrative proceedings, where necessary through the provision of interpretation or by other appropriate means;

PART IV

Article 14

Indigenous peoples have the right to all levels and forms of education. They also have the right to establish and control their educational systems and institutions providing education in their own languages;

313

Article 15

Indigenous peoples have the right to have the dignity and diversity of their cultures, traditions, histories and aspirations appropriately reflected in all forms of education and public information.

States shall take effective measures, in consultation with indigenous peoples, to eliminate prejudice and to promote tolerance, understanding and good relations;

Article 16

Indigenous peoples have the right to establish their own media in their own languages. They also have the right to equal access to all forms of non-indigenous media.

States shall take effective measures to ensure that public media duly reflect indigenous cultural diversity;

PART V

Article 17

Indigenous peoples have the right to participate fully, if they so wish, at all levels of decision-making in matters which may affect their rights, lives and destinies through representatives chosen by themselves in accordance with their own procedures;

Article 18

Indigenous peoples have the right to participate fully, if they so wish, through procedures determined in consultation with them, in devising legislative or administrative measures that may affect them.

States shall obtain the free and informed consent of the peoples concerned before adopting and implementing such measures;

Article 19

Indigenous peoples have the right to maintain and develop their political, economic and social systems, to be secure in the enjoyment of their own means of subsistence, and to engage freely in their traditional and other economic activities, including hunting, fishing, herding, gathering, forestry and cultivation. Indigenous peoples who have been deprived of their means of subsistence are entitled to just and fair compensation;

Article 20

Indigenous peoples have the right to special measures for the immediate, effective and continuing improvement of their economic and social conditions, including in the areas of employment, vocational training and retraining, housing, sanitation, health and social security.

Particular attention shall be paid to the special needs of indigenous elders, women, youth, children and disabled;

Article 21

Indigenous peoples have the right to determine and develop priorities and strategies for exercising their right to development. In particular, indigenous peoples have the right to determine and develop all health, housing and other economic and social programmes affecting them and, as far as possible, to administer such programmes through their own institutions;

Article 22

Indigenous peoples have the right to their traditional medicines and health practices, including the right to the protection of vital medicinal plants, animals, and minerals;

PART VI

Article 23

Indigenous peoples have the right to recognition of their distinctive spiritual and material relationship with their lands and territories, including the total environment of the lands, air, water, sea, sea-ice, flora and fauna and other resources which indigenous peoples have traditionally owned or otherwise occupied or used;

Article 24

Indigenous peoples have the collective and individual right to own, control and use their lands and territories. This includes the right to the full recognition of their laws, traditions and customs, land-tenure systems and institutions for the management of resources, and the right to effective measures by States to prevent any interference with or encroachment upon these rights;

Article 25

Indigenous peoples have the right to the restitution of lands and territories which have been confiscated, occupied, used or damaged without their free an informed consent, and where this is not possible, to just and fair compensation. Unless otherwise freely agreed upon by the peoples concerned, compensation shall take the form of lands and territories at least equal in quality, size and legal status;

Article 26

Indigenous peoples have the right to the recreation and protection of the total environment and the productive capacity of their lands and territories, as well as to the assistance for this purpose from States and through international cooperation. Military activities and the storage or disposal of hazardous materials shall not take place in the lands and territories of indigenous peoples, unless otherwise freely agreed upon by the peoples concerned.

Article 27

Indigenous peoples have the right to special measures to protect, as intellectual property, their sciences, technologies and cultural manifestations, including genetic resources, seeds, medicines, knowledge of the properties of fauna and flora, oral traditions, literatures, designs and visual and performing arts;

Article 28

Indigenous peoples have the right to require that States obtain their free and informed consent prior to the approval of any project affecting their lands and territories, particularly in connection with the development or exploitation of mineral or other resources. Pursuant to agreement with the indigenous peoples concerned, just and fair compensation shall be provided for any such activities and measures taken to mitigate adverse environmental, economic, social, cultural or spiritual impact;

PART VII

Article 29

Indigenous peoples, as a specific form of exercising their right to self-determination, have the right to autonomy or self-government in matters relating to their internal and local affairs, including culture, religion, education, information, media, health, housing, employment, social welfare, economic activities, land and resources management, environment and entry by non-members, as well as ways and means for financing these autonomous functions;

316

Article 30

Indigenous peoples have the right to determine the structures and to select the membership of their institutions in accordance with their own procedures;

Article 31

Indigenous peoples have the right to retain and develop their customs, traditions, laws and legal systems in accordance with internationally recognized human rights standards;

Article 32

Indigenous peoples have the right to determine the responsibilities of individuals to their communities;

Article 33

Indigenous peoples have the right to maintain and develop contacts, relations and cooperation, including activities for spiritual, cultural, political, economic and social purposes, in particular with other indigenous peoples across borders;

Article 34

Indigenous peoples have the right to the observance and enforcement of treaties, agreements and other constructive arrangements concluded with States or their successors, according to their original intent. Conflicts and disputes which cannot otherwise be settled should be submitted to competent international bodies agreed to by all parties concerned;

PART VIII

Article 35

States shall take effective and appropriate measures, in consultation with the indigenous peoples concerned, to give full effect to the provisions of this Declaration. The rights contained herein shall be adopted and included in national legislation in such manner that indigenous peoples can avail themselves of such rights in practice;

Article 36

Indigenous peoples have the right to adequate financial and technical assistance, from States and through international cooperation, to pursue freely their political, economic, social, cultural and spiritual development, and for the enjoyment of the rights and freedoms contained in this Declaration;

Article 37

Indigenous peoples have the right to have access to and prompt decision through mutually acceptable and fair procedures for the resolution of conflicts and disputes with States, as well as to effective remedies for all infringements of their individual and collective rights;

Article 38

The organs and specialized agencies of the United Nations system and other intergovernmental organizations shall contribute to the full realization of the provisions of this Declaration through the mobilization, _inter alia_, of financial cooperation and technical assistance. Ways and means of ensuring participation of indigenous peoples on issues affecting them shall be established;

Article 39

The United Nations shall monitor the implementation of this Declaration through a body at the highest level with special competence in this field and with the direct participation of indigenous peoples. United Nations human rights bodies shall promote respect for the provisions of this Declaration;

PART IX

Article 40

The rights contained herein constitute the minimum standards for the survival and well-being of the indigenous peoples of the world;

Article 41

Nothing in this Declaration may be interpreted as diminishing or extinguishing existing or future rights indigenous peoples may have or acquire;

Article 42

Nothing in this Declaration may be interpreted as implying for any State, group or person any right to engage in any activity or to perform any act contrary to the Charter of the United Nations or to the Declaration on Principles of International Law concerning Friendly Relations and Cooperation among States in accordance with the Charter of the United Nations.

Appendix 4:

Draft Declaration on the Rights of Indigenous Peoples, African Group Package, 30 August 2007

30.08.07

United Nations Declaration on the Rights of Indigenous Peoples

The ~~Human Rights Council~~ General Assembly,

Guided **by the purposes and principles of the Charter of the United Nations, and good faith in the fulfilment of the obligations assumed by States in accordance with the Charter,**

Affirming that indigenous peoples are equal to all other peoples, while recognizing the right of all peoples to be different, to consider themselves different, and to be respected as such,

Affirming also that all peoples contribute to the diversity and richness of civilizations and cultures, which constitute the common heritage of humankind,

Affirming further that all doctrines, policies and practices based on or advocating superiority of peoples or individuals on the basis of national origin, racial, religious, ethnic or cultural differences are racist, scientifically false, legally invalid, morally condemnable and socially unjust,

Reaffirming that indigenous peoples, in the exercise of their rights, should be free from discrimination of any kind,

Concerned that indigenous peoples have suffered from historic injustices as a result of, inter alia, their colonization and dispossession of their lands, territories and resources, thus preventing them from exercising, in particular, their right to development in accordance with their own needs and interests,

Recognizing the urgent need to respect and promote the inherent rights of indigenous peoples which derive from their political, economic and social structures and from their cultures, spiritual traditions, histories and philosophies, especially their rights to their lands, territories and resources,

Recognizing also the urgent need to respect and promote the rights of indigenous peoples affirmed in treaties, agreements and other constructive arrangements with States,

Welcoming the fact that indigenous peoples are organizing themselves for political, economic, social and cultural enhancement and in order to bring an end to all forms of discrimination and oppression wherever they occur,

Convinced that control by indigenous peoples over developments affecting them and their lands, territories and resources will enable them to maintain and strengthen their institutions, cultures and traditions, and to promote their development in accordance with their aspirations and needs,

Recognizing that respect for indigenous knowledge, cultures and traditional practices contributes to sustainable and equitable development and proper management of the environment,

Emphasizing the contribution of the demilitarization of the lands and territories of indigenous peoples to peace, economic and social progress and development, understanding and friendly relations among nations and peoples of the world,

319

Recognizing in particular the right of indigenous families and communities to retain shared responsibility for the upbringing, training, education and well-being of their children, consistent with the rights of the child,

~~*Recognizing* that indigenous peoples have the right freely to determine their relationships with States in a spirit of coexistence, mutual benefit and full respect,~~

Considering that the rights affirmed in treaties, agreements and constructive arrangements between States and indigenous peoples are, in some situations, matters of international concern, interest, responsibility and character,

Considering also that treaties, agreements and other constructive arrangements, and the relationship they represent, are the basis for a strengthened partnership between indigenous peoples and States,

Acknowledging that the Charter of the United Nations, the International Covenant on Economic, Social and Cultural Rights and the International Covenant on Civil and Political Rights **as well as the Vienna Declaration and Programme of Action,** affirm the fundamental importance of the right of self-determination of all peoples, by virtue of which they freely determine their political status and freely pursue their economic, social and cultural development,

Bearing in mind that nothing in this Declaration may be used to deny any peoples their right of self-determination, exercised in conformity with international law,

Convinced that the recognition of the rights of indigenous peoples in this Declaration will enhance harmonious and cooperative relations between the State and indigenous peoples, based on principles of justice, democracy, respect for human rights, non-discrimination and good faith,

Encouraging States to comply with and effectively implement all their obligations as they apply to indigenous peoples under international instruments, in particular those related to human rights, in consultation and cooperation with the peoples concerned,

Emphasizing that the United Nations has an important and continuing role to play in promoting and protecting the rights of indigenous peoples,

Believing that this Declaration is a further important step forward for the recognition, promotion and protection of the rights and freedoms of indigenous peoples and in the development of relevant activities of the United Nations system in this field,

Recognizing and reaffirming that indigenous individuals are entitled without discrimination to all human rights recognized in international law, and that indigenous peoples possess collective rights which are indispensable for their existence, well-being and integral development as peoples,

Recognizing also **that the situation of indigenous peoples varies from region to region and from country to country and that the significance of national and regional particularities and various historical and cultural backgrounds should be taken into consideration,**

Solemnly proclaims the following United Nations Declaration on the Rights of Indigenous Peoples as a standard of achievement to be pursued in a spirit of partnership and mutual respect:

Article 1

Indigenous peoples have the right to the full enjoyment, as a collective or as individuals, of all human rights and fundamental freedoms as recognized in the Charter of the United Nations, the Universal Declaration of Human Rights and international human rights law.

Article 2

Indigenous peoples and individuals are free and equal to all other peoples and individuals and have the right to be free from any kind of discrimination, in the exercise of their rights, in particular that based on their indigenous origin or identity.

Article 3

Indigenous peoples have the right of self-determination. By virtue of that right they freely determine their political status and freely pursue their economic, social and cultural development.

Article 4

Indigenous peoples, in exercising their right to self-determination, have the right to autonomy or self-government in matters relating to their internal and local affairs, as well as ways and means for financing their autonomous functions.

Article 5

Indigenous peoples have the right to maintain and strengthen their distinct political, legal, economic, social and cultural institutions, while retaining their rights to participate fully, if they so choose, in the political, economic, social and cultural life of the State.

Article 6

Every indigenous individual has the right to a nationality.

Article 7

1.   Indigenous individuals have the rights to life, physical and mental integrity, liberty and security of person.

2.   Indigenous peoples have the collective right to live in freedom, peace and security as distinct peoples and shall not be subjected to any act of genocide or any other act of violence, including forcibly removing children of the group to another group.

Article 8

1.   Indigenous peoples and individuals have the right not to be subjected to forced assimilation or destruction of their culture.

2. States shall provide effective mechanisms for prevention of, and redress for:

(a) Any action which has the aim or effect of depriving them of their integrity as distinct peoples, or of their cultural values or ethnic identities;

(b) Any action which has the aim or effect of dispossessing them of their lands, territories or resources;

(c) Any form of forced population transfer which has the aim or effect of violating or undermining any of their rights;

(d) Any form of forced assimilation or integration ~~by other cultures or ways of life imposed on them by legislative, administrative or other measures~~;

(e) Any form of propaganda designed to promote or incite racial or ethnic discrimination directed against them.

Article 9

Indigenous peoples and individuals have the right to belong to an indigenous community or nation, in accordance with the traditions and customs of the community or nation concerned. No discrimination of any kind may arise from the exercise of such a right.

Article 10

Indigenous peoples shall not be forcibly removed from their lands or territories. No relocation shall take place without the free, prior and informed consent of the indigenous peoples concerned and after agreement on just and fair compensation and, where possible, with the option of return.

Article 11

1. Indigenous peoples have the right to practise and revitalize their cultural traditions and customs. This includes the right to maintain, protect and develop the past, present and future manifestations of their cultures, such as archaeological and historical sites, artefacts, designs, ceremonies, technologies and visual and performing arts and literature.

2. States shall provide redress through effective mechanisms, which may include restitution, developed in conjunction with indigenous peoples, with respect to their cultural, intellectual, religious and spiritual property taken without their free, prior and informed consent or in violation of their laws, traditions and customs.

Article 12

1. Indigenous peoples have the right to manifest, practice, develop and teach their spiritual and religious traditions, customs and ceremonies; the right to maintain, protect, and have access in privacy to their religious and cultural sites; the right to the use and control of their ceremonial objects; and the right to the repatriation of their human remains.

2. States shall seek to enable the access and/or repatriation of ceremonial objects and human remains in their possession through fair, transparent and effective mechanisms developed in conjunction with indigenous peoples concerned.

Article 13

1.   Indigenous peoples have the right to revitalize, use, develop and transmit to future generations their histories, languages, oral traditions, philosophies, writing systems and literatures, and to designate and retain their own names for communities, places and persons.

2.   States shall take effective measures to ensure this right is protected and also to ensure that indigenous peoples can understand and be understood in political, legal and administrative proceedings, where necessary through the provision of interpretation or by other appropriate means.

Article 14

1.   Indigenous peoples have the right to establish and control their educational systems and institutions providing education in their own languages, in a manner appropriate to their cultural methods of teaching and learning.

2.   Indigenous individuals, particularly children, have the right to all levels and forms of education of the State without discrimination.

3.   States shall, in conjunction with indigenous peoples, take effective measures, in order for indigenous individuals, particularly children, including those living outside their communities, to have access, when possible, to an education in their own culture and provided in their own language.

Article 15

1.   Indigenous peoples have the right to the dignity and diversity of their cultures, traditions, histories and aspirations which shall be appropriately reflected in education and public information.

2.   States shall take effective measures, in consultation and cooperation with the indigenous peoples concerned, to combat prejudice and eliminate discrimination and to promote tolerance, understanding and good relations among indigenous peoples and all other segments of society.

Article 16

1.   Indigenous peoples have the right to establish their own media in their own languages and to have access to all forms of non-indigenous media without discrimination.

2.   States shall take effective measures to ensure that State-owned media duly reflect indigenous cultural diversity. States, without prejudice to ensuring full freedom of expression, should encourage privately owned media to adequately reflect indigenous cultural diversity.

Article 17

1.   Indigenous individuals and peoples have the right to enjoy fully all rights established under applicable international and domestic labour law.

2.   States shall in consultation and cooperation with indigenous peoples take specific measures to protect indigenous children from economic exploitation and

323

from performing any work that is likely to be hazardous or to interfere with the child's education, or to be harmful to the child's health or physical, mental, spiritual, moral or social development, taking into account their special vulnerability and the importance of education for their empowerment.

3. Indigenous individuals have the right not to be subjected to any discriminatory conditions of labour and, inter alia, employment or salary.

Article 18

Indigenous peoples have the right to participate in decision-making in matters which would affect their rights, through representatives chosen by themselves in accordance with their own procedures, as well as to maintain and develop their own indigenous decision-making institutions.

Article 19

States shall consult and cooperate in good faith with the indigenous peoples concerned through their own representative institutions in order to obtain their free, prior and informed consent before adopting and implementing legislative or administrative measures that may affect them.

Article 20

1. Indigenous peoples have the right to maintain and develop their political, economic and social systems or institutions, to be secure in the enjoyment of their own means of subsistence and development, and to engage freely in all their traditional and other economic activities.

2. Indigenous peoples deprived of their means of subsistence and development are entitled to just and fair redress.

Article 21

1. Indigenous peoples have the right, without discrimination, to the improvement of their economic and social conditions, including, inter alia, in the areas of education, employment, vocational training and retraining, housing, sanitation, health and social security.

2. States shall take effective measures and, where appropriate, special measures to ensure continuing improvement of their economic and social conditions. Particular attention shall be paid to the rights and special needs of indigenous elders, women, youth, children and persons with disabilities.

Article 22

1. Particular attention shall be paid to the rights and special needs of indigenous elders, women, youth, children and persons with disabilities in the implementation of this Declaration.

2. States shall take measures, in conjunction with indigenous peoples, to ensure that indigenous women and children enjoy the full protection and guarantees against all forms of violence and discrimination.

Article 23

Indigenous peoples have the right to determine and develop priorities and strategies for exercising their right to development. In particular, indigenous peoples have the right to be actively involved in developing and determining health, housing and other economic and social programmes affecting them and, as far as possible, to administer such programmes through their own institutions.

Article 24

1. Indigenous peoples have the right to their traditional medicines and to maintain their health practices, including the conservation of their vital medicinal plants, animals and minerals. Indigenous individuals also have the right to access, without any discrimination, to all social and health services.

2. Indigenous individuals have an equal right to the enjoyment of the highest attainable standard of physical and mental health. States shall take the necessary steps with a view to achieving progressively the full realization of this right.

Article 25

Indigenous peoples have the right to maintain and strengthen their distinctive spiritual relationship with their traditionally owned or otherwise occupied and used lands, territories, waters and coastal seas and other resources and to uphold their responsibilities to future generations in this regard.

Article 26

1. Indigenous peoples have the right to the lands, territories and resources which they have traditionally owned, occupied or otherwise used or acquired.

2. Indigenous peoples have the right to own, use, develop and control the lands, territories and resources that they possess by reason of traditional ownership or other traditional occupation or use, as well as those which they have otherwise acquired.

3. States shall give legal recognition and protection to these lands, territories and resources. Such recognition shall be conducted with due respect to the customs, traditions and land tenure systems of the indigenous peoples concerned.

Article 27

States shall establish and implement, in conjunction with indigenous peoples concerned, a fair, independent, impartial, open and transparent process, giving due recognition to indigenous peoples' laws, traditions, customs and land tenure systems, to recognize and adjudicate the rights of indigenous peoples pertaining to their lands, territories and resources, including those which were traditionally owned or otherwise occupied or used. Indigenous peoples shall have the right to participate in this process.

325

Article 28

1. Indigenous peoples have the right to redress, by means that can include restitution or, when this is not possible, of a just, fair and equitable compensation, for the lands, territories and resources which they have traditionally owned or otherwise occupied or used, and which have been confiscated, taken, occupied, used or damaged without their free, prior and informed consent.

2. Unless otherwise freely agreed upon by the peoples concerned, compensation shall take the form of lands, territories and resources equal in quality, size and legal status or of monetary compensation or other appropriate redress.

Article 29

1. Indigenous peoples have the right to the conservation and protection of the environment and the productive capacity of their lands or territories and resources. States shall establish and implement assistance programmes for indigenous peoples for such conservation and protection, without discrimination.

2. States shall take effective measures to ensure that no storage or disposal of hazardous materials shall take place in the lands or territories of indigenous peoples without their free, prior and informed consent.

3. States shall also take effective measures to ensure, as needed, that programmes for monitoring, maintaining and restoring the health of indigenous peoples, as developed and implemented by the peoples affected by such materials, are duly implemented.

Article 30

1. Military activities shall not take place in the lands or territories of indigenous peoples, unless justified by a ~~significant threat to~~ relevant public interest or otherwise freely agreed with or requested by the indigenous peoples concerned.

2. States shall undertake effective consultations with the indigenous peoples concerned, through appropriate procedures and in particular through their representative institutions, prior to using their lands or territories for military activities.

Article 31

1. Indigenous peoples have the right to maintain, control, protect and develop their cultural heritage, traditional knowledge and traditional cultural expressions, as well as the manifestations of their sciences, technologies and cultures, including human and genetic resources, seeds, medicines, knowledge of the properties of fauna and flora, oral traditions, literatures, designs, sports and traditional games and visual and performing arts. They also have the right to maintain, control, protect and develop their intellectual property over such cultural heritage, traditional knowledge, and traditional cultural expressions.

2. In conjunction with indigenous peoples, States shall take effective measures to recognize and protect the exercise of these rights.

Article 32

1. Indigenous peoples have the right to determine and develop priorities and strategies for the development or use of their lands or territories and other resources.

2. States shall consult and cooperate in good faith with the indigenous peoples concerned through their own representative institutions in order to obtain their free and informed consent prior to the approval of any project affecting their lands or territories and other resources, particularly in connection with the development, utilization or exploitation of their mineral, water or other resources.

3. States shall provide effective mechanisms for just and fair redress for any such activities, and appropriate measures shall be taken to mitigate adverse environmental, economic, social, cultural or spiritual impact.

Article 33

1. Indigenous peoples have the right to determine their own identity or membership in accordance with their customs and traditions. This does not impair the right of indigenous individuals to obtain citizenship of the States in which they live.

2. Indigenous peoples have the right to determine the structures and to select the membership of their institutions in accordance with their own procedures.

Article 34

Indigenous peoples have the right to promote, develop and maintain their institutional structures and their distinctive customs, spirituality, traditions, procedures, practices and, in the cases where they exist, juridical systems or customs, in accordance with international human rights standards.

Article 35

Indigenous peoples have the right to determine the responsibilities of individuals to their communities.

Article 36

1. Indigenous peoples, in particular those divided by international borders, have the right to maintain and develop contacts, relations and cooperation, including activities for spiritual, cultural, political, economic and social purposes, with their own members as well as other peoples across borders.

2. States, in consultation and cooperation with indigenous peoples, shall take effective measures to facilitate the exercise and ensure the implementation of this right.

Article 37

1. Indigenous peoples have the right to the recognition, observance and enforcement of treaties, agreements and other constructive arrangements concluded with States or their successors and to have States honour and respect such treaties, agreements and other constructive arrangements.

327

2. Nothing in this Declaration may be interpreted as to diminish or eliminate the rights of Indigenous Peoples contained in treaties, agreements and constructive arrangements.

Article 38

States in consultation and cooperation with indigenous peoples, shall take the appropriate measures, including legislative measures, to achieve the ends of this Declaration.

Article 39

Indigenous peoples have the right to have access to financial and technical assistance from States and through international cooperation, for the enjoyment of the rights contained in this Declaration.

Article 40

Indigenous peoples have the right to have access to and prompt decision through just and fair procedures for the resolution of conflicts and disputes with States or other parties, as well as to effective remedies for all infringements of their individual and collective rights. Such a decision shall give due consideration to the customs, traditions, rules and legal systems of the indigenous peoples concerned and international human rights.

Article 41

The organs and specialized agencies of the United Nations system and other intergovernmental organizations shall contribute to the full realization of the provisions of this Declaration through the mobilization, inter alia, of financial cooperation and technical assistance. Ways and means of ensuring participation of indigenous peoples on issues affecting them shall be established.

Article 42

The United Nations, its bodies, including the Permanent Forum on Indigenous Issues, and specialized agencies, including at the country level, and States shall promote respect for and full application of the provisions of this Declaration and follow up the effectiveness of this Declaration.

Article 43

The rights recognized herein constitute the minimum standards for the survival, dignity and well-being of the indigenous peoples of the world.

Article 44

All the rights and freedoms recognized herein are equally guaranteed to male and female indigenous individuals.

Article 45

Nothing in this Declaration may be construed as diminishing or extinguishing the rights indigenous peoples have now or may acquire in the future.

Article 46

1.	Nothing in this Declaration may be interpreted as implying for any State, people, group or person any right to engage in any activity or to perform any act contrary to the Charter of the United Nations **or construed as authorizing or encouraging any action which would dismember or impair totally or in part, the territorial integrity or political unity of sovereign and independent States.**

2.	In the exercise of the rights enunciated in the present Declaration, human rights and fundamental freedoms of all shall be respected. The exercise of the rights set forth in this Declaration shall be subject only to such limitations as are determined by law, and in accordance with international human rights obligations. Any such limitations shall be non-discriminatory and strictly necessary solely for the purpose of securing due recognition and respect for the rights and freedoms of others and for meeting the just and most compelling requirements of a democratic society.

3.	The provisions set forth in this Declaration shall be interpreted in accordance with the principles of justice, democracy, respect for human rights, equality, non-discrimination, good governance and good faith

———————

Appendix 5:

Declaration on the Rights of Indigenous Peoples, Adopted by the United Nations General Assembly, 13 September 2007

United Nations

A/RES/61/295

 **General Assembly**

Distr.: General
2 October 2007

Sixty-first session
Agenda item 68

Resolution adopted by the General Assembly

[*without reference to a Main Committee (A/61/L.67 and Add.1)*]

61/295. United Nations Declaration on the Rights of Indigenous Peoples

The General Assembly,

Taking note of the recommendation of the Human Rights Council contained in its resolution 1/2 of 29 June 2006,[1] by which the Council adopted the text of the United Nations Declaration on the Rights of Indigenous Peoples,

Recalling its resolution 61/178 of 20 December 2006, by which it decided to defer consideration of and action on the Declaration to allow time for further consultations thereon, and also decided to conclude its consideration before the end of the sixty-first session of the General Assembly,

Adopts the United Nations Declaration on the Rights of Indigenous Peoples as contained in the annex to the present resolution.

107th plenary meeting
13 September 2007

Annex

United Nations Declaration on the Rights of Indigenous Peoples

The General Assembly,

Guided by the purposes and principles of the Charter of the United Nations, and good faith in the fulfilment of the obligations assumed by States in accordance with the Charter,

Affirming that indigenous peoples are equal to all other peoples, while recognizing the right of all peoples to be different, to consider themselves different, and to be respected as such,

Affirming also that all peoples contribute to the diversity and richness of civilizations and cultures, which constitute the common heritage of humankind,

---

[1] See *Official Records of the General Assembly, Sixty-first Session, Supplement No. 53* (A/61/53), part one, chap. II, sect. A.

06-51207

Affirming further that all doctrines, policies and practices based on or advocating superiority of peoples or individuals on the basis of national origin or racial, religious, ethnic or cultural differences are racist, scientifically false, legally invalid, morally condemnable and socially unjust,

Reaffirming that indigenous peoples, in the exercise of their rights, should be free from discrimination of any kind,

Concerned that indigenous peoples have suffered from historic injustices as a result of, inter alia, their colonization and dispossession of their lands, territories and resources, thus preventing them from exercising, in particular, their right to development in accordance with their own needs and interests,

Recognizing the urgent need to respect and promote the inherent rights of indigenous peoples which derive from their political, economic and social structures and from their cultures, spiritual traditions, histories and philosophies, especially their rights to their lands, territories and resources,

Recognizing also the urgent need to respect and promote the rights of indigenous peoples affirmed in treaties, agreements and other constructive arrangements with States,

Welcoming the fact that indigenous peoples are organizing themselves for political, economic, social and cultural enhancement and in order to bring to an end all forms of discrimination and oppression wherever they occur,

Convinced that control by indigenous peoples over developments affecting them and their lands, territories and resources will enable them to maintain and strengthen their institutions, cultures and traditions, and to promote their development in accordance with their aspirations and needs,

Recognizing that respect for indigenous knowledge, cultures and traditional practices contributes to sustainable and equitable development and proper management of the environment,

Emphasizing the contribution of the demilitarization of the lands and territories of indigenous peoples to peace, economic and social progress and development, understanding and friendly relations among nations and peoples of the world,

Recognizing in particular the right of indigenous families and communities to retain shared responsibility for the upbringing, training, education and well-being of their children, consistent with the rights of the child,

Considering that the rights affirmed in treaties, agreements and other constructive arrangements between States and indigenous peoples are, in some situations, matters of international concern, interest, responsibility and character,

Considering also that treaties, agreements and other constructive arrangements, and the relationship they represent, are the basis for a strengthened partnership between indigenous peoples and States,

Acknowledging that the Charter of the United Nations, the International Covenant on Economic, Social and Cultural Rights[2] and the International Covenant on Civil and Political Rights,[2] as well as the Vienna Declaration and Programme of

---

[2] See resolution 2200 A (XXI), annex.

Action,[3] affirm the fundamental importance of the right to self-determination of all peoples, by virtue of which they freely determine their political status and freely pursue their economic, social and cultural development,

Bearing in mind that nothing in this Declaration may be used to deny any peoples their right to self-determination, exercised in conformity with international law,

Convinced that the recognition of the rights of indigenous peoples in this Declaration will enhance harmonious and cooperative relations between the State and indigenous peoples, based on principles of justice, democracy, respect for human rights, non-discrimination and good faith,

Encouraging States to comply with and effectively implement all their obligations as they apply to indigenous peoples under international instruments, in particular those related to human rights, in consultation and cooperation with the peoples concerned,

Emphasizing that the United Nations has an important and continuing role to play in promoting and protecting the rights of indigenous peoples,

Believing that this Declaration is a further important step forward for the recognition, promotion and protection of the rights and freedoms of indigenous peoples and in the development of relevant activities of the United Nations system in this field,

Recognizing and reaffirming that indigenous individuals are entitled without discrimination to all human rights recognized in international law, and that indigenous peoples possess collective rights which are indispensable for their existence, well-being and integral development as peoples,

Recognizing that the situation of indigenous peoples varies from region to region and from country to country and that the significance of national and regional particularities and various historical and cultural backgrounds should be taken into consideration,

Solemnly proclaims the following United Nations Declaration on the Rights of Indigenous Peoples as a standard of achievement to be pursued in a spirit of partnership and mutual respect:

Article 1

Indigenous peoples have the right to the full enjoyment, as a collective or as individuals, of all human rights and fundamental freedoms as recognized in the Charter of the United Nations, the Universal Declaration of Human Rights[4] and international human rights law.

Article 2

Indigenous peoples and individuals are free and equal to all other peoples and individuals and have the right to be free from any kind of discrimination, in the exercise of their rights, in particular that based on their indigenous origin or identity.

---

[3] A/CONF.157/24 (Part I), chap. III.

[4] Resolution 217 A (III).

3

332

Article 3

Indigenous peoples have the right to self-determination. By virtue of that right they freely determine their political status and freely pursue their economic, social and cultural development.

Article 4

Indigenous peoples, in exercising their right to self-determination, have the right to autonomy or self-government in matters relating to their internal and local affairs, as well as ways and means for financing their autonomous functions.

Article 5

Indigenous peoples have the right to maintain and strengthen their distinct political, legal, economic, social and cultural institutions, while retaining their right to participate fully, if they so choose, in the political, economic, social and cultural life of the State.

Article 6

Every indigenous individual has the right to a nationality.

Article 7

1.   Indigenous individuals have the rights to life, physical and mental integrity, liberty and security of person.

2.   Indigenous peoples have the collective right to live in freedom, peace and security as distinct peoples and shall not be subjected to any act of genocide or any other act of violence, including forcibly removing children of the group to another group.

Article 8

1.   Indigenous peoples and individuals have the right not to be subjected to forced assimilation or destruction of their culture.

2.   States shall provide effective mechanisms for prevention of, and redress for:

(*a*) Any action which has the aim or effect of depriving them of their integrity as distinct peoples, or of their cultural values or ethnic identities;

(*b*) Any action which has the aim or effect of dispossessing them of their lands, territories or resources;

(*c*) Any form of forced population transfer which has the aim or effect of violating or undermining any of their rights;

(*d*) Any form of forced assimilation or integration;

(*e*) Any form of propaganda designed to promote or incite racial or ethnic discrimination directed against them.

Article 9

Indigenous peoples and individuals have the right to belong to an indigenous community or nation, in accordance with the traditions and customs of the

4

333

community or nation concerned. No discrimination of any kind may arise from the exercise of such a right.

Article 10

Indigenous peoples shall not be forcibly removed from their lands or territories. No relocation shall take place without the free, prior and informed consent of the indigenous peoples concerned and after agreement on just and fair compensation and, where possible, with the option of return.

Article 11

1. Indigenous peoples have the right to practise and revitalize their cultural traditions and customs. This includes the right to maintain, protect and develop the past, present and future manifestations of their cultures, such as archaeological and historical sites, artefacts, designs, ceremonies, technologies and visual and performing arts and literature.

2. States shall provide redress through effective mechanisms, which may include restitution, developed in conjunction with indigenous peoples, with respect to their cultural, intellectual, religious and spiritual property taken without their free, prior and informed consent or in violation of their laws, traditions and customs.

Article 12

1. Indigenous peoples have the right to manifest, practise, develop and teach their spiritual and religious traditions, customs and ceremonies; the right to maintain, protect, and have access in privacy to their religious and cultural sites; the right to the use and control of their ceremonial objects; and the right to the repatriation of their human remains.

2. States shall seek to enable the access and/or repatriation of ceremonial objects and human remains in their possession through fair, transparent and effective mechanisms developed in conjunction with indigenous peoples concerned.

Article 13

1. Indigenous peoples have the right to revitalize, use, develop and transmit to future generations their histories, languages, oral traditions, philosophies, writing systems and literatures, and to designate and retain their own names for communities, places and persons.

2. States shall take effective measures to ensure that this right is protected and also to ensure that indigenous peoples can understand and be understood in political, legal and administrative proceedings, where necessary through the provision of interpretation or by other appropriate means.

Article 14

1. Indigenous peoples have the right to establish and control their educational systems and institutions providing education in their own languages, in a manner appropriate to their cultural methods of teaching and learning.

2. Indigenous individuals, particularly children, have the right to all levels and forms of education of the State without discrimination.

5

3.   States shall, in conjunction with indigenous peoples, take effective measures, in order for indigenous individuals, particularly children, including those living outside their communities, to have access, when possible, to an education in their own culture and provided in their own language.

Article 15

1.   Indigenous peoples have the right to the dignity and diversity of their cultures, traditions, histories and aspirations which shall be appropriately reflected in education and public information.

2.   States shall take effective measures, in consultation and cooperation with the indigenous peoples concerned, to combat prejudice and eliminate discrimination and to promote tolerance, understanding and good relations among indigenous peoples and all other segments of society.

Article 16

1.   Indigenous peoples have the right to establish their own media in their own languages and to have access to all forms of non-indigenous media without discrimination.

2.   States shall take effective measures to ensure that State-owned media duly reflect indigenous cultural diversity. States, without prejudice to ensuring full freedom of expression, should encourage privately owned media to adequately reflect indigenous cultural diversity.

Article 17

1.   Indigenous individuals and peoples have the right to enjoy fully all rights established under applicable international and domestic labour law.

2.   States shall in consultation and cooperation with indigenous peoples take specific measures to protect indigenous children from economic exploitation and from performing any work that is likely to be hazardous or to interfere with the child's education, or to be harmful to the child's health or physical, mental, spiritual, moral or social development, taking into account their special vulnerability and the importance of education for their empowerment.

3.   Indigenous individuals have the right not to be subjected to any discriminatory conditions of labour and, inter alia, employment or salary.

Article 18

Indigenous peoples have the right to participate in decision-making in matters which would affect their rights, through representatives chosen by themselves in accordance with their own procedures, as well as to maintain and develop their own indigenous decision-making institutions.

Article 19

States shall consult and cooperate in good faith with the indigenous peoples concerned through their own representative institutions in order to obtain their free, prior and informed consent before adopting and implementing legislative or administrative measures that may affect them.

Article 20

1.   Indigenous peoples have the right to maintain and develop their political, economic and social systems or institutions, to be secure in the enjoyment of their own means of subsistence and development, and to engage freely in all their traditional and other economic activities.

2.   Indigenous peoples deprived of their means of subsistence and development are entitled to just and fair redress.

Article 21

1.   Indigenous peoples have the right, without discrimination, to the improvement of their economic and social conditions, including, inter alia, in the areas of education, employment, vocational training and retraining, housing, sanitation, health and social security.

2.   States shall take effective measures and, where appropriate, special measures to ensure continuing improvement of their economic and social conditions. Particular attention shall be paid to the rights and special needs of indigenous elders, women, youth, children and persons with disabilities.

Article 22

1.   Particular attention shall be paid to the rights and special needs of indigenous elders, women, youth, children and persons with disabilities in the implementation of this Declaration.

2.   States shall take measures, in conjunction with indigenous peoples, to ensure that indigenous women and children enjoy the full protection and guarantees against all forms of violence and discrimination.

Article 23

Indigenous peoples have the right to determine and develop priorities and strategies for exercising their right to development. In particular, indigenous peoples have the right to be actively involved in developing and determining health, housing and other economic and social programmes affecting them and, as far as possible, to administer such programmes through their own institutions.

Article 24

1.   Indigenous peoples have the right to their traditional medicines and to maintain their health practices, including the conservation of their vital medicinal plants, animals and minerals. Indigenous individuals also have the right to access, without any discrimination, to all social and health services.

2.   Indigenous individuals have an equal right to the enjoyment of the highest attainable standard of physical and mental health. States shall take the necessary steps with a view to achieving progressively the full realization of this right.

Article 25

Indigenous peoples have the right to maintain and strengthen their distinctive spiritual relationship with their traditionally owned or otherwise occupied and used lands, territories, waters and coastal seas and other resources and to uphold their responsibilities to future generations in this regard.

Article 26

1. Indigenous peoples have the right to the lands, territories and resources which they have traditionally owned, occupied or otherwise used or acquired.

2. Indigenous peoples have the right to own, use, develop and control the lands, territories and resources that they possess by reason of traditional ownership or other traditional occupation or use, as well as those which they have otherwise acquired.

3. States shall give legal recognition and protection to these lands, territories and resources. Such recognition shall be conducted with due respect to the customs, traditions and land tenure systems of the indigenous peoples concerned.

Article 27

States shall establish and implement, in conjunction with indigenous peoples concerned, a fair, independent, impartial, open and transparent process, giving due recognition to indigenous peoples' laws, traditions, customs and land tenure systems, to recognize and adjudicate the rights of indigenous peoples pertaining to their lands, territories and resources, including those which were traditionally owned or otherwise occupied or used. Indigenous peoples shall have the right to participate in this process.

Article 28

1. Indigenous peoples have the right to redress, by means that can include restitution or, when this is not possible, just, fair and equitable compensation, for the lands, territories and resources which they have traditionally owned or otherwise occupied or used, and which have been confiscated, taken, occupied, used or damaged without their free, prior and informed consent.

2. Unless otherwise freely agreed upon by the peoples concerned, compensation shall take the form of lands, territories and resources equal in quality, size and legal status or of monetary compensation or other appropriate redress.

Article 29

1. Indigenous peoples have the right to the conservation and protection of the environment and the productive capacity of their lands or territories and resources. States shall establish and implement assistance programmes for indigenous peoples for such conservation and protection, without discrimination.

2. States shall take effective measures to ensure that no storage or disposal of hazardous materials shall take place in the lands or territories of indigenous peoples without their free, prior and informed consent.

3. States shall also take effective measures to ensure, as needed, that programmes for monitoring, maintaining and restoring the health of indigenous peoples, as developed and implemented by the peoples affected by such materials, are duly implemented.

Article 30

1.   Military activities shall not take place in the lands or territories of indigenous peoples, unless justified by a relevant public interest or otherwise freely agreed with or requested by the indigenous peoples concerned.

2.   States shall undertake effective consultations with the indigenous peoples concerned, through appropriate procedures and in particular through their representative institutions, prior to using their lands or territories for military activities.

Article 31

1.   Indigenous peoples have the right to maintain, control, protect and develop their cultural heritage, traditional knowledge and traditional cultural expressions, as well as the manifestations of their sciences, technologies and cultures, including human and genetic resources, seeds, medicines, knowledge of the properties of fauna and flora, oral traditions, literatures, designs, sports and traditional games and visual and performing arts. They also have the right to maintain, control, protect and develop their intellectual property over such cultural heritage, traditional knowledge, and traditional cultural expressions.

2.   In conjunction with indigenous peoples, States shall take effective measures to recognize and protect the exercise of these rights.

Article 32

1.   Indigenous peoples have the right to determine and develop priorities and strategies for the development or use of their lands or territories and other resources.

2.   States shall consult and cooperate in good faith with the indigenous peoples concerned through their own representative institutions in order to obtain their free and informed consent prior to the approval of any project affecting their lands or territories and other resources, particularly in connection with the development, utilization or exploitation of mineral, water or other resources.

3.   States shall provide effective mechanisms for just and fair redress for any such activities, and appropriate measures shall be taken to mitigate adverse environmental, economic, social, cultural or spiritual impact.

Article 33

1.   Indigenous peoples have the right to determine their own identity or membership in accordance with their customs and traditions. This does not impair the right of indigenous individuals to obtain citizenship of the States in which they live.

2.   Indigenous peoples have the right to determine the structures and to select the membership of their institutions in accordance with their own procedures.

Article 34

Indigenous peoples have the right to promote, develop and maintain their institutional structures and their distinctive customs, spirituality, traditions, procedures, practices and, in the cases where they exist, juridical systems or customs, in accordance with international human rights standards.

Article 35

Indigenous peoples have the right to determine the responsibilities of individuals to their communities.

Article 36

1.   Indigenous peoples, in particular those divided by international borders, have the right to maintain and develop contacts, relations and cooperation, including activities for spiritual, cultural, political, economic and social purposes, with their own members as well as other peoples across borders.

2.   States, in consultation and cooperation with indigenous peoples, shall take effective measures to facilitate the exercise and ensure the implementation of this right.

Article 37

1.   Indigenous peoples have the right to the recognition, observance and enforcement of treaties, agreements and other constructive arrangements concluded with States or their successors and to have States honour and respect such treaties, agreements and other constructive arrangements.

2.   Nothing in this Declaration may be interpreted as diminishing or eliminating the rights of indigenous peoples contained in treaties, agreements and other constructive arrangements.

Article 38

States in consultation and cooperation with indigenous peoples, shall take the appropriate measures, including legislative measures, to achieve the ends of this Declaration.

Article 39

Indigenous peoples have the right to have access to financial and technical assistance from States and through international cooperation, for the enjoyment of the rights contained in this Declaration.

Article 40

Indigenous peoples have the right to access to and prompt decision through just and fair procedures for the resolution of conflicts and disputes with States or other parties, as well as to effective remedies for all infringements of their individual and collective rights. Such a decision shall give due consideration to the customs, traditions, rules and legal systems of the indigenous peoples concerned and international human rights.

Article 41

The organs and specialized agencies of the United Nations system and other intergovernmental organizations shall contribute to the full realization of the provisions of this Declaration through the mobilization, inter alia, of financial cooperation and technical assistance. Ways and means of ensuring participation of indigenous peoples on issues affecting them shall be established.

10

Article 42

The United Nations, its bodies, including the Permanent Forum on Indigenous Issues, and specialized agencies, including at the country level, and States shall promote respect for and full application of the provisions of this Declaration and follow up the effectiveness of this Declaration.

Article 43

The rights recognized herein constitute the minimum standards for the survival, dignity and well-being of the indigenous peoples of the world.

Article 44

All the rights and freedoms recognized herein are equally guaranteed to male and female indigenous individuals.

Article 45

Nothing in this Declaration may be construed as diminishing or extinguishing the rights indigenous peoples have now or may acquire in the future.

Article 46

1.   Nothing in this Declaration may be interpreted as implying for any State, people, group or person any right to engage in any activity or to perform any act contrary to the Charter of the United Nations or construed as authorizing or encouraging any action which would dismember or impair, totally or in part, the territorial integrity or political unity of sovereign and independent States.

2.   In the exercise of the rights enunciated in the present Declaration, human rights and fundamental freedoms of all shall be respected. The exercise of the rights set forth in this Declaration shall be subject only to such limitations as are determined by law and in accordance with international human rights obligations. Any such limitations shall be non-discriminatory and strictly necessary solely for the purpose of securing due recognition and respect for the rights and freedoms of others and for meeting the just and most compelling requirements of a democratic society.

3.   The provisions set forth in this Declaration shall be interpreted in accordance with the principles of justice, democracy, respect for human rights, equality, non-discrimination, good governance and good faith.

CPSIA information can be obtained
at www.ICGtesting.com
Printed in the USA
LVIC04n1753261014
410568LV00005BA/28